SEW A BEAUTIFUL GIFT

Claire B. Shaeffer

• • •

Photographs by Robert A. Keeran

Sterling Publishing Co., Inc.   **New York**

Also by Claire B. Shaeffer

The Complete Book of Sewing Shortcuts, Sterling Publishing Co., Inc., New York, 1981.

Edited by Barbara Busch

Library of Congress Cataloging-in-Publication Data

Shaeffer, Claire B.
  Sew a beautiful gift.

  Includes index.
  1. Sewing.   2. Gifts.   I. Title.
TT715.S53   1986   646.2   86-1796
ISBN 0-8069-6340-9
ISBN 0-8069-6314-X (pbk.)

Copyright © 1986 by Claire B. Shaeffer
Published by Sterling Publishing Co., Inc.
Two Park Avenue, New York, N.Y. 10016
Distributed in Australia by Capricorn Book Co. Pty. Ltd.
Unit 5C1 Lincoln St., Lane Cove, N.S.W. 2066
Distributed in the United Kingdom by Blandford Press
Link House, West Street, Poole, Dorset BH15 1LL, England
Distributed in Canada by Oak Tree Press Ltd.
% Canadian Manda Group, P.O. Box 920, Station U
Toronto, Ontario, Canada M8Z 5P9
Manufactured in the United States of America
All rights reserved

CONTENTS

For Ma-Ma, Lottie Davis Sumner, the most wonderful grandmother in the world

ACKNOWLEDGMENTS

Thank you—

Elizabeth Lawson, Marcy Tilton, Bobbie Carr, Betty Bennett, Susan Schleif, Sandra Neiger, John Monteith, Karyl Garbow, and Charlotte Ezra for your many words of wisdom.

Lucy Spector, Martha Pullen, Linda Williams, Julie Lewis, Shirley Mattis, Honor Donor, Clotilde, Barney Sofro and Donann Creedon for your support.

Lisa Urban, Dorcas Caldwell, Tony Morucci, Sharmin Spector, Beverly Spector, Dianne Giancola, Maureen Gilligan, Jean Accardi, Milton Taylor, and Elisabeth J. Vandermey for filling my many requests.

Jeanne Weaver and Marcy Tilton for sharing your sewing talents.

Britex Fabrics, Martha Pullen Co., The Fabric Carr, Caswell-Massey Co. Ltd., Fairfield Processing Corporation, Gingher, Inc., Stacy Fabrics Corporation, Seams Great Products, Inc., Pelle Leathers, Daisy Kingdom, Inc., Ghee's, Donner Designs, IBC Notions, Fiskars Manufacturing Corporation, Blue Magic Products, Inc., Sew Easy Industries, Coats & Clark, C.M. Offray & Son, Inc., Solar-Kist Corp., Salem Industries, Inc., Risdon Corp., Dan River, Inc., Pentapco, Inc., Johnson/Hirscher, Inc., and Banar Designs for supplying fabrics sewing supplies, and tools.

My sons, Charles and James, for sharing their expertise with the gift selection and designs.

My parents, Louie and Juanita Brightwell, for their help during the final days of editing.

Charlie, for everything.

Readers unable to locate suppliers in their areas, who carry the materials recommended by the author, should contact: Customer Service, Sterling Publishing, Inc., Two Park Avenue, New York, NY 10016.

ABOUT THE BOOK

This book gives you patterns and step-by-step instructions for making over 150 gifts. Specific materials and directions are included for each gift; however, there is general information that applies to all of them.

The Gifts

Each project is a timeless gift, which can be completed in a short period at a minimal cost. With a little imagination, the design possibilities are unlimited. By varying the fabric, changing the appliqué or adding embroidery, you can create fashionable and original gifts for many years.

Materials

The requirements, listed at the beginning of each gift project, describe the exact amount of yardage needed for a minimum of waste.

Since many gifts require small amounts of fabrics, fabric requirements are frequently described as remnants with specific measurements to indicate their exact size. This is particularly helpful for quantity sewing, and it might be helpful also when you're looking through your own scrap box.

However, when you are considering scraps, be selective. Just because the scrap is the right size doesn't mean it is the right one for your gift.

The fabric notes describe the specific fabric used for the book sample and suggest other suitable fabrics.

In a few instances, trade names have been mentioned. These are products which produced optimal results.

Cutting Directions

Most of the patterns in this book are simple rectangles or squares. The simplest designs have no pattern pieces, only measurements. A few patterns have been reduced in size but most are full-scale.

For simple patterns—rectangles, squares, and strips—the dimensions are provided in the Cutting Directions. The pattern piece width is always described first. For example, a 14″ × 10″ rectangle is 14″ wide and 10″ long; a 10″ × 14″ rectangle is 10″ wide and 14″ long.

To decide which would be better during the pattern-making process, I considered fabric economy and fabric design as well as the overall gift design. In most instances, gifts would be unaffected if fabric sections were cut on the opposite grain.

Unless otherwise indicated, all patterns include seam allowances.

No cutting layouts are given for most projects.

Sewing Directions

The step-by-step directions are clear and concise. Frequently used construction methods for zippers, hems, straps, and appliqués are described in Gift-Making Basics.

SEAM AND HEM ALLOWANCES

The seam and hem allowances are always given in step one. Seam allowance widths vary from ¼″ to 1″. Hem allowance widths vary from ½″ to 4″.

Narrow seam allowances are used when accuracy is particularly important and to eliminate unnecessary trimming.

Wider widths are frequently used for applied sections, such as pockets, since they are easier to press before stitching. They are also used in some strap designs for strength and appearance.

The frequently used narrow machine hem is inconspicuous and easy to sew on straight edges and gentle curves. Wider widths are used for casings and decorative hems.

DIAGRAMS

The line drawings are screened to make them easy to read. They have also been simplified; and even though the directions may indicate pins, generally pins are not shown in the diagrams.

Right side of fabric	
Wrong side of fabric	
Right side of lining or felt	
Wrong side of lining	
Fusible web, fleece and interfacing	

Illus. 1

GIFT-MAKING BASICS

One of the great pleasures of gift-making is the simplicity of it. With a few basic tools and a little skill, you can create distinctive, one-of-a-kind gifts.

This chapter includes a summary of frequently used information which will be helpful.

Tips and Techniques for Patterns

ENLARGING PATTERNS

Patterns, too large to fit into the book's format, are reduced in size and printed over a square grid. The grid scale (1 sq. = 1″; 1 sq. = 2″) indicates how much the pattern is to be enlarged.

Work on 1″ grid graph paper or pattern cloth. Copy the pattern, one square at a time, until complete.

Claire's Hint: If you have a cutting mat or board with a grid pattern, tape a plain translucent paper over it. The grid on the mat will show through for easy copying.

ENLARGING APPLIQUÉS

When enlarging an appliqué design, you can change the designated scale to make the design larger or smaller, if you choose. The football helmet design used on the stroller bag would make an interesting bib, quilt, or place mat appliqué. One would be much smaller than the design on the stroller bag and the other might be larger.

Claire's Hint: When working with appliqués, I cheat a lot and use a copying machine that enlarges and reduces the designs.

TRACING DESIGNS

Some designs and pattern sections are drawn full size and must be transferred to your fabric.

Trace the design onto tracing paper or stabilizer. This step can be eliminated with some marking methods. However, it will preserve the book and it has the added advantage of being reversible. This is extremely important when tracing onto the wrong side of the fabric.

If most of your work is done at night, use your dining-room table with a lamp placed beneath it. Open the table about 10″ to insert a leaf. Cover the opening with an 11″ × 14″ piece of glass. (Cover the edges of the glass with masking tape to avoid cutting yourself.)

TRANSFERRING PATTERNS

Transferring by Direct Marking

When working on light-colored fabrics, trace directly onto the fabric. If the fabric is opaque, pin it to the tracing paper design; hold it up to a window and trace.

Transferring with Dressmaker's Carbon

When working with dark-colored fabrics, place light-colored dressmaker's carbon between the tracing paper and the fabric; then trace the design using a ballpoint pen or an orange stick.

Using a Transfer Pencil

Trace the design onto tracing paper; then, with a transfer pencil, trace again on the reverse side of the tracing paper. Iron the design on the fabric.

MAKING PATTERNS

Rectangular Patterns

To cut rectangles accurately, use a see-through ruler.
1. Cut one side on the straight grain or use the selvage.
2. To draw the corners, align one of the crosslines on the ruler with the straight grain. Using a marking pen or soap sliver draw the corners and sides to the desired length. If you don't have a see-through ruler, use the corner of a magazine or record album.
3. Draw the remaining two corners to finish the pattern.

Circular Patterns

1. Cut a piece of paper several inches larger than the circle diameter.
2. Fold the pattern paper into quarters.
3. Mark the radius (½ the circle diameter) on a tape measure.
4. Pin the marked point to the circle center—the folded corner.
5. Mark the radius on the pattern paper, moving the tape measure as needed. (Illus. 2)
6. Cut on the marked line.

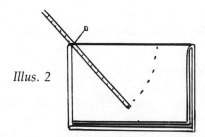

Illus. 2

Cutting Techniques

ROTARY CUTTERS

Rotary cutters are particularly useful in gift-making. To avoid damaging the cutting table, always use a cutting mat. Mats are available in a variety of sizes from 6″ × 18″ to 4′ × 8′.

To cut smoothly, hold the fabric firmly.

For straight lines, align the edge of a see-through ruler with the cutting line. Hold the ruler firmly with one hand and cut with the other.

For curved lines, use the index and middle fingers on your left hand to hold the fabric tautly. Place your fingers behind the rotary cutter and just before the beginning of the cutting line. Press with your fingers to keep the fabric from slipping when you cut. Reposition your fingers as needed.

APPLIQUÉ SCISSORS

To trim an appliqué, position the large blade between the appliqué and base fabric. Clip to all inward corners and sharp curves; then trim close to the stitched line.

To trim a hem, position the large blade under the hem allowance so that the blade holds the hem allowance away from the item itself. Trim.

CLIPPING

To clip to a corner, use scissors which are very sharp all the way to the ends of the points. Position the points of the scissors exactly where the clip is to be; clip.

TRIMMING

Corners

To reduce bulk, trim away the seam allowances at the corners. (Illus. 3a) Sharp points need to be trimmed even more. (Illus. 3b)

Seams

Since narrow seam allowances are used in gift-making, few seams will need trimming.

When trimming is indicated, trim close (⅛″–¼″) to the stitching line.

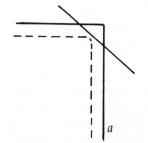

Illus. 3

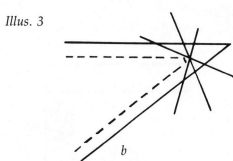

General Sewing Techniques

BACKTACK

Stitch forward ½″, then backwards, then forward again. To stitch backwards, reverse the machine or pull the work forward to prevent the fabric from feeding normally.

BIAS

True bias is cut at a 45° angle to the grainline. To determine the true bias, mark a point on the selvage close to one end. Using a see-through ruler, draw a line at right angles to the selvage. Mark one end of the bias strip on that line. Mark the other end of the bias on the selvage an equal distance from the original point. Use a ruler to connect the points. (Illus. 4)

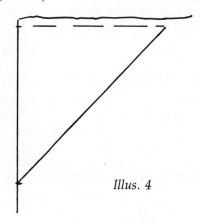

Illus. 4

Claire's Hint: When the fabric is folded diagonally, the lengthwise grain of the upper layer is parallel to the cross-grain on the lower layer.

Joining Bias

For best results, join bias strips on the lengthwise grain. Use this easy method to avoid a jog.
1. Square off the ends of the strips.
2. Right sides together, position the strips at right angles to each other.
3. Stitch across the corner on the grainline. (Illus. 5)

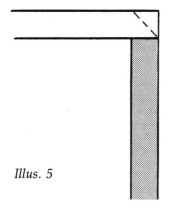

Illus. 5

Use a very short stitch (1.25mm or 20 spi) to join strips without backstitching.

Bindings

Bias binding and ribbon are frequently used to finish the edges of gift projects. No hem or seam allowances are allowed on edges to be bound.

RIBBON BINDING

This technique can also be used on double-fold bias binding.
1. Wrong sides together, press the ribbon almost *but not quite* in half lengthwise.
2. Using the steam iron, shape to the general shape of the edge. (Illus. 6a)

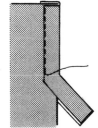

Illus. 6   *b*

3. Right sides up, encase the raw edge with the ribbon.
4. Topstitch or zigzag the ribbon in place. (Illus. 6b)

Claire's Hint: Zigzag stitching doesn't have to be as precise as straight-stitching and fewer "holidays" occur.

BINDING CORNERS
Outward Corners
1. Bind one edge. Stop and break the threads when you reach the edge.
2. Fold the ribbon to make a mitre at the corner; pin. (Illus. 7)
3. Continue stitching until all edges are finished.

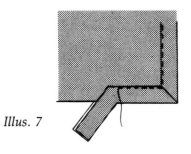

Illus. 7

Inward Corners
1. Reinforce the stitching line at the corner. Clip. (Illus. 8a)
2. Bind one edge to the corner. Pull the corner open so clip spreads. Bind the corner and adjacent edge. (Illus. 8b)
Claire's Hint: For a neat finish, stitch a small dart on the underside.

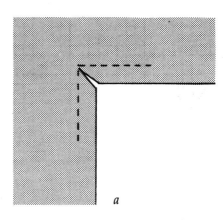

a

Illus. 8

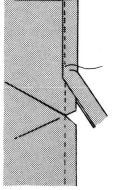

b

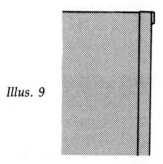

Illus. 9

Finishing the Ends
1. Right sides up, fold the ribbon end over the fabric end. (Illus. 9)
2. Fold the ribbon wrong sides together; stitch.

Joining the Ends
1. This is a flat, inconspicuous join for bias bindings and ribbons that won't fray. Overlap the ends ½", leaving them exposed and raw.
2. Use this join for fabrics that fray and for neatness. Fold under the end ¼" and overlap the beginning ½". (Illus. 10a)
3. For a very inconspicuous join, seam the ends together. Leave 2" tails at the beginning and end. (Illus. 10b)

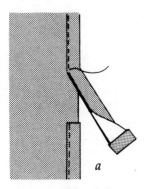

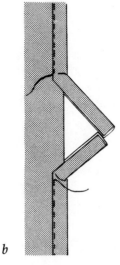

Illus. 10

Stitch the ends together. Trim and complete the unstitched section.
On double-fold bias binding, unfold the bias and join on the lengthwise grain.

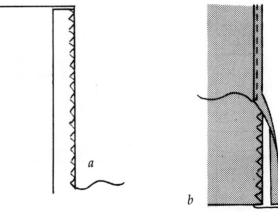

Illus. 11

BIAS BINDING
1. Open out the binding. Wrong sides up with the binding on top, join the binding and fabric with a ¼" seam. Use a zigzag stitch for the join. (Illus. 11a)
2. Wrap the binding around the raw edge. Fold the raw edge of the binding under and press.
3. Right sides up, edgestitch. (Illus. 11b)

Binding Corners
The seam allowance on narrow commercial bias bindings is ¼"; it is ⅜" on wide commercial binding. Corners are easier to handle when the binding strip is on the bottom.

Outward Corners
1. To bind outward corners, begin right sides up with the fabric on top. Stitch towards the corner, stopping ¼" or ⅜" (the seam width) before reaching the edge. Backtack and break your threads. (Illus. 12a)

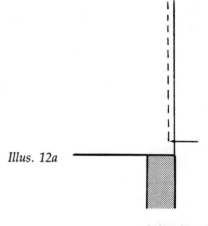

Illus. 12a

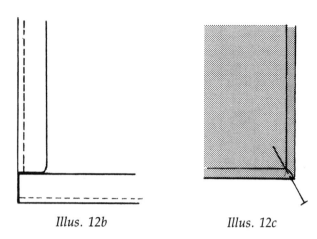

| Illus. 12b | Illus. 12c |

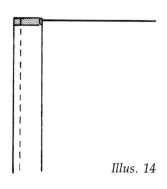

Illus. 14

2. On narrow bindings, fold the binding diagonally so the outer fold is even with the raw edge. Begin stitching at the binding fold, continue to the end of the strip. The diagram shows the reverse side. (Illus. 12b)

On wide bindings, fold the binding so the outer fold is a generous ⅛" beyond the raw edge. Continue as above.

3. Wrap the binding around the raw edges. Fold the raw edge of the binding under and press.

4. Mitre the corner on the right side in the opposite direction. Use the point of a needle to push it into place; pin. (Illus. 12c)

5. Right sides up, edgestitch the binding in place.

Inward Corners
1. Right sides up, reinforce the stitching line at the corner. Clip.
2. Stitch to the corner, stopping with the needle down at the end of the clip. Align the next edge with the binding and continue stitching. (Illus. 13)

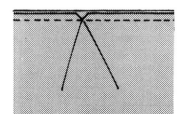

Illus. 13

3. Wrap and press the binding over the raw edges.
4. Mitre the corner.
5. Turn under the raw edge of the binding.
6. Right sides up, edgestitch.

Finishing the Ends
1. Open the bias flat.
2. Wrong sides together, fold under ½". The diagram shows the reverse side. (Illus. 14)
3. Apply as above.

BOXING
To form the boxing at the bottom of a bag, fold the corners, right sides together, matching the side and bottom seam lines. To make a 1" box, mark a point ¾" from the corner on each folded edge.

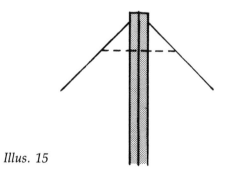

Illus. 15

Draw a line to connect the marked points. Stitch on the line. (Illus. 15) Use this chart to make a larger box.

Box	Distance from Corner
2"	1⅜"
3"	2⅛"
4"	2⅞"
5"	3½"
6"	4⅛"
8"	5¾"

CLOSE THE OPENING
Handbag linings, pillows, sachets, pot holders, and place mats frequently need small openings to turn the article right side out. These openings can be closed by hand or machine.

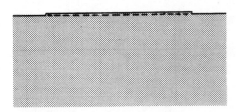

Illus. 16

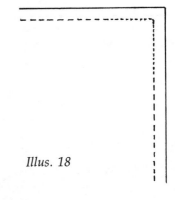

Illus. 18

By Machine
Push the seam allowances to the wrong side. Align the seam line folds, and edgestitch. (Illus. 16) This is an excellent method for pillow forms, handbag linings and flat pot holders and place mats.

By Hand
Make a ladder or slipstitch (see page 14) to close the opening inconspicuously.

CORDING
Sometimes called piped cording or piping, cording is frequently used to outline the edges of gifts. In garment construction, cordings and pipings are made from bias strips since the bias-cut is easier to manipulate on curved seams and edges. In gift construction, the strips can be cut on either the cross grain or straight as well as on the bias.

Making the Cording
1. Select a small-size cord, such as postal twine, and preshrink it.
   To preshrink the cord, wind several yards onto a piece of cardboard. Fold the cardboard in half and place in a basin of very hot water. Let the water cool. Remove the cord and let it dry.
2. Cut fabric strips 1½" wide unless otherwise indicated.
3. Wrap the fabric around the cord, wrong sides together.
4. Using a zipper foot, stitch close to the cord.
5. Trim the seam allowances on the cording to ¼" unless otherwise indicated. (Illus. 17)

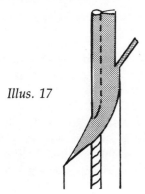

Illus. 17

CORNERS
To achieve a well-formed point at a corner, shorten the stitch 1" before reaching the corner. At the corner, make one or more stitches diagonally across the corner. (Illus. 18)

Bulky and thick fabrics require a greater diagonal than lightweight, thin materials. Trim as needed.

GATHERING
Choose one of these methods for easy, frustration-free gathering.

Loosen the Tension
1. Fill the bobbin with a strong cord such as topstitching thread or buttonhole twist.
2. Loosen the upper tension so that the bobbin thread will be tight.
3. Set the stitch length at 2.5mm (10 spi).
4. Right side up, stitch almost *but not quite* on the seam line. Stitch again midway between the seam line and raw edge. This positions the gathering rows on the right side of the fabric for seams which will be stitched right sides together. If the seam will be stitched right sides up, position the gathering rows on the right side of the fabric.
5. Pull up the bobbin threads.
6. Fasten the bobbin threads at the beginning and end by winding them around a pin in a figure eight.

Zigzag over Cord
This method works better on heavier fabrics.
1. Knot the end of a strong cord, such as buttonhole twist.
2. Zigzag (W,2-L,2) over the cord on the seam line and again midway between the seam line and raw edge. Stitch wrong side up for seams which will be stitched right sides together. (Illus. 19)

Claire's Hint: If you can't avoid stitching on the cord, increase the stitch width.

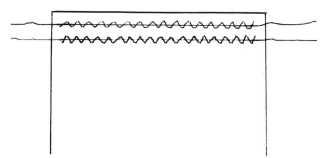

Illus. 19

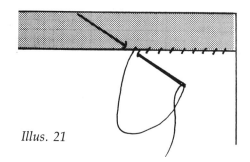

Illus. 21

GAUGE-STITCHING

To gauge-stitch, stitch almost *but not quite* on the seam line. Use this stitched line as a guide for pressing the seam or hem allowance to the wrong side.

HAND-STITCHES

Slipstitch or Ladder Stitch

Working from right to left, take a ¼" stitch in one folded edge, then a stitch in the other folded edge. Make several stitches, forming a ladder then pull the thread taut. (Illus. 20)

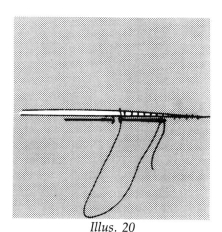

Illus. 20

To make the stitches inconspicuous, the second stitch must begin exactly opposite the end of the first stitch, making the stitches between the two layers straight, not slanted. After all, you wouldn't want a ladder with crooked steps.

Hemming Stitch

Working right to left and wrong side up, take a tiny stitch in the gift; bringing the needle up through the edge of the hem. (Illus. 21)

HEMMING BY MACHINE

Narrow Machine Hems

Wrong side up, fold ¼" to the wrong side; fold over ¼" again; edgestitch. (Illus. 22a)

To overlap the hem at corners, stitch the hem on one edge, stopping about 1" before reaching the end. Fold the first few inches of the hem on the next edge in place; pin. Stitch a triangle at the corner; and continue. (Illus. 22b)

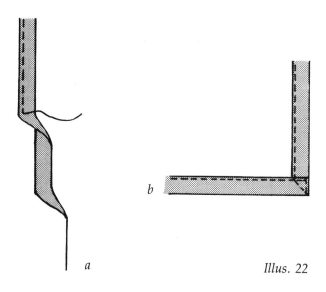

b

a   Illus. 22

Double Hems

Wrong side up, press the hem allowance to the wrong side; fold the raw edge to the pressed line; and press again. Pin or baste. Edgestitch close to the fold line. (Illus. 23)

Claire's Hint: Gauge-stitch to mark the hem allowance width for quicker, easier pressing. Stitch *almost but not quite* on the hemline. Fold next to the gauge-stitching, positioning the stitched line on the underside.

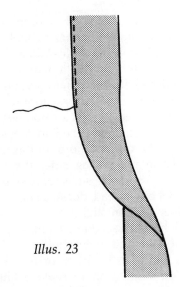

Illus. 23

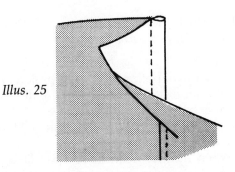

Illus. 25

MITRE

1. Press the hem allowances to the wrong side.
2. Clip the raw edges where they meet and mark the corner with a marking pen.
3. Refold the corners, right sides together. Stitch from the clips to the corner. (Illus. 24)
4. Trim as needed. Press.
5. Turn right side out.

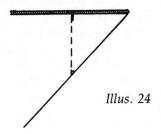

Illus. 24

SEAMS

French Seams

   A seam within a seam, a French seam is used when the appearance of the inside or wrong side of the item is important.
1. Wrong sides together, stitch a narrow ¼" seam.
2. Press and trim to remove any whiskers.
3. Right sides together, stitch a wide ¼" seam. (Illus. 25)
Claire's Hint: When stitching the first seam, align the raw edges with the edge of the presser foot and set the needle position to the extreme right. When stitching the second seam, align the first seam line with the edge of the presser foot and set the needle position to the extreme left.

Hairline Seams

   Despite their fragile appearance, these seams are very sturdy.
1. Right sides together, stitch on the seam line.
2. Trim to ⅛".
3. Zigzag (W,2-L,1) over the trimmed edge, allowing the needle to swing off the fabric each time it swings to the right. (Illus. 26)

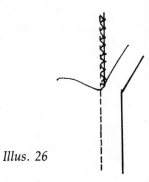

Illus. 26

STRAPS, TIES, TABS AND HANDLES

   This frequently used technique is particularly useful for making strong, smooth strips.
   Wrong sides together, press in half lengthwise; fold the raw edges to the pressed line; and press again. (Illus. 27)

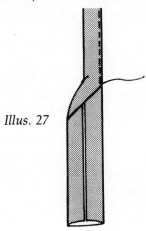

Illus. 27

Edgestitch the folds together. If desired, edge-stitch the other side of the strip.

ZIPPERS

The zipper application for gift projects is much easier than for garments. Use these directions for the gifts unless directed otherwise.

1. Right sides together, join the gift and the zipper with a ¼" seam. (Illus. 28a)
2. When the gift is lined, join the lining to the zipper. Right sides together with the zipper sandwiched between, stitch through all layers.
3. Right sides up, press the fabric away from the zipper.
4. Edgestitch through all layers close to the seam line. (Illus. 28b)

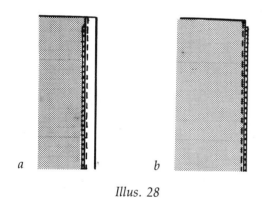

Illus. 28

Techniques for Machine Appliqué

GENERAL TIPS

Fabric Notes: Firmly woven fabrics are the easiest to use.

Preshrink the appliqué and background fabrics before stitching, using the same laundering method planned for the item. Preshrinking also removes fabric finishes, which sometimes cause skip-stitching.

Press with spray starch or fabric finish to add body to limp fabrics.

1. Use an embroidery foot. An open-toed foot allows better visibility, but a regular embroidery foot holds the fabric more securely. A regular zigzag foot will cause a thread jam.
2. Universal ballpoint needles work well on most fabrics. The size varies with the material and thread; however, always use the smallest size that doesn't cause skipped stitches.

To avoid skipped stitches, always start with a new needle.

3. To satin-stitch, set the stitch length so the stitches are close enough together to look like a solid line. This will probably be less than .5mm.
4. Set the stitch width between 2mm and 4mm so that the stitch will be wide enough to cover the raw edges and hold them securely forevermore.
5. Loosen the upper tension for a smoother, prettier satin stitch or tighten the bobbin tension by turning the screw ¼ turn (or more) to the right.
Claire's Hints: From the wrong side, the needle thread will show on both sides of the bobbin thread. If the bobbin thread doesn't show at all, tighten the upper tension slightly.

Consider purchasing a second bobbin case to use for machine appliqué and embroidery.

6. Clean the machine every three or four hours. Use a brush and canned air to remove lint and fibres that collect between the throat plate and feed dog. The old saying, "Cleanliness is next to godliness" applies to your sewing machine.

Often, a small appliqué will have as many stitches as an entire garment.

7. Use good-quality machine embroidery thread. To prevent disappointment, avoid cheap bargains.

Use white darning cotton in the bobbin unless otherwise indicated.

8. Place a piece of stabilizer between the background fabric and the machine base to prevent tunnelling and skipped stitches.
9. Stitch slowly and evenly to reduce puckering. If your machine has a low gear, shift down.
10. Always guide the work without pulling it or holding it back.

STITCHING TECHNIQUES

Turning Outward Corners

Stitch to the corner. Take one stitch off the appliqué, stopping with the needle in the right-hand position. Pivot and continue stitching. (Illus. 29)

The stitches will overlap at the corner.

Illus. 29

Turning Inward Corners

Stitch to the corner. Continue stitching into the appliqué for a distance equal to the stitch width. For example: A 3mm stitch width is ⅛″ wide; 4mm is about 3⁄16″.

Stop with the needle in the left-hand position. Pivot and continue stitching. (Illus. 30)

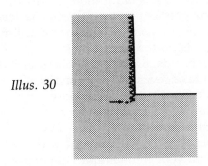

Illus. 30

Stitching Points

Reduce the stitch width when approaching a point. Pivot at the point. Increase the stitch width when stitching away from a point. (Illus. 31)

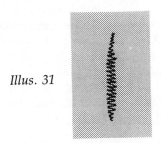

Illus. 31

Stitching Curves

For outward curves, pivot only when the needle is in the right-hand position and off the edge of the appliqué. For smooth curves, pivot frequently. (Illus. 32)

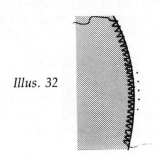

Illus. 32

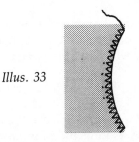

Illus. 33

For inward curves, pivot only when the needle is in the left-hand position and on the appliqué. For smooth curves, pivot frequently. (Illus. 33)

Claire's Hint: To help you remember where the needle should be for pivoting: On outward curves, pivot "outside" the fabric; on inward curves pivot in the fabric.

APPLYING APPLIQUÉS

There are more than a dozen different techniques for applying machine appliqués. In this book, only two were used—the Fusing Method and the Upside-Down Method.

If this is your first experience with machine appliqué, you'll find these techniques quick and easy to master. If you are experienced and prefer another method, use it instead.

The Fusing Method

The Fusing Method—utilizing a release sheet—differs from some other fusing methods.

When the appliqué is fused to the background, it becomes a little stiff and rarely puckers when you satin-stitch, even if you don't use a stabilizer or an embroidery hoop.

There are two major disadvantages. When appliqués are fused to quilted fabrics, the quilting shows through. And the weight, heat and/or moisture required for the fusing process will damage some appliqués.

1. Using a release sheet (*see Glossary*), bond fusible web to the wrong side of the appliqué fabric(s).
Claire's Hint: An Elnapress is a wonderful aid when fusing.
2. Trace the design(s) on the fabric(s) and cut out.
3. Right sides up, fuse the appliqué(s) to the background fabric.
4. Satin-stitch around the appliqué.
5. Press.

The Upside-Down Method

In the Upside-Down Method, the appliqués retain their tactile quality.

1. Trace the appliqué design on the wrong side of the fabric. If it is a dark-colored fabric, trace it onto paper or stabilizer which can be pinned to the fabric.
2. Cut a square appliqué patch at least one inch wider and longer than the appliqué.
3. Right sides up, pin the appliqué square to the background fabric, placing the pins near the perimeter of the appliqué patch to avoid stitching over them.
4. Shorten the stitch length to 1.5mm (18 spi).
5. Wrong side up, stitch on the design lines.
6. Right side up, use appliqué scissors to trim the appliqué patch close to the stitched line.
7. Satin-stitch around the appliqué.
8. Press.

Techniques for Machine Embroidery

SIMPLE ZIGZAG EMBROIDERY

Machine embroidery doesn't have to be difficult or complicated. The embroidery on the Toy Bag and matching pillow (page 150) as well as the monogram on the Corduroy Tote Bag (page 95) is done with a zigzag machine.

Review the General Tips for Machine Appliqué as well as the Stitching Techniques and practise a little before beginning.

FREEHAND EMBROIDERY

For many machine artists, freehand embroidering is more fun than eating. The gift projects in this book—the Pet Neckerchief (page 180) and the Sunshine Pot Holder (page 46)—feature the simplest of designs, just to introduce you to this exciting art form.

Freehand embroidery is done without a zigzag, embroidery, or all-purpose presser foot.
1. Stretch the fabric in a machine embroidery hoop. Put the large ring—with the screw—on the table. Place the fabric, right side up, on top.
Claire's Hint: To hold the fabric snugly, wrap the outer ring with twill tape or flat bias strips. Cover with the small ring. Close the rings with the inner ring about ⅛" below the outer one. Tighten the screw.

To prevent skip-stitching, use a piece of stabilizer between the large ring and the fabric. Experienced stitchers sometimes stitch without stabilizer; I like the insurance.
2. Lower or cover the feed dogs; or set the stitch length at 0.

3. Remove the presser foot and replace it with the darning foot or darning spring. Or you can sew without the foot, if you can keep your fingers out of the way.
4. Loosen the upper tension or tighten the bobbin tension.
5. Slide the hoop in place. Some of my hoops are too thick to slide under the foot easily. Position the hoop while the foot is off.
6. Lower the presser foot lever. When the lever is up, there is no tension and the thread will make balls and knots on the underside.
7. Lock the threads. Bring the bobbin thread to the surface and take several stitches in place.
Claire's Hint: Do not cut off the ends until after you've embroidered an inch or two.
8. Set the stitch width to 4mm.
9. Rest your arms on the machine bed and hold the hoop with your thumbs and little fingers.
10. Write the desired name on the fabric with a pencil.
11. Stitch, moving the hoop smoothly either sideways or back and forth. Do not rotate the hoop. And try to relax.
Claire's Hints: To prevent skip-stitching, use your middle fingers to press the fabric against the machine.

To avoid breaking needles, don't move the fabric too far, too quickly; and don't pull the work forward when you've finished.

Practise, practise, practise.

Techniques for Heirloom Machine-Stitching

The techniques called Heirloom Machine-Stitching or French Hand-Sewing by Machine, feature beautiful laces, insertions, and fine fabrics which can be new or antique, matched designs or assorted, handmade or purchased.

For centuries, the art of French hand-sewing was used to create exquisite undergarments and dressing gowns. It reached its height between 1870 and 1910 when tea gowns and elaborate blouses were popular. Today only a few devoted artisans practise this beautiful art.

Fortunately for those of us who like this look of yesteryear, but don't have the time or patience to pursue the art of hand-sewing, a simple zigzag machine can be used to make those time-consuming hand-stitches and create elaborate gifts in a fraction of the time.

STITCHING TECHNIQUES

1. Finish the edge. Some directions call this turn and stitch or roll and whip; a few eliminate this step. To eliminate fraying and preserve the life of the gift, all edges should be finished before being joined to entredeux or lace.

Fold the seam allowance to the wrong side and zigzag (W,1-L,1) over the edge of the fabric. Trim close to the zigzag stitching, using appliqué scissors for a close trim.

2. Join entredeux and fabric. Finish the edge; trim away the fabric on one side of the entredeux. Right sides up, butt the edges of the fabric and entredeux together. Zigzag (W,2-L,1) to join them.

Claire's Hint: It's very difficult to distinguish the right and wrong sides of entredeux. According to lace expert and importer, Martha Pullen, "if it takes more than 15 seconds, it doesn't matter."

3. Join entredeux and lace. Right sides up, butt the edges together and zigzag (W,2-L,1). To avoid stretching the lace, stitch entredeux to fabric, before joining it to lace.

4. Join lace insertions. Right sides up, butt the edges together; zigzag (W,2-L,1).

5. Join ribbon strips to each other or lace. Butt the edges together; zigzag (W,2-L,1).

6. Apply lace galloons and medallions. Right sides up, baste the lace in place. Zigzag (W,1-L,.5) the edge to the fabric. Wrong sides up, trim close to the stitched line to remove the fabric under the lace. (Illus. 34)

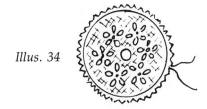

Illus. 34

7. Gather the lace. When the lace has a heavy thread at the edge, pull this thread to gather the lace. When there is no heavy thread, machine-stitch (12 spi or 2mm) close to the edge; then pull up the bobbin thread. Generally, lace is gathered 1½ times for fullness.

8. Join gathered lace to straight lace, entredeux, or fabric. Right sides up, butt the edges together. Adjust the gathers with the point of a needle as you stitch.

9. Puffed strips. Machine-stitch two rows on each side of the strip—one on the seam line and the

Illus. 35

other ⅜" from the raw edge. Pull up the bobbin threads until the strip is the desired length and adjust the gathers. Fold and stitch (W,1-L,1) at the seam line. Trim close to the zigzag stitches. (Illus. 35)

10. Pin tucks. Pull a thread to mark the location of each tuck. Wrong sides together, fold the fabric on the tuck line. Press and stitch close to the edge, using the inside of the straight-stitch presser foot as a guide. (Illus. 36)

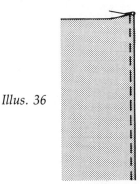

Illus. 36

11. Scalloped tucks. Set the machine for a hemming stitch (W,3-L,1). With the bulk of the fabric to the *right* of the needle, stitch so that the needle swings off the edge of the tuck to form a scallop. (Illus. 37)

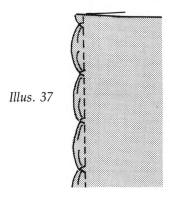

Illus. 37

GENERAL TIPS

Fabric Notes: Firmly woven, natural-fibre fabrics such as handkerchief linen, Swiss batiste, pima cotton, lawn, and silk broadcloth are preferred. However, there are also some beautiful cotton/polyester blends for easy-care gifts.

Generally, imported laces and trims are much more beautiful than domestic ones. Some are available in all cotton; others are 90% cotton and 10% nylon. Most require ironing.

1. Preshrink all fabric and trims before cutting them, especially when sewing on natural fibres.

To preshrink trims, place each trim in a separate nylon stocking. Tie the top of the stocking; machine-wash and dry.

2. Use small machine needles (Sizes: 8/60, 10/70, or 12/80).

3. Experiment with the stitch length-width if those suggested don't give the desired results. Machines and materials vary and some fine tuning may be needed.

4. When beginning to stitch, hold the needle and bobbin threads securely to prevent the lace and fabric from being pulled into the needle hole. If you are still having problems, stitch 2"–3" on a piece of paper or nonwoven stabilizer before stitching onto the lace and/or fabric.

5. Use French seams, hairline seams and insertions to join fabrics.

6. Cut fabric and lace strips about 2" longer than needed to avoid being caught short; or, join the lace to the corresponding section; then cut.

7. Mark matchpoints on lace, entredeux, and fabric with a fadeaway marking pen.

COOKS' CORNER

POSH PICNIC BASKET

This elegant picnic basket will make any picnic outing a special occasion. Outfit one for a wedding gift or a handsome hostess gift; and, of course, you'll want one for family outings and tailgate parties.

The large basket has been lined and outfitted with a 44" square tablecloth, one wine-bottle bag, a silverware caddy, 4 wineglasses in their own individual storage bags, 4 napkins, silverware, a cutting board, knife, can opener, and corkscrew.

Finished Sizes: Basket, 15" × 11" × 13"; Picnic cloth, 44" square; Napkins, 17½" square; Wine-bottle bag, 13" × 4" cylinder; Wineglass bags, 5½" × 10½"; Silverware caddy, 6" × 16"

Materials

Material requirements are for a completely outfitted picnic basket. Individual requirements are listed with the Sewing Directions.
Basket, 15" × 11" × 13"
Fabric A, quilted (basket liner, wine-bottle bag, and silverware caddy), 1⅜ yard, 45" wide
Fabric B (picnic cloth and wineglass bags), 1⅞ yard, 45" wide
Fabric C (napkins and silverware caddy lining), 1 yard, 45" wide
Fleece or needlepunch insulation, one piece 18" × 15" Ribbon, 2½ yards, ¼" wide

Bias binding, 2 yards
Double-sided hem tape or Rug-N-Carpet tape, 1 pkg.

Other items:
Wineglasses, 4
Silverware for four
Cutting board
Knife
Can opener
Corkscrew

QUILTED BASKET LINER

The quilted basket liner is sized for a rattan mini-trunk. Directions are included for cutting a lining to fit a different kind or size basket.
Finished Size: 15" × 11" × 13"

Materials

Basket, one 15" × 11" × 13"
Fabric A, quilted, 1⅜ yards, 45" wide
Double-sided tape, such as hem tape or Rug-N-Carpet tape, 1 pkg.

Cutting Directions

1. From Fabric A (quilted), cut one bottom 36½" × 32" and one top 18½" × 15".
2. If your basket is a different size, measure the inside of the basket to determine the liner size.

Begin at one side of the basket, measure to the bottom, across the bottom, and up the other side; add 2" to this measurement.

To determine the liner length: Begin at the front of the basket, measure to the bottom, across the bottom, and up the other side; add 2".
Claire's Hint: Save the large scraps to make pot holders and hot-mats (page 101).

Sewing Directions

1. Make the liner for the basket. Right sides together, pin a triangle at each corner of the basket liner 11″ from the corner. (Illus. 38)
2. Place the liner in the basket with the wrong side up to check the fit.

The distance around the top of the liner should be exactly the same as the inside of the basket. The liner should extend 1″ above the top of the basket to allow for turning the raw edges in. If the liner is larger or smaller than the basket, repin the corners so that the liner will fit properly.
3. Stitch the triangles as pinned; then trim the seam allowances to ½″.
4. Fold the 1″ extension at the top to the wrong

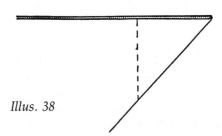

Illus. 38

side and stitch ¼″ from the edge. Position the liner in the basket, using a double-sided tape like hem tape or Rug-N-Carpet tape to secure it.
5. Make liner for the basket top. Pin a triangle 2″ from each corner. Check to be sure it fits; then stitch. Fold the raw edge under 1″ and stitch ¼″ from the fold. Tape the liner in place.

• • •

WINE-BOTTLE BAG

Finished Size: 13″ × 4″ cylinder

Materials

Remnant A (quilted), one 18″ × 15″
Fleece or needlepunch, one 13½″ × 13″
Ribbon, ½ yard, ¼″ wide
Fabric Notes: I used the leftovers from the basket liner to make the wine-bottle bag. Both fleece and needlepunch insulation provide extra protection against breakage. I prefer needlepunch because it insulates better.

Cutting Directions

1. From the quilted fabric, cut one rectangle 13½″ × 15″ and one 4½″ circle for the bottom.
2. From the fleece or needlepunch, cut one rectangle 13½″ × 13″.

Sewing Directions

1. All seam allowances are ¼″.

2. Pin the fleece to the wrong side of the bag. To avoid unnecessary bulk, the fleece is 2″ shorter.
3. Place a horizontal buttonhole 2⅜″ from the top of the bag for the casing ribbon. Position it about 3″ from one side and make it ½″ long.
4. Right sides together, stitch the bag from top to bottom.
5. Press and turn right side out.
6. At the top of the bag, fold 2″ to the wrong side, enclosing the raw edge of the fleece. The buttonhole will be on the outside of the bag ⅜″ below the fold line. Topstitch around the top ¾″ from the fold and again 1½″. Press.
7. Join the bag and bottom, right sides together, pin and stitch. Before you join the two sections, place a row of gauge-stitching at the bottom of the bag ¼″ from the raw edge. Clip the seam allowance to the stitched line every ½″; then pin the sections together. You'll be surprised how easy this makes a difficult-to-stitch seam.
8. Turn right side out and insert an 18″ casing ribbon.

• • •

NAPKINS

Finished Size: 17½″ square

Materials

Remnant C, one 36″ square

Directions

1. Cut four 18" squares.
2. Finish the edges of the napkins with a narrow satin stitch. Fold under ¼" and satin-stitch (W,2.5) over the folded edge. As you finish each side of the napkin, trim away the excess hem allowance. Stitch and trim until the napkin is finished.

Claire's Hints: Generally, use an embroidery foot. However, if you have a Bernina, use the buttonhole foot; if you have an Elna, use foot B.

To save time, stitch one side on each napkin; trim; then stitch the next side on each napkin. Repeat until all four napkins are finished.

Use appliqué scissors to get a really close trim.

• • •

PICNIC CLOTH

Finished Size: 44" square

Materials

Fabric B, 1¼ yards, 45" wide

Directions

1. From Fabric B, cut the tablecloth 45" square.
2. Finish all edges with a narrow hem.

• • •

WINEGLASS BAGS

Finished Size: 5½" × 10½"

Materials

Remnant B, four 11" × 11½"
Ribbon, 2 yards, ¼" wide

Sewing Directions

1. All seam allowances are ¼".
2. Place a horizontal buttonhole 1¼" from the top of the bag for the casing ribbon. Position it about 3" from one side and make it ½" long.

3. Make the bag. Fold the bag section in half lengthwise with the right sides together. Stitch across the bottom and up the side. Turn the bag right side out.
4. Make the casing at the top of the bag. Fold 1" to the inside—the buttonhole should be ¼" below the fold line. Turn the raw edge under ¼"; stitch the casing. Press.
5. Repeat for the other bags.
6. Cut the ribbon into 18" lengths and thread into the casings.

• • •

SILVERWARE CADDY

Finished Size: 6" × 16"

Materials

Remnant A, quilted (caddy), one 12" × 16"
Remnant C (caddy lining), one 6" × 16"
Bias binding, 1⅝ yards

Cutting Directions

1. From Remnant A (quilted), cut one 6" × 16" rectangle and one 6" square.
2. From Remnant C, cut one 6" × 16" lining.

Sewing Directions

1. Round all corners on the quilted rectangle. Wrong sides together, glue-baste the caddy and lining. (Illus. 39) Do not, however, round the lining corners until after stitching.

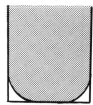

Illus. 39

2. Bind the top of the pocket.
3. Join the pocket and caddy. Pin the pocket to the lined section. Zigzag (W,2-L,2) all the layers together, following the outline of the section with rounded corners.
4. Trim all corners.
5. Bind the edges. To make the binding-join inconspicuous, I begin binding even with the top edge of the pocket.

6. Make the ties. Fold ¾ yard of the bias binding in half and zigzag (W,2-L,2) down the center of the strip. Center and pin a tie to the quilted side of the top and bottom. Stitch it in place.
7. Divide the pocket in half and stitch the center of the pocket.
Claire's Hint: Use a fadeaway marking pen to mark the stitching line.

• • •

NO-NONSENSE APRON

This no-nonsense apron has three handy pockets and ties long enough to tie in front so the chef can tuck a towel in the waist. It also provides a perfect background for an appliqué design.
Finished Size: 30″ × 31″

Materials

Fabric A, 1 yard, 45″ wide
Twill tape, 3 yards, 1″ wide
D-rings, 1 pair ¾″

Cutting Directions

1. Enlarge the apron pattern. (Illus. 40)
2. From the fabric, cut one apron and one 8½″ × 31″ pocket.

Sewing Directions

1. All seam allowances are ¼″; the pocket hem allowance is 1″; all other hem allowances are ½″.
2. Hem the pocket. Press 1″ to the wrong side; fold the raw edge under ¼″ and edgestitch.

Photo also shows pot holders on pp 43–45 and scalloped cocktail napkins on p. 32.

3. Right sides together, align the bottom and sides of the apron with the hem and sides of the pocket. Stitch the seam at the bottom of the pocket. (Illus. 41)

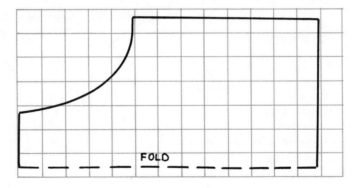

Illus. 40. ¼″ = 2″

FOLD

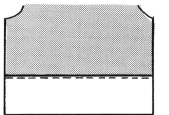

Illus. 41

4. Complete the pocket. Fold and press the pocket into place; baste the sides of the pocket and apron together. Divide and stitch the pocket into three equal sections.

Claire's Hint: Use a fadeaway marking pen to indicate the stitching lines.

5. Make the neck ties. Cut two strips of twill tape—3″ and 23″ long. Thread the shorter piece into the D-rings; fold in half to make a loop and baste both ends together.

6. Set the neck ties to the wrong side of the apron. Matching the raw edges to the top of the apron; baste.

7. Set the waist ties. Cut the remaining tape into two equal pieces. Wrong sides up, pin to the apron sides about ½″ below the curve.

8. Make a narrow machine hem around the apron, folding the ties into place as you stitch.

9. Press.

• • •

CHEF'S DELIGHT

This special apron is perfect for the man who likes to cook. He'll particularly enjoy wearing it for picnics and backyard barbecues.

Materials

Remnant A (apron vest, pockets, ties), one 40″ × 27″
Remnant B (apron skirt), one 31″ × 25″
Bias binding, 4 yards
Buttons, four ½″ or ⅝″
Fabric Notes: Select a firmly woven easy-care fabric.

Cutting Directions

1. Enlarge the pattern for the apron top. (Illus. 42)
2. From Remnant A, cut the apron vest, two 5″ × 4½″ pocket welts, and two 4″ × 27″ ties.
3. From Remnant B, cut a 31″ × 25″ apron skirt.

Sewing Directions

1. Seam allowances are ½″ except as noted; hem allowances are ½″.
2. Make the pockets. Right sides together, fold the pocket welts in half, crosswise. Stitch a ¼″ seam at each end. Turn right side out; press.
3. Right sides together, match the welt raw edges and the pocket-placement line; stitch a ¼″ seam. (Illus. 43)

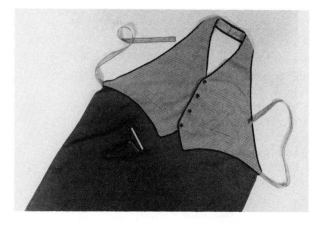

4. Fold the pockets into place and edgestitch the ends.
5. Right sides together, join the back neckline seam on the vest. Press.

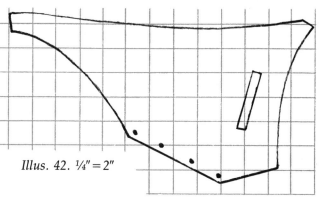

Illus. 42. ¼″ = 2″

6. Bind the edges of the vest.

7. Make the ties. Wrong sides together, press the ties in half; fold the raw edges in to the fold line; and edgestitch both sides of the ties.

8. Pin the vest sections together, overlapping them 1½" at the center front. Sew the buttons on, catching both layers. Remember, men's vests lap left over right.

9. Right sides together, stitch the ties to the sides of the vest.

10. Hem the sides and bottom of the skirt with a narrow machine hem. Pink the top edge.

11. Right sides up, place the skirt on a flat surface. Cover the pinked edge with the vest, overlapping ½". Pin and stitch following the edge of the vest. Press.

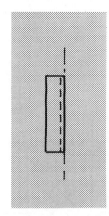

Illus. 43

• • •

COUNTRY APRON

This colorful calico apron should delight any country lover.

Materials

Fabric A (skirt and straps), 1¼ yards, 45" wide
Fabric B, quilted (apron bib), one 6¾" × 10"
Narrow bias binding, ½ yard

Cutting Directions

1. From Fabric A, cut one 45" × 27" skirt, two 34" × 3" straps, three 24" × 3" waistband strips, and one 7½" × 14½" pocket. (Illus. 44)

Sewing Directions

1. All seam and hem allowances are ½".

2. Make the pocket. Wrong sides together, fold the pocket in half crosswise and stitch the sides and bottom. Trim the corners. Make a 2"–3" slash in the center of the pocket. (Illus. 45a) Turn right side out through the slash. Press.

3. Edgestitch the pocket to the skirt 11½" from the bottom and 10" from the right side.

4. Hem the skirt sides and bottom with a narrow machine hem.

5. Right sides together, join the three waistband strips.

6. Gather the top of the skirt. Right sides up and the skirt on top, pin and stitch the skirt to the center section of the waistband.

Claire's Hints: To distribute the gathers evenly, divide and mark the skirt and center waistband section into quarters; match and stitch.

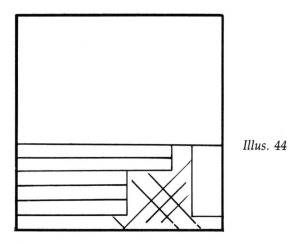

Illus. 44

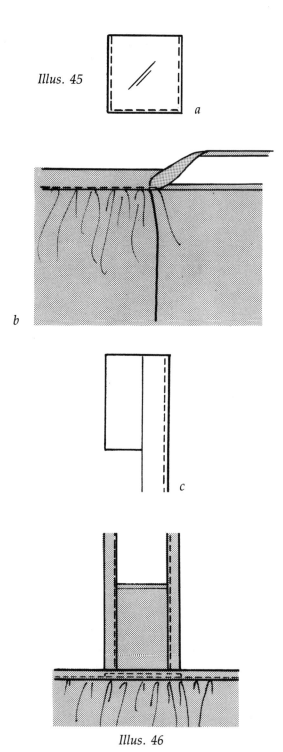

Illus. 45

a

b

c

Illus. 46

To make the gathering rows: Use a heavy thread, such as buttonhole twist. Right side up, zigzag (W,2-L,2) over the thread; and pull up to gather. Make a knot at the beginning so the thread won't pull through.

7. Finish the skirt waistband. Press the waistband seam allowance towards the band. Fold the band to the right side of the skirt; fold the raw edge under ½"; pin. Wrong sides together, fold ties in half lengthwise; with the seam allowances in between and the folded edges aligned, pin. Edgestitch the ties and band. (Illus. 45b)

8. Make the apron bib. Bind the top and bottom of the bib with bias binding.

9. Finish the bib. Fold the ends of both straps under ½"; glue-baste.

10. Wrong sides up, stitch the straps to the sides of the bib. (Illus. 45c)

11. Finish the straps like the skirt waistband.

12. Right sides up, center the bib under the skirt, overlapping the edge 1¼". Pin.

13. Right sides up, stitch a rectangle on the waistband to secure the apron bib. (Illus. 46)

EYELET HOSTESS APRON

This elegant apron can be worn year-round on festive occasions; yet it is practical enough for every day. Made in embroidered eyelet, this is a lovely gift for Mother's Day or for someone special.

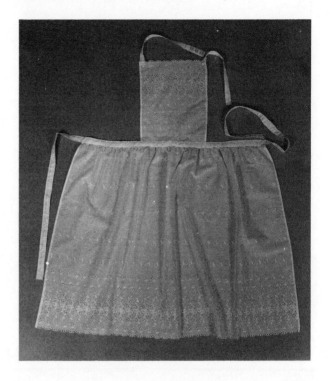

Materials

Eyelet, 1½ yards, 45" wide
Eyelet trim, 2⅝ yards, ¾" wide
Satin ribbon, ⅝ yard, 1" wide
Buttons, three ½"
Fabric Notes: I selected an easy-care, cotton/polyester eyelet.

Cutting Directions

1. Cut one 25" × 43" skirt, aligning one long edge with the eyelet scallops. (Illus. 47)
2. Cut one 11½" × 11" bib, aligning one short edge with the eyelet scallops.
3. Cut two 1¾" × 36" waistband facings.
4. Cut two strips of eyelet trim—72" and 22½" long.

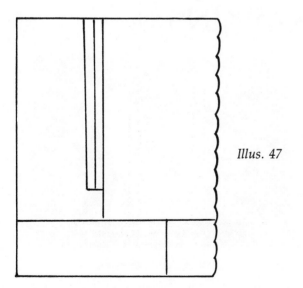

Illus. 47

Sewing Directions

1. All seam and hem allowances are ½".
2. Finish the sides of the bib and skirt with a narrow hem.
3. Place two rows of gathering stitches along the upper edge of the apron skirt. Use buttonhole twist on the bobbin; loosen the upper tension; and set the stitch length to 8 spi (3mm). Wrong side up, stitch twice—first ½" from the edge and again midway between the seam line and raw edge.

When adjusting the gathers, the heavy bobbin thread will pull up easily without breaking.
4. Right sides together, join the two waistband facings. (For fabric economy, there is a seam at the center front.)
5. Divide and mark the top of the skirt into quarters.
6. Using short snips, mark the waistband facing 6" and 12" from the center front on each side.
7. Join the skirt and facing. Right sides up and the skirt on top, match and pin the marked points. Pull up the gathering threads and adjust the gathers. To secure the gathering thread, place a pin at each end of the gathering rows. Wrap the thread around the pin in a figure-eight pattern. Stitch.
8. Join the bib and waistband facing. Right sides up with the bib on top, match the centers; pin and stitch.
9. Press all seam allowances towards the waistband facing. Press the seam allowances on the sides and ends of the band to the wrong side ½". (Illus. 48)

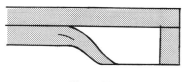

Illus. 48

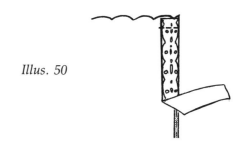

Illus. 50

10. Finish the waistband. Pin the eyelet trim to the facing, covering all the raw edges. Turn under the seam allowance at each end. Edgestitch all edges. (Illus. 49)

Illus. 49

11. Make the straps. Wrong sides together, stitch the eyelet trim to the ribbon. Cut into two straps: 10½″; 12″.

12. Join the straps and apron. Wrong sides together, match the raw edge of the strap to the scal-loped edge of the bib. Pin and stitch ½″ from the top. (Illus. 50)

13. Trim the seam allowance on the strap to ¼″. Fold the strap over the raw edge and stitch again through all layers.

14. Repeat for the other strap.

15. Zigzag (W,2-L,1) the ends of the strap to prevent fraying.

16. Make one ½″ buttonhole on the end of the short strap.

17. Sew the buttons on the other strap, spacing them about ½″ apart.

• • •

BORDERED NAPKINS

Finished with double hems and mitred corners, these napkins are especially attractive when made in organdy and voile.
Finished Size: 18″ square

Materials

Material requirements are for four napkins.
Remnant A, one 26″ × 104″ (approximately 3 yards)
Fabric Notes: Select a fabric which doesn't have an obvious wrong side. These napkins are particularly attractive in sheer fabrics. I used a polyester/cotton voile.

Cutting Directions

1. Cut four 26″ squares.
2. Using the pattern, shape the corners on each napkin. (Illus. 51)
3. To make a larger-size napkin or tablecloth, cut the fabric 8″ wider and longer than the desired finished size.

Sewing Directions

1. To mitre the corners, stitch right sides together. (Illus. 52)
Claire's Hint: To save time, chain-stitch from one corner to the next without breaking threads until all the corners are completed.
2. Turn right side out. Press.
3. Fold in the raw edges; press; and edgestitch. (Illus. 53)

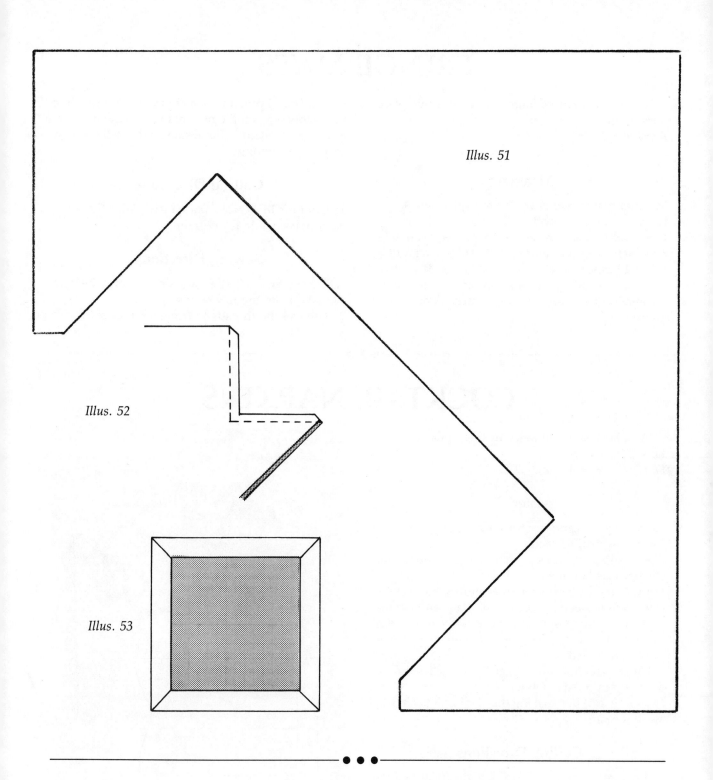

Illus. 51

Illus. 52

Illus. 53

FRINGE MATS

For informal entertaining, these attractive place mats are sure to be a hit.
Finished Size: 18″ × 12½″

Materials

Material requirements are for four place mats.
Fabric, ¾ yard, 45″ wide
Fabric Notes: Select an easy-to-fringe, easy-care fabric which looks the same on both sides. The multicolored stripe which I used had heavy decorative yarns in the filling (cross grain) and small black, inconspicuous yarns in the warp (lengthwise grain).

Claire's Hint: Spray the mats with one of the fabric protectors now on the market to make them water- and soil-repellent. This coating will last through several launderings.

Cutting Directions

1. Cut four 18″ × 12½″ place mats. Pull a thread to be sure each side is on-grain.

Sewing Directions

1. Zigzag (W,2-L,2) the short sides ¾″ and the long sides ¼″ from the raw edges.
2. Unravel the threads to fringe all four sides.

• • •

COCKTAIL NAPKINS

Most hostesses will welcome these practical napkins.
Finished Size: 8″ square

Materials

Fabric requirements are for four napkins.
Fabric, ¼ yard, 45″ wide
Bias binding, 4 yards or remnant 30″ square for custom bias bindings.
Fabric Notes: Fabrics like piqué, shirtings and polyester/cotton blends, which don't have an obvious right and wrong side are particularly nice. Trim them with a fancy binding. Or you may prefer print fabrics with solid trim.

These napkins are especially attractive when made up in holiday fabrics.
Claire's Hint: When making the bias bindings, try to avoid a seam.

Cutting Directions

1. Enlarge the pattern, placing both straight edges on a fold. (Illus. 54)
2. Cut 4 napkins.

Sewing Directions

1. Baste the bias around the napkin edge. Allow

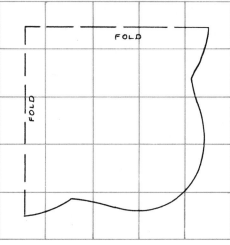

Illus. 54.
½″ = 1″

Above: This elegant picnic basket will make any outing a special occasion. Outfit one for a wedding or hostess gift. Left: These cleverly designed, easy-to-make pillows are made from bandanas.

French bread warmer, coasters, a basket liner, pot holders and reversible place mats make practical presents.

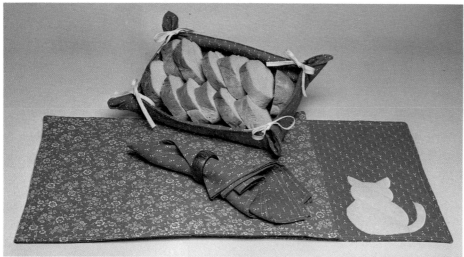

Cat fanciers will love this place mat/napkin ensemble. The bread basket shown also doubles as a casserole jacket.

Designed originally for a friend who wanted to match her place mats to her stonewear, these will brighten any table. The sunshine pot holder will do the same for the kitchen.

B

The sturdy demim knap-sack and sailcloth tote bag are perfect for youngsters of all ages.

A quilted overnight bag, an appliquéd beach bag and a take-along duffel are all practical.

D

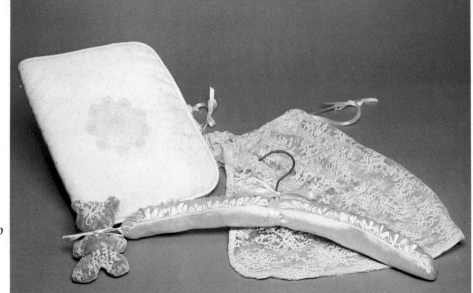

Top: Even the plainest stationery will look fancy in this elegant folder; with this lingerie bag, the most delicate underthings can go in the washing machine; and sachets are always sweet—especially in the form of teddy bears.

Bottom: That special woman deserves a set of ultra feminine closet accessories to treasure for years to come. Luxurious hangers, shoe stuffers, garment covers and a lingerie keeper will protect and preserve a wardrobe.

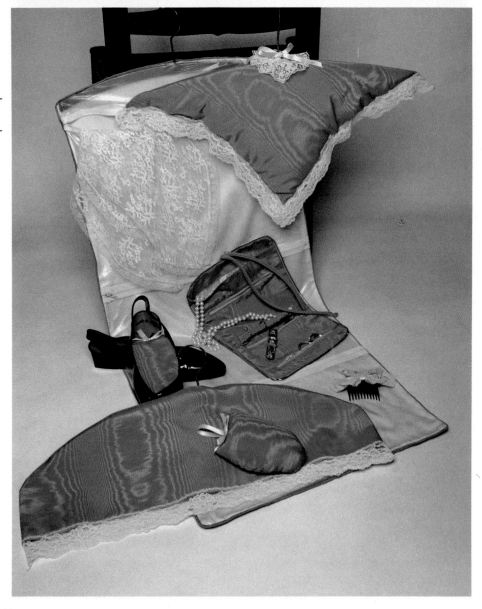

Opposite page: Just right for a weekend in the country or an overnight business trip, this travel ensemble includes a hanging garment bag and a weekend duffel.

E

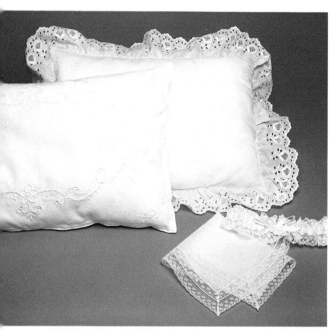

Top left: The pillowcases in white are perfect for a bride; the handkerchief and garter are intended for one. Top right: the flange and the decorator pillow are both simple to make. Bottom: This exquisite pillow is aptly named the heirloom pillow; the camisole will make any lady feel special; the needle book is a nice present for anyone who enjoys sewing.

F

Chic and contemporary, these lively pillows will brighten any room. What's more they can be made in fifteen minutes or less.

These beautiful towels look like Seminole patchwork, and they are—with a difference.

Add a touch of country with these easy-to-make towel sets.

G

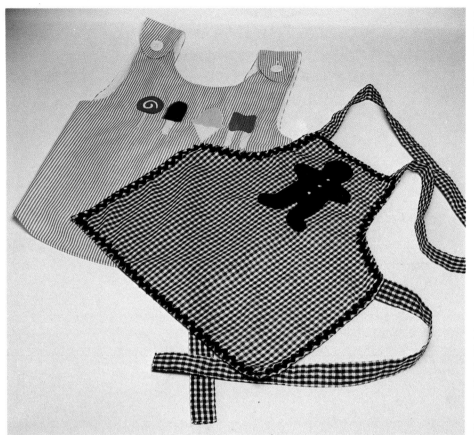

They're never too young to learn to cook and your favorite small chef will love either of these two appliquéd aprons.

There is also a pattern for a burping cloth to protect mom's or dad's shoulder which makes these bibs or the receiving blanket with them an ideal gift for a baby shower.

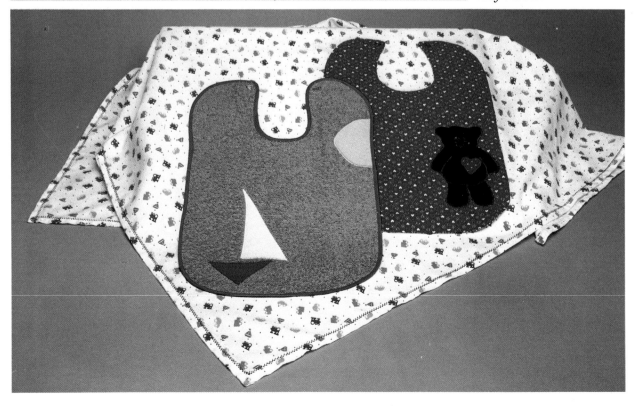

H

for a 1″ overlap at the end; cut off the excess. Fold the end under ¼″.

Claire's Hints: Fold and press the bias binding in half lengthwise to make it easier to shape.

To save time and temper when working with scallops, hand-baste the bias binding.
2. Stitch the binding in place.

* * *

OVERLOCKED NAPKINS

If you have one of the new home sergers, this is an excellent design with which to practise turning corners, as well as a gift that's always welcome.
Finished Size: Dinner Napkins, 18″ square; Luncheon, 15″ square

Materials

Material requirements for four 18″ napkins
Fabric A, 1 yard
Requirements for six 15″ napkins
Fabric A, ⅞ yard, 45″ wide

Sewing Directions

1. Cut out the napkin squares.
2. Following the directions with your machine, set it to make a narrow rolled hem.

3. Beginning at one corner, overlock one edge, slowing down as you reach the corner. Turn the handwheel manually to continue sewing until you make one stitch off the fabric. Raise the presser foot; turn the fabric and stitch the next edge. Continue until all sides are finished.

Claire's Hint: Serger expert Leonora Johnson taught me this trick for smooth corners. When you reach the edge, lift the needle and presser foot; pull the needle thread just below the tension disc to make the thread slack; then pull the thread chain off the back of the stitch finger.

Practise this technique several times to determine how much extra slack and thread is needed.
4. Seal the last corner with a dab of fray retardant to prevent ravelling.

* * *

APPLIQUÉ PLACE MATS

Designed originally for a friend who wanted to match her place mats to her Marimekko stoneware, these place mats will brighten any table.
Finished Size: 14½″ circle

Materials

Fabric requirements are for 6 place mats.
Fabric A (place mats), double-faced quilted, ⅞ yard, 45″ wide
Remnant B (blue flowers), six 4½″ squares
Remnant C (yellow flowers), six 4½″ squares
Remnant D (red flowers), six 4½″ squares
Remnant E (green stems), six 7″ squares
Wide bias binding, 9 yards
Stabilizer, 28″ × 42″

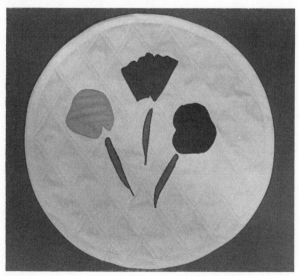

Machine embroidery thread: blue, yellow, red, green

Fabric Notes: If the quilted fabric you like isn't double-faced, purchase an equal amount of contrast fabric to line the mats.

Cutting Directions

1. From Fabric A, cut six 14″ circles for place mats.
2. From the stabilizer, cut six 14″ circles.
3. Enlarge and trace the patterns onto the stabilizer. (Illus. 55)

Sewing Directions

1. Wrong side up, pin the stabilizer to the place mat.
2. Right sides up, pin the Fabric B square to the place mat. From the wrong side, stitch around the design, using a short stitch. Turn the mat over and trim close to stitched line.

Claire's Hint: To save time, stitch all Fabric B appliqués to all the mats before stitching the other parts of the design.

3. Using embroidery thread, satin-stitch (W,2) around the design. Use the same color thread in the bobbin so that the wrong side will be as attractive as the right.
4. Repeat for each part of the appliqué until all mats are finished.
5. Bind the edges, beginning and ending at one side. Press.

Claire's Hint: Stitch the binding to the wrong side of the place mat first with a ⅛″ seam. Fold and press the binding to the right side and edgestitch in place.

Illus. 55

¾″ = 1″

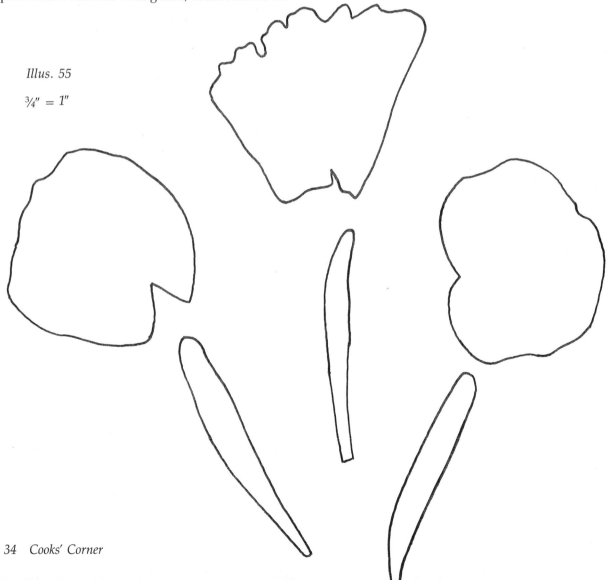

REVERSIBLE MATS

This country kitchen ensemble will brighten any table. The oval place mats reverse to a contrasting print.
Finished Size: Place mats, 18″ × 13″; Napkins, 17½″ square

Materials

Material requirements are for four place mats and four napkins.
Fabric A, quilted (place mat tops), ¾ yard, 45″ wide
Contrast B (linings), ¾ yard, 45″ wide
Contrast C (napkins), one 36″ square
Wide bias binding, 6 yards
Fusible web, 1½ yards, 18″ wide
Fabric Notes: When quilted fabrics aren't available, fuse fleece to the wrong side of Fabric A before cutting out.

Cutting Directions

1. Enlarge the place mat pattern and set it aside. (Illus. 56)

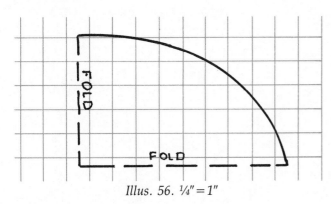

Illus. 56. ¼″ = 1″

2. From Fabric A, cut four 18″ × 13″ rectangles for the place mat tops.
3. From Contrast B, cut four 18″ × 13″ rectangles for the place mat linings.
4. From the fusible web, cut four 18″ × 13″ rectangles.

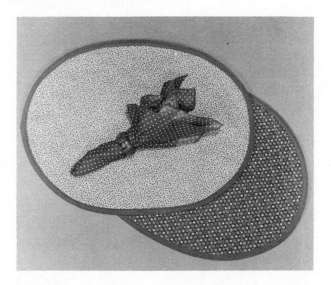

5. From Contrast C, cut four 18″ squares for the napkins.

Sewing Directions

PLACE MATS
1. Right sides out, make a sandwich with the fusible web between the place mat tops and linings. Fuse all layers together.
2. Using the place mat pattern, cut four mats from the fabric sandwiches. (Illus. 56)
3. Bind the edges with bias, beginning and ending at one side.

NAPKINS
1. Finish the edges with a narrow satin stitch. Fold under ¼″ and satin-stitch over the folded edge. Stop when you finish one side and trim away the excess hem allowance. Stitch and trim until the napkin is finished.
Claire's Hint: To save time, stitch one side of all four napkins; trim all napkins, and repeat the stitch-and-trim process on each napkin until all are finished.
2. Dab a little fray retardant at each napkin corner, using a toothpick to apply it.

CAT FANCIER ENSEMBLE

Cat fanciers will love this place mat/napkin ensemble. The feline design is an easy-to-make appliqué and should be a hit.

Finished Sizes: Place mats, 12" × 18"; Napkins, 17" square

Materials

Fabric requirements are for two place mats and two napkins.

Fabric A, quilted (place mat tops), ⅜ yard, 45" wide

Contrast B (linings), ⅜ yard, 45" wide

Contrast C (napkins), one 36" × 18"

Remnant D (appliqué—white), one 9" × 18"

Fabric Notes: I used a quilted fabric which had two

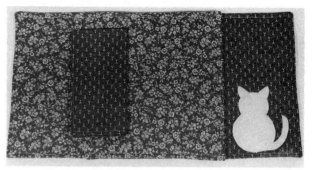

unquilted, companion prints. If the quilted fabric you select has only one companion print, cut the napkins and lining to match. When quilted fabric is unavailable, fuse a piece of polyester fleece to the wrong side of a plain fabric.

Illus. 57

Cutting Directions

1. Enlarge and trace the appliqué. (Illus. 57)
2. From Fabric A, cut two 13″ × 19″ place mat tops.
3. From Contrast B, cut two 13″ × 19″ linings.
4. From Contrast C, cut two 18″ square napkins.

Sewing Directions

PLACE MATS

1. All seam allowances are ½″.
2. Appliqué the designs to the quilted mat sections using the upside-down appliqué technique.
3. Right sides together, stitch each place mat and lining together, leaving one side open about 6″.
6. Turn right side out.
7. Fold the seam allowances in at the opening and topstitch ¼″ from the edge. Continue topstitching around the mat.

NAPKINS

1. All hem allowances are ½″.
2. Hem all edges with a narrow, machine hem.

• • •

EASY, ELEGANT PLACE MATS

These place mats are a sophisticated version of an old standby. Never out of style and always in good taste, make them for all your favorite hostesses.
Finished Size: 18″ × 12″

Materials

Fabric requirements are for four place mats.
Fabric, 1½ yards, 45″ wide
Craft-Fuse, ¾ yard
Fabric Notes: Choose a firmly woven fabric to coordinate with the decor. I used a linen/silk blend.

Cutting Directions

1. Enlarge the place mat pattern. (Illus. 58)
2. Cut four 19″ × 13″ lining rectangles.
3. Fuse the Craft-Fuse to the back of the remaining fabric; then, using the place mat pattern, cut four 19″ × 13″ tops.

Sewing Directions

1. All seam allowances are ½″.
2. Make the mats. Right sides together, join the top and lining, leaving 4″ open on one long side. Repeat for all mats.
3. Trim away the excess lining and trim all corners.
4. Turn the mats right side out; press.

Claire's Hint: Press the seam allowances of the unstitched section in and align the folded edges.
5. Edgestitch all edges, closing the unstitched section as you stitch; press.

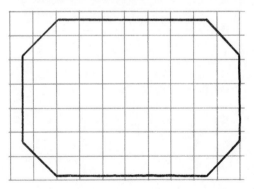

Illus. 58.
¼″ = 2″

COUNTRY MATS

Perfect for a country kitchen, this place mat set is certain to be a hit. Completely reversible with mitred corners, the lining material makes an attractive band around the mats.
Finished Size: Place mats, 19″ × 12½″; Napkins, 17″ square

Materials

Fabric requirements are for four place mats and four napkins.
Fabric A, quilted (tops), ¾ yard, 45″ wide
Contrast B (linings and napkins), 2⅛ yards, 45″ wide
Optional: Fleece, one 25″ × 40″
Fabric Notes: Select two coordinated fabrics. I used a quilted material for the tops; however, if the fabric selected isn't quilted, use fleece to back them.

Cutting Directions

1. From Fabric A, cut four 18¾″ × 12¼″ tops.
2. From Contrast B, cut four 23″ × 16½″ linings.
3. From Contrast B, cut four 18″ square napkins.
4. *Optional:* From the fleece, cut four 18¾″ × 12¼″ backings.

Sewing Directions

PLACE MATS

1. All seam allowances are ¼″; hem allowances are 2″.
2. Right sides together, mitre the corners on the lining sections.
3. Turn right side out and press.

4. *Optional:* If the top isn't quilted, glue-baste the fleece to the wrong side of the tops.
5. Wrong sides together, insert and pin the top into the lining. Straight-stitch ½″ from the raw edge of the band; press. Check to be sure the top is flat and the band even before stitching.
6. Trim close to the stitched line.
7. Zigzag over the raw edge (W,4-L,1). (Illus. 59)

NAPKINS

1. Hem all edges with a satin-stitch hem.

Illus. 59

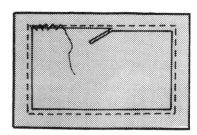

UNDERSTATED ELEGANCE

This elegant set makes a magnificent gift or addition to your own entertaining. As practical as they are beautiful, the place mats and hot-pads are made like pillow shams. Inside, needlepunch insulation inserts will protect the finest table.

The fine hemstitched design is created with a decorative stitch and a special wing-needle.

Finished Sizes: Place mats, 19″ × 13″; Napkins, 20″ square; Hot-pads, 8″ square

Materials

Fabric requirements are for four place mats, four napkins, and two hot-pads. Individual requirements are in parentheses.

Fabric, 2¾ yards, 45″ wide (Place mats, 1½ yards; Napkins, 1¼ yards; Hot-pads, ¼ yard)

Needlepunch insulation, ⅝ yard, 45″ wide

Machine embroidery thread

Wing-shaped needle

Fabric Notes: The hemstitching design will be more pronounced on crisp fabrics such as linen, organdy, or muslin (calico). I used a soft Swiss batiste, which I spray-starched when I pressed.

If the embroidered design doesn't feature hemstitching, select a print or solid-colored fabric to coordinate with the room or china.

Cutting Directions

1. *Place mats:* Cut four 19½″ × 13½″ tops, four 3½″ × 13½″ lining sections, and four 17½″ × 13½″ lining sections.
2. *Napkins:* Cut four 22″ squares.
3. *Hot-pads:* Cut two 9″ square tops, two 3½″ × 9″ lining sections, and two 7″ × 9″ lining sections.
4. From the needlepunch, cut four 16″ × 10″ mat interlinings and two hot-pad interlinings, 6″ square.

Sewing Directions

PLACE MATS AND HOT-PADS

1. All seam allowances are ¼″.
2. Make a narrow hem on one 13½″ end of all place mat linings and on one 9″ end of all hot-mat linings.
3. Right sides together, pin the large lining section and top together. Cover with the small lining section, wrong side up; repin and stitch.

4. Turn right side out and press. (Spray-starch if using a soft fabric.)
5. Change to the wing-shaped needle and select a decorative zigzag stitch. Using matching embroidery thread on the needle and bobbin, embroider all mats 1″ from each edge.

Claire's Hints: I used Elna-disc 140 to make the hemstitched design. If you have a different machine, select a pattern which allows the needle to sew into the same hole several times. Or, if you prefer, use a regular needle and the decorative stitch of your choice.

To reduce puckering, use strips of stabilizer under all embroidery and stitch at a moderate speed. For this project, I used strips of Ziploc (2mm) freezer bags.

6. Press and insert the interlinings.

NAPKINS

1. All hem allowances are 1″.
2. Press all hem allowances to the wrong side of the napkins.
3. Mitre all corners.
4. Turn right side out and press.

Claire's Hint: The napkins will be more attractive if you arrange the corner seams evenly without trimming.

5. Embroider the napkins ½″ from the edge. Trim away the excess hem.
6. Press.

PLACE MAT CADDY

This practical place mat caddy is the perfect answer for storing place mats. Designed to keep them clean and wrinkle-free, place mats are ready to use on a moment's notice.

Materials

Fabric, 1¼ yards, 45" wide
Wide bias binding, 7 yards
Cardboard, 14" × 19"
Fabric Notes: Select a lightweight, firmly woven fabric. I used a nylon organdy in white; however, prints and pastels would be equally attractive.

Cutting Directions

1. Cut five 20" × 15" rectangles to make one caddy bottom, two A-flaps and two B-flaps.
2. Cut one 18¾" × 15" pocket.

Sewing Directions

1. Hem allowances are 1".
2. Bind one short end of the caddy pocket with bias binding.
3. Right sides up, align the short ends and machine-baste the pocket to the caddy bottom. (Illus. 60)

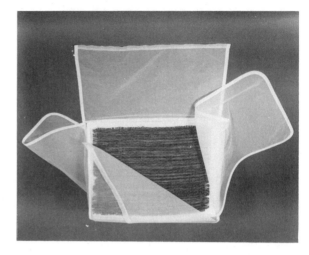

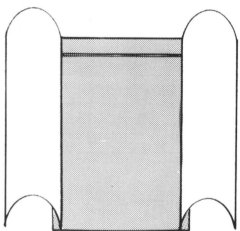

Illus. 61

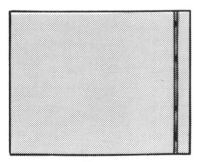

Illus. 60

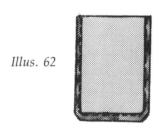

Illus. 62

4. Join the A-flaps and caddy bottom. Right sides up, machine-baste one long edge of one A-flap to the caddy bottom stack; bind the edge. Fold the flap out of the way and join the other flap to the other long edge; bind the edge. (Illus. 61)
5. Bind three sides of the remaining two flaps. (Illus. 62) For easy binding, round the corners on one end.

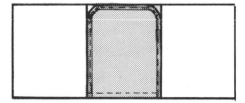

Illus. 63

6. Apply the B-flaps. Right sides up, place one B-flap on top of the caddy, matching the raw edges on one short end. Baste. (Illus. 63)
7. Join the remaining flap to the other short end.
8. Bind the ends, beginning with one A-flap, continuing across the B-flap/pocket section, and ending with the other A-flap. (Illus. 64)
9. Hem all unfinished edges with a double ½" hem.
10. Insert the cardboard into the pocket.

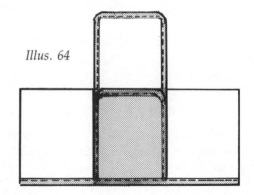

Illus. 64

TABLE PROTECTORS

Used under beautiful embroidered or lace mats, this very utilitarian gift is a true table saver. Treat yourself and all your friends to a set.
Finished Size: 8" circles

Materials

Fabric requirements are for four.
Needlepunch insulation, one 32" × 8"

Fabric Notes: If needlepunch insulation is unavailable, substitute two layers of fleece.

Directions

1. From the needlepunch, cut four 8" circles; or cut eight circles from the fleece.
2. No sewing is required for the needlepunch. When using fleece, zigzag (W,4-L,2) two layers together around the edges.

CASSEROLE JACKET

This easy-to-make casserole jacket is perfect for a kitchen shower or bread-and-butter gift. It not only transforms the plainest dish into an elegant serving container, it also protects the table and keeps the food warm. And, if you don't like casseroles, the jackets are great for bread or fruit baskets.

Make several for yourself to use every day or to create a special theme for a party buffet.
Finished Size: 15" × 11" to fit a 1½ quart glass dish

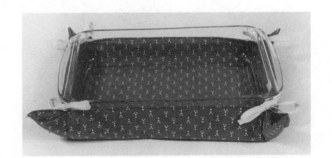

Materials

Remnant A, one 32″ × 12″
Needlepunch insulation, one 28″ × 10″
Narrow bias binding, 2 yards

Cutting Directions

1. From the fabric, cut two 16″ × 12″ rectangles.
2. From the needlepunch, cut two 14″ × 10″ rectangles.
3. To determine the finished jacket size for a different-size casserole, measure the outside of the casserole, beginning at the rim. Measure down the side, across the bottom, and up the other side. Cut the jacket sections 2¼″ larger than the casserole measurements. Cut the needlepunch 1″ larger.

Sewing Directions

1. All seam allowances are ⅜″.
2. Make the ties. Fold the bias binding in half lengthwise and zigzag (W,2-L,2) down the center. Cut into eight 9″ lengths.
3. Mark each side of one rectangle 2½″ from the end.
4. Right side up, pin and stitch the ties at each mark. (Illus. 65)
5. Right sides together, join the sections, leaving one end open between the ribbons.
6. Trim away the bulk at the corners; turn right side out; and press.
7. Insert the needlepunch sections, adjusting as needed until smooth.

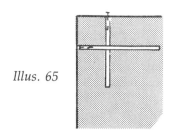

Illus. 65

8. Close the opening. Fold the seam allowances in and edgestitch. Continue edgestitching around the edge.
9. Topstitch 2″ from each edge through all fabric layers. (Illus. 66)
10. Tie the ribbons at each corner.

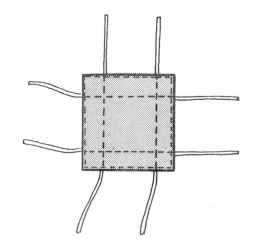

Illus. 66

● ● ●

POT HOLDERS AND HOT-MATS

Have you priced pot holders lately? All the pretty decorative ones are terribly expensive. Fortunately, home-sewers can make pot holders for a fraction of their cost. Make one or several for shower, housewarming and bread-and-butter gifts.

Several different construction techniques have been used to make a variety of pot-holder designs. All are easy to make and most can be made in 15 minutes or less. And, of course, the size and shape can be tailored to fit your scraps and preferences.

Photographs of the designs can be seen on page 25.

The same designs can be used to make practical hot-mats for the table.

Fabric Notes: Firmly woven cotton blends are the best choices. Needlepunch insulation is the insulating material I prefer because it provides greater protection. If you have to use polyester fleece, add an extra layer or two. Test to be sure you have enough protection.

Each of these designs has one quilted square. If your fabric isn't quilted, use an additional layer of needlepunch insulation.

TRAPUNTO HEART

Finished Size: 8″ square

Materials

Remnant A (quilted), one 9″ square
Contrast B, one 9″ square
Contrast C for heart, white, one 4″ square
Needlepunch insulation, one 9″ square
Fibrefill
Embroidery thread, white
Plastic ring, one 1″

Sewing Directions

1. All seam allowances are ½″.
2. Trace the pattern. (Illus. 67)
3. Appliqué the heart to Remnant B.
Claire's Hint: I used the upside-down appliqué technique. Do not fuse.
4. Wrong side up, slash the background fabric about 2″. Fill the heart with a soft layer of fibrefill; and close the slash by hand.
5. Place the appliquéd top, right side up, on the needlepunch; pin and zigzag (W,3-L,2) the edges together.
6. Right sides together, join the pot-holder squares, leaving a 3″ opening on one side.
7. Trim the seam allowances to ¼″ and trim off a triangle at the corners.

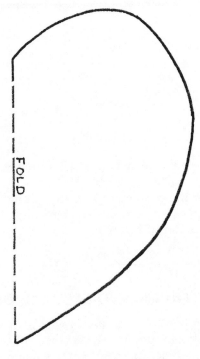

Illus. 67

8. Turn the pot holder right side out; pin the opening together; and edgestitch all edges.
9. Wrong side up, place the ring at one corner. Zigzag (W,4-L,0) over it.
Claire's Hints: Use transparent tape to hold the ring in position and stitch slowly to avoid breaking the needle.

Eliminate the ring when making hot-pads for the table.

• • •

HEARTS AND FLOWERS

This pot holder looks much more complicated than it is. The mitred border is actually part of the pot-holder back. This is a particularly good design to use in mastering mitred corners.
Finished Size: 7″ square

Materials

Remnant A (quilted), one 7″ square
Contrast B, one 11″ square
Needlepunch insulation, one 7″ square
Plastic ring, one 1″

Cutting Directions

1. Check the remnants to be sure they are square and even.
Claire's Hint: When making a different size pot holder, cut Remnant A and the needlepunch the same size; cut Contrast B 4″ longer and 4″ wider than the finished pot holder.

Sewing Directions

1. All seam allowances are ¼″.
2. Right sides together, mitre the corners. (Illus. 68)

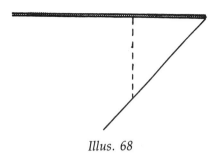

Illus. 68

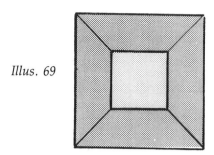

Illus. 69

3. Press the seams open and turn right side out. Press.

4. Pin the needlepunch to the wrong side of the quilted square and position both inside the mitred square. Pin. (Illus. 69)

5. Stitch the band in place ¼" from the raw edges. Trim close to the stitched line.

6. Satin-stitch (W,3) over the raw edge of the band.

7. On the wrong side of the pot holder, place the ring at one corner. Zigzag (W,4-L,0) over it.

• • •

QUICK-AND-EASY BORDER

This pot holder is even easier than the Hearts and Flowers design. Again, the border is part of the pot-holder back; but, instead of mitred corners, the border is turned under twice and edgestitched. *Finished Size:* 7" square

Materials

Remnant A (quilted), one 7" square
Contrast B, one 9" square
Needlepunch insulation, one 7" square
Plastic ring, one 1"

Cutting Directions

1. Check the remnants to be sure they are square and even.
Claire's Hint: When making a different size pot holder, cut Remnant A and the needlepunch the same size; cut Contrast B 2" longer and 2" wider than the finished pot holder.

Sewing Directions

1. Center the needlepunch on the wrong side of the large square. Cover it with the small square, right side up. Pin. (Illus. 70)
2. Right side up, fold the back over the raw edge; turn under ½"; and edgestitch. Repeat for all sides. (Illus. 70b) To avoid breaking threads and starting again, stitch a triangle at each corner. (Illus. 70c)
3. Wrong side up, place the ring at one corner. Zigzag (W,4-L,0) over it.

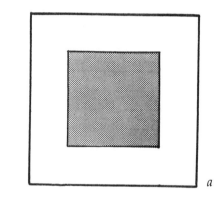

a

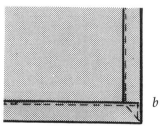

b

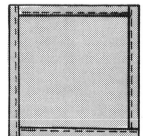

Illus. 70   *c*

Claire's Hint: This is one of the designs I use to revive old pot holders in my own kitchen. Use two unquilted fabrics and substitute the old pot holder for the needlepunch.

PLAIN AND SIMPLE

Materials

Remnant A (quilted), one 8" square
Contrast B, one 8" square
Needlepunch insulation, one 8" square
Plastic ring, one 1"

Cutting Directions

1. Check the remnants to be sure they are square and even. When making a different-size pot holder, cut the remnants and needlepunch insulation the same size.

Sewing Directions

1. All seam allowances are ½".
2. Pin the needlepunch to the wrong side of the unquilted square. Stitch all sides almost *but not quite* ½" from the raw edges.

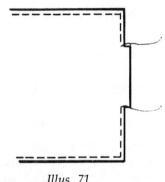

Illus. 71

3. Right sides together, join the two squares, leaving a 3" opening in the center of one side.
4. Trim the seam allowances *except* at the opening. Trim the corners and turn the pot holder right side out. (Illus. 71)
5. Fold in the seam allowances at the opening and topstitch around the pot holder ¼" from the edge.
6. Wrong side up, place the ring at one corner. Zigzag (W,4-L,0) over it.

• • •

FIVE-MINUTE POT HOLDER

If you're one of the lucky home-sewers who has a home serger, this pot holder was designed for you.
Finished Size: Approximately 7"

Materials

Remnant A (quilted), one 8" square
Contrast B, one 8" square
Needlepunch insulation, one 8" square

Sewing Directions

1. Using a 7"–7½" plate, draw a circle on Remnant A with a fadeaway pen.
2. Stack the layers with the fabrics right sides out and the needlepunch in between. Carefully pin them together, placing the pins at least ½" from the marked line. If you have difficulty handling three separate layers, machine-stitch them together on the marked line.
3. Overlock the pot holder on the marked line. Sew around the pot holder, stopping ½" before reaching the starting point. To finish the edge, turn the handwheel manually and guide the fabric carefully to avoid cutting the first stitches.

Overlap the stitching for ½". Turn the pot holder and stitch off the fabric. Clip the threads, leaving a 2" tail. Thread the tail into a large-eyed needle, such as a tapestry needle, and hide the thread ends in the stitched edge.
Claire's Hint: When stitching around a curved edge, use your left hand to guide the fabric back of the presser foot while using your right to guide the layers in front.

• • •

SUNSHINE POT HOLDER

This sunny pot holder will brighten any day. Novice and expert embroiderers alike will enjoy this design.

Finished Size: Approximately 9" circle

Materials

Fabric A (yellow), one 6" square
Contrast B (orange), two 12" squares
Needlepunch insulation, two 12" squares
Stabilizer
Machine embroidery thread: yellow, orange, black, red

Cutting Directions

1. Enlarge the pattern. (Illus. 72a)
2. From Contrast B, cut one 1" × 3" loop.
3. Using a release sheet, bond the fusible web to the wrong side of Fabric A.
4. From Fabric A, cut one 5" circle for the face.
5. Trace the design onto the face. (Illus. 72b)

Illus. 72a. ¼" = 1"

Illus. 72b

Claire's Hint: Trace the design onto paper first. Cover with fabric and hold up to a window for easy tracing.

Sewing Directions

1. Right sides up, fuse the face to the center of one orange square.
2. Set the machine for embroidering, changing to an embroidery foot. Loosen the upper tension slightly so the top thread color will show on the wrong side.

Set the stitch width to 4 and the stitch length almost to 0. Experiment a little with various stitch lengths and a wide stitch width (W,4) until you're happy with the appearance of the satin stitch.
3. Pin stabilizer to the wrong side of the square.
4. Satin-stitch the eyebrows, nose, and mouth:

Eyebrows (black): Satin-stitch (W,3.5) on the line.

Nose (black): Satin-stitch (W,2), turning the work as needed to follow the design.

Mouth (red): Satin-stitch (W,2) around the mouth. Beginning at the left corner, stitch across the top; stop at the right corner with the needle in the left-hand position; pivot and stitch the bottom of the mouth.
5. Complete the remainder of the face with free-hand embroidery.

Remove the embroidery foot and lower the feed dogs and the presser foot bar.

Change the stitch width (W,4); using a side stitch, fill in the mouth. To make a side stitch, keep the work horizontal and move the fabric slowly to the right then back to the left until the mouth is finished.

Claire's Hints: Use a machine embroidery hoop.

To prevent tangling at the beginning, bring the bobbin thread up through the fabric. Hold the top thread and turn the handwheel manually until the bobbin thread comes up. Hold both threads firmly to one side and make a couple of stitches in place before beginning.
6. Using the pattern as a guide, draw the pot holder and sunrays on the embroidery square.
7. Satin-stitch (W,3.5) the sunrays. Taper the ends by narrowing the stitch width.
8. Make a pot-holder sandwich. Right sides out and the needlepunch between, pin the layers together.
9. Right side up, outline the pot holder with a short, straight stitch (L,1.5). Trim close to the stitched line.
10. Satin-stitch (W,4) around the pot holder and face.
11. Make the loop. Fold under the long edges ¼" and satin-stitch (W,2). Trim.
12. Set the loop to the wrong side of the pot holder. Wrong sides together, fold the loop in half crosswise; pin at the top. Right sides up, satin-stitch (W,4).

● ● ●

FELINE POT HOLDER

The scraps from the Cat Fancier Mats and Napkins (page 36) were just the right size to make one pot holder. I sometimes make the pot holder first to practise my appliqué techniques before using them on the place mats.

Materials

Remnant A, quilted (top), one 7" square
Contrast B (back), one 8" × 13"
Remnant C (appliqué—white), one 5" × 6"
Needlepunch insulation, one 7" square
Plastic ring, one 1"

Cutting Directions

1. Trace the appliqué pattern (page 36).
2. From Contrast B, cut one 7" square and four 1½" × 9" strips.

Sewing Directions

1. Appliqué the cat to the quilted square using the upside-down appliqué technique.
2. Right sides out, make a pot-holder sandwich with the needlepunch sandwiched between the two squares.

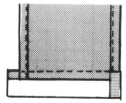

Illus. 73

3. Zigzag (W,2-L,2) the raw edges together. This retards ravelling on the quilted fabric and makes the three layers easier to control.
4. Bind each edge separately. When you bind the first side, leave both ends raw. When you bind the second and third sides, fold under ¼" at the beginning. When you bind the last side, fold under ¼" at the beginning and end. (Illus. 73)
Note: Since the edges are absolutely straight, this is one of the few occasions when the strips don't have to be bias-cut.
5. Sew the plastic ring to the upper left corner. This can be done easily by machine. Use a wide zigzag (W,4) with the feed dogs down.

• • •

COASTERS

QUICK-AND-EASY COASTERS

Even a novice can stitch these coasters. The simplest stitching skills and ordinary materials are all that's required to create this practical gift. Packaged in a small basket, they'll delight any hostess.
Finished Size: 5" circle

Materials

Material requirements are for 4 coasters.
Remnant A (double-faced quilted), 12" square, 1 (or four 6" squares)
Machine embroidery thread
Stabilizer
Fabric Notes: If your fabric is not double-faced, purchase an equal amount of contrast fabric and fusible web. Bond the layers together before stitching.

Sewing Directions

1. Draw four 5" circles on the fabric. I used a small fruit dish as a pattern. Any bowl 4½" or 5½" will be fine.
2. Stitch (L,1 or 20 spi) on the marked line. Trim close to the stitching. Fill the bobbin with matching thread so the bottom will be almost as pretty as the top.

Photo also shows basket liner.

3. Using an embroidery foot, loosen the upper tension; and satin-stitch (W,4) around the coaster.
4. Tear away the stabilizer. If using Ziploc as a stabilizer, you can leave it on the coaster as an added protection.

SCALLOPED COASTERS

These coasters are slightly more difficult to sew than the Quick-and-Easy Coasters, but make excellent small hostess gifts when patio entertaining is in season.

Finished Size: Approximate 5" circle

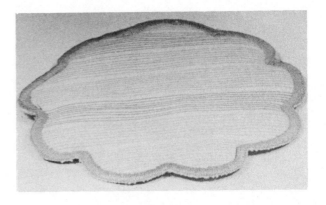

Materials

Material requirements are for 4 coasters.
Remnant A for the coaster top, one 12" square (or four 6" squares)
Contrast B for the coaster bottom, one 12" square (or four 6" squares)
Fleece, one 12" square (or four 6" squares)
Machine embroidery thread
Cardboard, 5" square
Stabilizer

Cutting Directions

1. Trace the pattern. (Illus. 74)
2. Using the pattern, cut out a cardboard template.

Sewing Directions

1. Using the cardboard template, trace around four coasters on the right side of Remnant A. Leave some space between each coaster and the raw edges.
2. Make a sandwich with Remnants A and B, right sides out, and the fleece between. Pin the layers together. Place the pins in the center of each coaster with the points towards the edges to eliminate removing the pins when stitching.
3. Place the sandwich on top of the stabilizer and stitch (L,1 or 20 spi) on the marked line. Trim close to the stitched line.
Claire's Hint: Fill the bobbin with matching thread so the coaster will be reversible.
4. Using an embroidery foot, loosen the upper tension; and satin-stitch (W,4).
Claire's Hints: When stitching around the small concave or inner curves, pivot frequently with the needle in the left-hand position. (Illus. 75) For convex or outside curves, pivot with the needle in the right-hand position.
   To pivot, stop with the needle down; lift the presser foot; reposition the fabric; lower the foot; and continue.

5. Tear away the stabilizer. If it is Water-Soluble Stabilizer, remove by spraying with a plant mister.

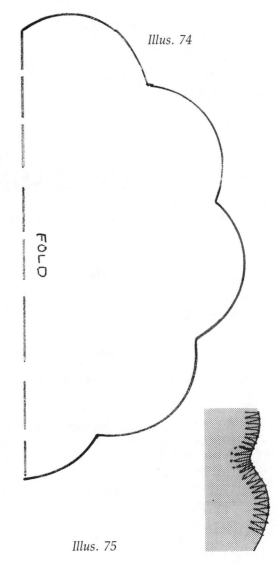

Illus. 74

FOLD

Illus. 75

BOUND COASTERS

Materials

Material requirements are for 4 coasters.
Remnant A, quilted (coaster tops), one 10″ square (or four 5″ squares)
Remnant B (coaster bottoms), one 10″ square (or four 5″ squares)
Narrow bias binding, 2 yards
Machine embroidery thread
Stabilizer

Cutting Directions

1. From Remnant A, cut four 5″ circles.
2. From Remnant B, cut four 5″ squares.

Sewing Directions

1. Wrong sides together, pin and zigzag (W,4-L,2) around the circles. Trim away the excess fabric.
2. Bind the edges, overlapping the ends ¼″ where they join. Press.

Claire's Hints: For a smooth finish, use a steam iron to shape the binding before stitching.

To avoid "holidays" (unstitched sections), zigzag (W,2-L,2).

To eliminate bulk where the ends overlap, do not turn the ends under. The raw edge won't ravel and will be inconspicuous.

• • •

BASKET LINER

Finished Size: 15″ × 12″ oval; fits a small baked potato basket 7″ × 4″ × 2¼″

Materials

Remnant A, one 15″ × 12″
Narrow elastic, ½ yard

Cutting Directions

1. Round the corners on the remnant to make an oval.
2. To make a pattern for a different size basket: Take all measurements on the outside of the basket. Beginning at the base, measure the widest part of the basket to the rim, across the top, and back to the base. Repeat to measure the narrowest part of the basket. To determine the width and length of the rectangle, add 3″ to both measurements.

Examples: For a 10½″ × 7½″ × 3″ basket, cut a 19½″ × 16½″ rectangle. For a circular basket 10″ × 3″, cut a 19″ circle.

Sewing Directions

1. The hem allowance is 1″.
2. Fold the hem allowance to the wrong side. Turn the raw edge under ¼″ and edgestitch, leaving a ½″ opening at the end.

Claire's Hint: Crimp the liner ¼″ from the edge so the excess fullness will be easy to control. To crimp, hold your index finger firmly behind the presser foot when stitching so the fabric will pile up between the foot and your finger. This makes small pleats in the fabric and gathers it into the stitched line. (Illus. 76)

Illus. 76

3. Thread the elastic into the casing and stitch the ends together. To avoid bulk, overlap the elastic ends.
4. Machine-stitch the opening closed, if desired.

MUSHROOM BAG

Delight your mushroom-loving friends with this bag to keep mushrooms fresh.
Finished Size: 13″ × 12¾″ square

Materials

Remnant A, one 30″ × 13½″
Remnant B, one 3″ square
Remnant C, one 3″ square
Remnant D, one 3″ square
Fusible web, three 3″ squares
Machine embroidery thread: medium brown
Fabric Notes: I used unbleached muslin to make the bag and trimmed it with an assortment of brown print and solid-colored mushrooms.

Cutting Directions

1. Trace the appliqués. (Illus. 77)
2. Cut two 13½″ bag sections and two 1¼″ × 13½″ ties.
3. Using a release sheet, bond the fusible web to the wrong sides of Remnants B, C, and D.
4. Cut out the mushrooms.

Sewing Directions

1. All seam allowances are ¼″ and hem allowances are ½″.
2. Appliqué the mushrooms to the bag. Embroider as needed to complete the design.
Claire's Hint: Center and fuse the mushrooms on one bag section about 2″ from the bottom. Using an embroidery foot, outline each mushroom with a satin stitch (W,3). Straight-stitch the underside of mushroom C.
3. Make the ties. Right sides together, fold the strip in half lengthwise and stitch ⅜″ from the fold line. Turn right side out; press.
4. Pin the ties to the right side of the bag about 3″ from the top.
5. Right sides together, join the sides and bottom.
6. Turn the bag right side out; and hem the top. Press.

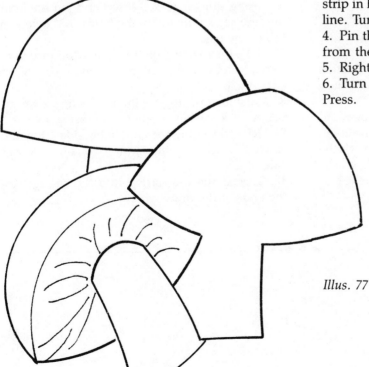

Illus. 77

STAY-FRESH BREAD BAG

Amazing as it seems, this easy-to-make bread bag actually keeps French bread fresher longer. Decorated with appliqués or made up in a pretty print, this bag will be an attractive accessory in any kitchen.

Finished Size: 7¾" × 26"

Materials

Fabric, ½ yard, 36" wide
Plastic (soft), ½ yard
Optional: Alphabet borders, B, R, E, A, D, 1 each
Fabric Notes: Select a firmly woven fabric. If you're using the hand-screened letters, choose a plain color. I used unbleached muslin.

The Alphabet borders (Banar Designs) are iron-on appliqués.

Cutting Directions

1. From the fabric, cut one bag 27" × 17" and one drawstring 27" × 1".
2. From the plastic, cut one lining 26" × 16½".
3. Cut away the excess from the letter appliqués.

Sewing Directions

1. All seam allowances are ¼"; the hem allowance is 1".
2. *Optional:* Apply the letters to the bag. Position them 2¾" from one long side and ½" apart. Fuse the letters in place.
Claire's Hint: Using a fadeaway marking pen and see-through ruler, draw a line parallel to the edge. Beginning 6½" below the top of the bag, mark the location for the top of the letter B.
3. Make the bag. Right sides together, join the bottom and side seams.

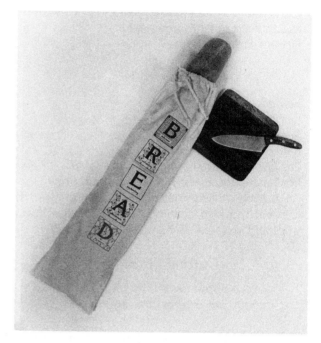

4. Press and turn right side out.
5. Make the lining by joining the bottom and side seams.
6. Wrong sides together, insert and pin the lining into the bag so the top of the lining is 1" below the top of the bag.
7. Make the casing. Fold the hem allowance to the wrong side, fold the raw edge under ¼", pin, and edgestitch.
8. Make the opening for the tie. Using a seam ripper, unpick the side seam in the casing area.
9. Make the drawstring. Right sides together, stitch a ¼" wide tubing. Trim to ⅛" and turn right side out.
10. Thread the drawstring into the casing. Knot the ends of the drawstring.

FRENCH BREAD WARMER

A French bread warmer is a practical "little" gift that solves the age-old dilemma of how to keep those long loaves warm.
Finished Size: 25" × 17"; fits French loaves 18" long

Materials

Remnant, one 31" × 13½"
Optional: Ribbon, 1½ yards, ⅜" wide

Cutting Directions

1. Cut one 31" × 13½" warmer.
2. Cut two 31" × 1¼" ties.

Sewing Directions

1. Hem allowances on the long sides are ½"; hem allowances on the ends are 3".
2. Finish the two long sides with a narrow machine hem.
3. At one end, fold 3" to the wrong side. Turn under the raw edge ¼" and edgestitch close to the inside fold. Stitch again ⅝" from the fold to make the ribbon casing. Press. Repeat on the other end. (Illus. 78)
4. Make the ties.

5. Using a safety pin, thread the ties into the casings.
6. Draw up the ties and make bows at each end.

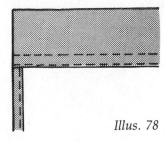

Illus. 78

FLOP BOX

The uses for these handy boxes are limited only by your imagination. Fill one with pot holders for a shower gift or cookies for a shut-in.

Flat when untied, they're great for travellers and picnickers.
Finished Sizes: Small, 6" × 6" × 2"; Medium, 8" × 8" × 2"; Large, 9" × 12" × 2"

Materials

Material requirements are for the small box; requirements for the medium and large boxes are in parentheses.
Remnant A, one 12" square (14" square, 15" × 18")
Contrast B, one 12" square (14" square, 15" × 18")
Ribbon or narrow bias binding, 1⅝ yards, ⅛"–¼" wide

Poster cardboard, one 10″ square, 12″ square, 13″ × 16″ (available from stationery and art suppliers)

Cutting Directions

1. On Fabric A, mark the placement for the ribbon strips with a short snip 2⅞″ from each end.
2. For each box, cut eight strips of ribbon or bias binding 7″ long. When using bias binding, zigzag (W,2-L,2) down the center before cutting into short strips.
3. From the cardboard, cut one 6″ square (8″ square; 9″ × 12″) and four 2″ × 6″ rectangles (four 2″ × 8″ rectangles; two 2″ × 9″ rectangles and two 2″ × 12″ rectangles).

Sewing Directions

1. All seam allowances are ⅜″.
2. Right sides up, pin the ribbon strips to Fabric A, matching the cut edges. (Illus. 79)
3. Right sides together, join the fabric sections, leaving one side open between the ribbons on one end.

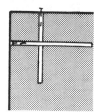

Illus. 79

4. Trim the corners, turn right side out; and press.
5. Edgestitch around the outside edge, beginning and ending at each side of the opening.
6. Insert the cardboard sections, positioning pins between them to hold the cardboard in place and mark the stitching lines. Use a zipper foot or straight-stitch presser foot to stitch between the cardboard sections. Stitch the fabric layers together

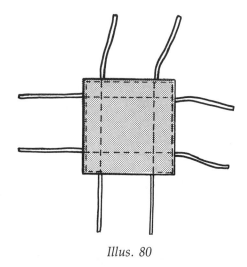

Illus. 80

along the marked lines. Stop as needed; break your threads; and start again. (Illus. 80)
7. Close the opening. Fold the raw edges in and edgestitch.
8. Tie the ribbons at each corner to form box.

For the Home

COUNTRY TOWEL SET

Add a touch of country with these easy-to-make towel sets. Trimmed with three different calico prints, you'd think it took hours to coordinate them. Instead, they're all from a single striped fabric.

Materials

Material requirements are for a set of two.
Bath towels, 2
Hand towels, 2
Face cloths, 2
Fabric, 1 yard, 45" wide
Eyelet or lace, 2½ yards
Fabric Notes: Select a firmly woven fabric with several different patterned stripes. I used a vertical-stripe fabric.

Cutting Directions

1. Preshrink the towels and all fabrics before cutting.
Claire's Hint: The exact width of all strips is determined by the stripe pattern. Add ½" seam allowance to each side of the selected stripes before cutting.
2. For the bath towels, cut 2 matching bands 3"–4" × 27". (Mine were 3½" wide.)
3. For the hand towels, cut 2 matching bands 2½"–3½" × 18". (Mine were 2⅞".)
4. For the face cloths, cut 2 matching bands 1¾"–2" × 18". (Mine were 2".)

Sewing Directions

TOWELS

1. All seam allowances are ½".
2. Press the seam allowances on all bands to the wrong side; press.
Claire's Hint: Gauge-stitch for accuracy.
3. Right sides up, pin the eyelet to the bottom of each towel with 1" extensions at each end. Stitch. (Illus. 81)
Claire's Hint: Be sure the nap is going the same way on all towels and the woven stripes on all towels will be covered.

4. Right sides up with 1" extensions at each end, pin the band in place so it covers the raw edge of the eyelet on the towels and the woven band on the face cloths. Edgestitch both sides.
5. Finish the ends. Wrap the eyelet and band extensions around the sides of the towel; fold under the raw edge; and stitch.
6. Repeat for all towels and face cloths.

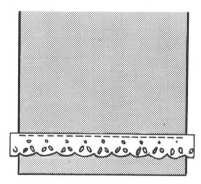

Illus. 81

TOWELS WITH SEMINOLE PATCHWORK TRIM

These beautiful towels look like Seminole patchwork, and they are—with a difference. To make the bands look more complex with a minimum of seaming, I used a striped fabric.

Seminole patchwork originated at some time during the late 19th century with the Seminole Indians in Florida and has always been made by machine.

By varying the strip patterns and colors, the number and width of strips, and the widths, angles, and offsets of the pieces, an infinite number of designs can be created. The finished bands on this towel set vary in width from 2¾" wide on the bath towels to 1⅞" wide on the face cloths.

Materials

Bath towels, 2
Hand towels, 2
Face cloths, 2
Fabric A, solid color, ¾ yard, 45" wide
Fabric B, vertical stripe, 1 yard, 45" wide
Fabric Notes: For easy sewing and easy care, choose firmly woven, medium-weight fabrics in cotton/polyester blends.
(*Note:* Although strips cut on the lengthwise grain will stretch less and be easier to handle, strips can also be cut on the cross grain for fabric economy or design.)

For a coordinated look, select a striped fabric with two or more sets of stripes so the bands on each kind of towel will match. For example, the bands on the bath towels should match; however, they don't have to be identical to those on the hand towels or face cloths.

If you want to substitute print fabrics for the solid strips, make some sample combinations; then look at them from a distance of six to eight feet before making a final decision.

Cutting Directions

1. Preshrink the towels and all fabrics before cutting.
2. If the fabric tears easily, tear the strips to ensure

an even width. If it doesn't tear easily, use a see-through ruler as a guide to mark the cutting lines accurately.
Caution: If the strips are uneven in width, the finished bands will be unattractive.
3. Cut or tear the solid-color fabric into sixteen 1⅝" × 45" strips.
4. Cut or tear two matching strips, 3¼" wide, from the striped fabric for the bath towels; two, 2" wide, for the hand towels; and two, 1½" wide, for the face cloths.

Sewing Directions

THE PATCHWORK
1. All seam allowances are ¼".
Claire's Hint: Seams must be stitched precisely. Even slight inaccuracies will be noticeable on the finished bands.
2. Shorten the stitch length to 20–25 spi (1mm).
3. Join the strips. Right sides together, stitch the striped strip between the two solid strips. (Illus. 82)

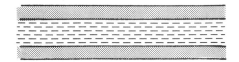

Illus. 82

4. Press all the seam allowances down.
5. Mark and cut the seamed strips into pieces 1¼" wide. Accuracy is extremely important! Measure, mark, and cut the pieces carefully so each piece is

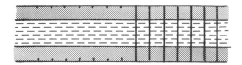

Illus. 83

exactly the same width and the cutting lines are parallel to each other and perpendicular to the seam lines. (Illus. 83)
6. Offset the pieces ¾". To do this, pin two pieces together so the top on the upper piece is ¾" below the top of the lower piece; stitch. (Illus. 84)

Illus. 84

7. Sew the pieces together in pairs stitching continuously from one pair to the next. When all the pairs have been stitched, check to be sure that each is properly aligned; clip them apart. Then sew the pairs together; again, check and clip. Repeat until

all the pieces make a band 1" longer than the towel width.
Note: The offset on this particular design is the same as the finished width of the individual patches so the solid-colored triangles at the top and bottom of the bands have two sides the same length.
8. Check one more time to be sure there are no major inaccuracies; then sew the ends together to make a circle. Cut through the circle to form the straight ends for the band.
9. Press all seam allowances in one direction; then steam-press from the right side.
10. Trim the patchwork strip. Trim the top and bottom edges to make a straight line.
11. Bind the edges of the patchwork. Right sides together, stitch the top to a solid color band. Repeat on the bottom. Press; wrap the band around the raw edges and fold to the wrong side. Pin.

TRIM THE TOWELS
1. Position the patchwork band on the towel, covering the woven design or stripe. If the towels have a nap, check to be sure the nap is running down when the towel is hung.
2. Fold under the ends of the band, hiding the ends between the band and the towel. Carefully pin the long edges and ends in place, checking to be sure the band is not stretched out of shape.
3. Topstitch the band in place.
Claire's Hint: To topstitch evenly, use a zipper foot.

• • •

TABLE COVER AND CARDCASE

If your friends like to play cards, give them this luxurious table cover and cardcase. The table cover eliminates the embarrassment of cards sailing into someone's lap and the cardcase is the perfect organizer for cards and score pad.

Materials

Fabric A, 1¼ yards, 45" wide
Ribbon, 5 yards, 1" wide
Ribbon, 5 yards, ½"–⅝" wide
Fabric Notes: Choose fabrics such as suede cloth, corduroy, velveteen, brushed denim, and even canvas. Avoid fabrics with busy patterns. I used a beautiful muted wool plaid.

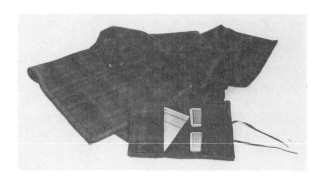

Cutting Directions

Even the edges and check to be sure you have a perfect square.

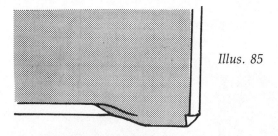

Illus. 85

Sewing Directions

1. All hem allowances are ½".
2. Press the hem allowance to the right side on each of the four edges.
3. Mitre the corners, if desired. To save time when sewing medium- or lightweight fabrics, simulate a mitre by folding one corner under. (Illus. 85)
4. Center the narrow ribbon on the wide ribbon and edgestitch in place.
5. Stitch the ribbon to the cover. Right sides up, cover the raw edges with ribbon, aligning the edges; pin; and edgestitch. (Illus. 86)

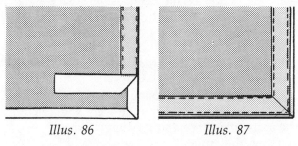

Illus. 86   *Illus. 87*

Claire's Hints: If the wrong side of the fabric is also attractive, position the ribbon about ⅛" from the edge. (Illus. 87)

To mitre the corner on the ribbon, stitch the outside of the ribbon first, pivoting at each corner. Fold and press the ribbon into a mitre at each corner; then edgestitch the other side of the ribbon.

CARDCASE

Finished Size: Closed, 6" × 8½"; Open, 12" × 8½"

Materials

Fabric A, ¼ yard, 45" wide
Fleece, one 20" × 9"
Ribbon, Color A, 1 yard, ⅛" wide
Ribbon, Color B, 1 yard, ⅛" wide
Fabric Notes: The cardcase is lined with the same fabric as the outside cover. For design variety or fabric economy, use a contrast lining. You'll need two 20½" × 9" remnants.

Cutting Directions

1. From the fabric, cut one 20½" × 9" cover and one 20" × 8¾" lining.
2. From the fleece, cut one 20" × 9" rectangle.

Sewing Directions

1. All seam allowances are ¼".
2. Pin and stitch the fleece to the wrong side of the cover.
3. Join the cover and lining. Right sides together, pin the cover and lining together. Stretch the lining, aligning the raw edges. Pin and stitch, leaving a 3" opening on one long side. (Illus. 88)

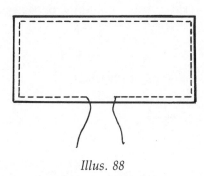

Illus. 88

4. Turn the case right side out.
5. Fold in the seam allowances at the opening and edgestitch, continuing around the rectangle. Press.
6. Make the pockets. Lay the case out flat, lining side up. Fold 3½" to the inside at each end. Pin and stitch the top and bottom of the case ⅜" from the edge. (Illus. 89)

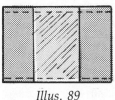

Illus. 89   *Illus. 90*

7. Stitch the pockets for the card decks. Divide the pocket at one end in half; stitch from the fold line to the top of the pocket. (Illus. 90)
8. Turn the case over and stitch the center of the ribbon to the center of the case.
9. Fill the case with two decks of cards and a score pad. Close the case and tie the ribbon.

SILVER CARE BAGS

These practical silver bags are just the answer for the hostess who likes to use her silver hollow ware but hates to polish it. The bags are made from specially treated Pacific Cloth which prevents tarnishing, protects against scratching, and eliminates dusting.

Although these bags can be custom-sized for any piece of silver, the directions are for a 16″ square bag. This size will accommodate a variety of silver trays, bowls, tea- and coffeepots.

If this is a gift for a special friend, give her a "gift certificate" for one bag in the size of her choice. *Note:* Silver care bags should *not* be washed.
Finished Size: 16″ × 16″ square

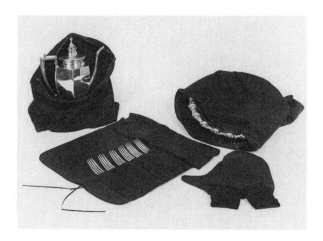

Materials

Pacific Cloth, ½ yard
Zipper, one brown, 16″

Cutting Directions

1. Cut two 16½″ square bag sections.
2. When making a custom-sized bag, add ½″ to the desired finished width and length measurements to determine the unstitched bag size.

Since Pacific Cloth is only 38″ wide, it is frequently more economical and less wasteful to cut several different-sized bags.

Sewing Directions

1. All seam allowances are ¼″.
2. Set the zipper. Place the zipper face down on one side of the Pacific Cloth—there isn't a right and wrong side. Align the edge of the zipper and the raw edge of the bag; using a zipper foot, stitch a ¼″ seam. Press.

Repeat to stitch the other side of the zipper in place.
3. With the bag "right" side up, stitch along both sides of the zipper ⅛″ from the seam line, catching the seam allowance and the zipper tape.
4. Open the zipper.
5. "Right" sides together, stitch the sides and bottom of the bag.
6. Turn right side out.

● ● ●

SILVERWARE ROLLS

Silver rolls are a true work-saver. Polishing silver flatware is such a chore. Best of all, you can make several of these utilitarian rolls on your overlock machine for the brides—new and not-so-new—on your list. If your sewing equipment doesn't include an overlock machine, use the alternate directions.
Finished Size: Small, 14″ × 14″ to hold 8 pieces; Large, 20″ × 14″ to hold 12 pieces

Materials

Material requirements are for a large roll; requirements for a small roll are in parentheses.
Pacific Cloth, one 20″ × 19½″ (14″ × 19½″)
Ribbon, ½ yard, ⅛″ or ¼″ wide

Cutting Directions

1. Cut one 20″ × 14″ (14″ × 14″) rectangle. Round three corners.

2. Cut one 18″ × 5½″ (12″ × 5½″) pocket. Round one corner on the pocket.

Sewing Directions

1. Finish the top and side of the pocket. Using the overlock machine, finish the two edges on each side of the rounded corner. Zigzag (W,3-L,3) or pink all edges if you don't have a home overlock.
2. Set the pocket to the rectangle. Aligning the square corners, pin. (Illus. 91) Beginning at the corner, overlock all edges. Place the pins about 1″ from the edges so they won't have to be removed when stitching.
3. Divide and mark the pocket into twelve 1½″ wide sections. Using a regular sewing machine, stitch the end and pockets.
Claire's Hint: Use a sliver of soap to mark the stitching lines.
4. Sew the ribbon on the reverse side of the roll. Pin and stitch it at the end of the pocket. (Illus. 92)

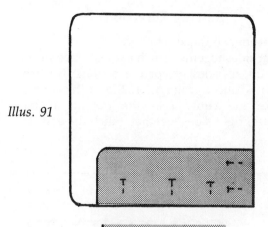

Illus. 91

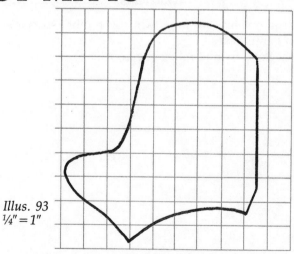

Illus. 92

• • •

SILVER DUST MITTS

This is one of those great gifts that is much more wonderful than you initially think. The first dust mitts I made were to utilize some odd pieces of Pacific Cloth which I couldn't bear to discard. After using them, I was convinced that they were terrific! I can dust my silver without scratching it; and I can buff it between polishings to restore the shine. The mitts won't remove tarnish, but they will restore that "showcase gleam." Also, the tarnish doesn't seem to build up as quickly.

Their unique back-to-front, right-to-left, inside-outside construction will provide 8 different polishing surfaces that can be used over and over again.

Note: The article to be dusted should always be completely dry. The silver dust mitts should *not* be washed.

Materials

Pacific Cloth, ¼ yard or 4 remnants 8″ × 9″
Ribbing, two 5″ × 7″ or ribbed cuffs, 1 pair

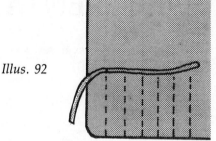

Illus. 93
¼″ = 1″

Pattern and Cutting Directions

1. Enlarge the mitt pattern. (Illus. 93)
2. Using the pattern, cut four mitts. (This is one of the few times you can cut off grain without affecting the finished product.)
3. From the ribbing, cut two 5″ × 7″ cuffs.

Sewing Directions

1. All seam allowances are ¼".
2. Right sides together, stitch two mitt sections together on all sides except the bottom. Trim the seam to ⅛" and zigzag (W,3-L,2) over the edge.
3. Make the cuffs. Fold the ribbing in half crosswise, right sides together: Stitch the ends together to make a circle. Then fold the ribbing, wrong sides together; match and pin the raw edges.
4. Join the cuff and mitt. Right sides together, pin the cuff and mitt together, stretching the ribbing as needed. Stitch. Trim to ⅛" and zigzag (W,3-L,2).

• • •

CONTINENTAL QUILT COVER

This practical gift is particularly easy to sew since it's made from two sheets. (Illus. 94)

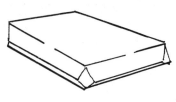

Illus. 94

Materials

Requirements are for a twin cover; other sizes are in parentheses.
Sheets, 2 twin (2 full; 2 queen; 2 king)

Velcro fastening tape, 1 yard (1¼ yds., 1½ yds., 1¾ yds.)

Sewing Directions

1. All seam allowances are ½".
2. Cut the Velcro into 6 (7, 7, 9) equal-length strips.
3. Set the Velcro to one sheet. Pin and stitch it to the wrong side of the wide hem.
Claire's Hint: Place the first and last strip about 2" from the side with 5¼" (5⅜", 5⅜", 5") between the strips.
4. Set the Velcro to the other sheet.
5. Join the two sheets. Right sides together, pin and stitch the sides and bottom. Press.
6. Turn right side out.

PILLOW POTPOURRI

BANDANA PILLOW

Soft and squeezable, this is one of the cleverest designs you'll ever see.
Finished Size: 20″ square

Materials

Bandanas, two 22″ squares, Color A
Bandanas, two 22″ squares, Color B
Pillow form, one 20″

Sewing Directions

1. All seam allowances are ⅛″.
2. Make the pillow top. Right sides together, pin together one bandana of each color. Begin at one corner and stitch 10″. Backstitch. Repeat on the other two bandanas.
3. Right sides together, pin the two sections together matching the seams at the center. Stitch, beginning and ending 10″ from the center. (Illus. 95) To prevent slipping, use a needle to pin the seams together at the center.
4. To finish the pillow, repeat all of the above on the opposite corners.
5. Insert the pillow form into one of the openings. Align the pillow corners with the bandana openings.
6. Tie the ends of the bandanas.

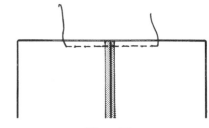

Illus. 95

• • •

ONE-PIECE PILLOW

Designed by sewing-machine expert Betty Bennett, this is one of the cutest and easiest-to-make pillows I've ever seen.
Finished Size: 13″ square (10″ square bandana)

Materials

One square bandana, scarf, or fabric remnant, any size

Two 1" buttons
Polyester batting
Fabric Notes: I particularly like bandanas, scarves, and fabrics with square designs; however, the design must be a perfect square. The diagonal seaming is also very attractive on plain fabrics.

Sewing Directions

1. All seam allowances are ¼". Except when using a hemmed bandana or scarf, match the pattern and disregard the seam allowance width.
2. Right sides together, fold the square in half and stitch the short ends. Press. (Illus. 96a)
3. Right sides together with the center seams matched, stitch the remaining seam, leaving 4"–5" open for turning and filling. (Illus. 96b) To make the opening less conspicuous on the finished pillow, begin it about 3" from one end.
4. Stuff the pillow with fibrefill.
5. Slipstitch the opening closed.
Claire's Hint: For an inconspicuous seam, make the slipstitch a perfect ladder. (Illus. 97)

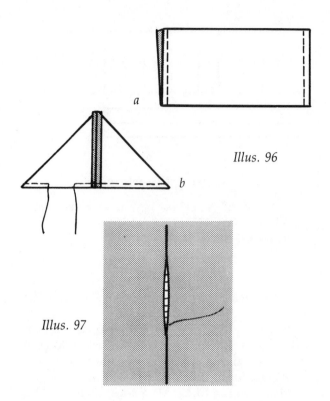

Illus. 96

Illus. 97

• • •

HEIRLOOM PILLOW

Fit for a queen or a princess, this exquisite pillow is certain to become an heirloom. Make this gift for someone extra special.

The pillow utilizes most of the heirloom sewing techniques; and, if this is your first experiment with this beautiful art form, it can serve as a sampler. You'll be surprised how quickly and easily you'll learn the methods and finish the gift.
Finished Size: 13" × 12"

Materials

Fabric, ⅝ yard, 45" wide
Lace edging, 2⅞ yards, ½" wide
Lace insertion, 1¼ yards, ½" wide
Eyelet insertion, ⅝ yard, ¾" wide
Entredeux, 1¼ yards
Ribbon, ⅝ yard, ½" wide

Fabric Notes: Select the best-quality fabrics and trims you can find. The fine thread count and glazed finish on some Swiss batistes are particularly lovely for this gift.

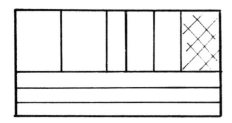

Illus. 98

Cutting Directions

1. Cut two 10″ × 11″ backs, one 4″ × 11″ center panel, two 6″ × 11″ tucking strips, three 45″ × 3″ ruffle strips. (Illus. 98)

Sewing Directions

1. All seam allowances are ½″; hem allowances are 1″.
2. Finish both sides of the center panel and one side of each tucking strip. Fold the seam allowance under and zigzag (W,1-L,1) over the folded edge. Trim close to the stitching.
3. Make the pin tucks. Mark tuck locations. Measure and mark the first tuck ¾″ from the finished edge; mark the other two, spacing all ¾″ apart. To ensure accuracy, pull a thread to mark the tuck lines. Stitch ⅛″ wide tucks. Press the tucks away from the finished edge.
4. Assemble the pillow top. Beginning with the center panel, join a row of entredeux, the lace insertion, the embroidered insertion, another row of lace insertion, a row of entredeux, and the tucking strip.

   Right sides up, butt the edges together and zigzag (W,2-L,2). Press. (Illus. 99)
Claire's Hints: Trim the entredeux before joining to the fabric. Always join the entredeux to fabric, then lace.
5. Measure the pillow top. If it is not 14″ × 11″ trim as needed.

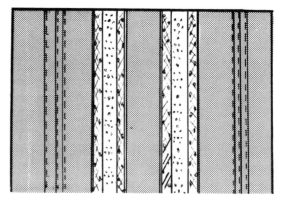

Illus. 99

6. Make the ruffle. French-seam the ruffle pieces to form a strip approximately 100″ long. Finish one edge.
7. Join the lace edging to the ruffle. Right sides up, zigzag (W,2-L,2), stopping and starting 1″ from the end.
8. Make a hairline seam at the ends of the lace and join the lace to the ruffle.
9. Divide and mark the ruffle into quarters. Divide and mark the midpoints on all sides of the pillow top.
10. Gather the ruffle. Make two gathering rows on the ruffle, placing them ½″ and ¼″ from the raw edge. Wrong sides up, zigzag over buttonhole twist. Break the threads at the marked points.
11. Join the ruffle and the pillow top. Right sides together, match the marked points on the ruffle to the centers. Pull up the gathering rows, distribute the fullness evenly, and stitch.
12. Hem the pillow backs. Make a double ½″ hem on one long side of each back.
13. Assemble the pillow. Right sides together, pin one back to the top; pin the other back in place. Stitch.
14. Turn right side out and press.
15. Insert a pillow form.

FIFTEEN-MINUTE PILL

Chic and contemporary, these lively pillows will jazz up any room. A great project for beginners, they're all made from fabric rectangles, and each takes less than 15 minutes to complete.

BULL'S-EYE PILLOW

Bursting with color, this striking pillow looks complicated. The secret is the fabric selection—a boldly colored fabric with a horizontal design.
Finished Size: 12″ diameter

Materials

Fabric, ⅜ yard, 45″ width
Round pillow form, one 12″
Fleece scraps
Cardboard scrap
Fabric Notes: Select a fabric with horizontal stripes; or, if the fabric you like has vertical stripes, cut it on the lengthwise grain. To do this, purchase 1¼ yards or use a remnant 13½″ × 45″.

Cutting Directions

1. From the fabric, cut one rectangle 41″ × 13½″ and two 3½″ circles.
2. From the fleece, cut two 2″ circles.
3. From the cardboard, cut two 1¼″ circles.

Sewing Directions

1. All seam allowances are ½″.
2. Right sides together, join the short ends to make a continuous loop.
3. Place a gathering row ¼″ from each raw edge. Right side up, zigzag (W,3-L,3) over a strong cord

such as dental floss, fishing-tackle line, or buttonhole twist.
4. Pull up the gathering thread on one edge as much as possible; and knot. If the hole is still larger than 1¼″, sew it together by hand to make it smaller. Don't cut the cord used to pull up the gathers. Thread it into a needle and sew the hole together enough for the button to cover it.
5. Insert and adjust the pillow form so the hole is at the center of the pillow.
6. Pull up the gathering thread on the other edge; knot; and sew the hole closed.
7. To make the buttons, baste around each fabric circle. Place the fleece circle, then the cardboard circle in the center. Pull up the basting thread tightly; fasten the thread.
8. Sew the buttons to the pillow.

• • •

CANDY WRAPPER PILLOW

Shaped like a Tootsie Roll candy, this quick-and-easy pillow is particularly attractive in candy stripes and bright solids. With a touch of imagination the possibilities are limitless.
Finished Size: Approximately 28″ × 7¾″; fits a 5″ × 16″ bolster

Materials

...e 31½" × 18"
...ibbon, 1 yard, ¼"–½" wide
...orm, 1
  Notes: Any soft, firmly woven fabric is suit-
...e. I used a stripe.

Cutting Directions

1. Cut one 29" × 18" pillow cover.
2. Cut two 1¼" × 18" ties.

Sewing Directions

1. All seam and hem allowances are ½".
2. Make narrow machine hems on both short ends.
3. Right sides together, join the long sides; press.
4. Turn right side out and insert the pillow form.
5. Make the ties. Instead of fabric ties, you can use ¼"–½" wide ribbon.
6. Tie the strips tightly at each end of the bolster.

• • •

SLEEPING-BAG PILLOW

This pillow looks like a sleeping bag. It's really an easy-to-sew pillowcase with a drawstring at one end.
Finished Size: 30" × 11"; fits a 26" × 20" standard-size pillow

Materials

Remnant, one 30" × 22½"
Drawstring, ribbon, or rope, 1¼ yard
Standard-size pillow, one

Sewing Directions

1. All seam allowances are ¼"; the casing allowance is 1".
2. Right sides together, fold the fabric in half lengthwise and join the end and sides. Turn right side out and press.
3. Make the casing. Fold the hem to the wrong side. Turn under the raw edge ¼" and edgestitch. Press.
4. Fold a standard-size pillow crosswise and insert into the pillow cover.

• • •

SHISHADAR PILLOW

This one-of-a-kind design features a piece of Indian *shishadar* (mirrorwork embroidery) which I purchased at a flea market. Bias binding ties are used to close the pillow at the top.

Shishadar is one of the most popular forms of embroidery in India. Small pieces of silvered glass or mica are attached to the background fabric by a web of embroidery around their edges. The designs and colors are frequently connected to Hindu religious belief, and they believe that the mirrored glass will frighten away evil spirits. Mirrorwork is frequently used on decorative items as well as clothing.

Don't be discouraged if you don't have an attractive piece of ethnic embroidery. Look through your collectibles to find an interesting fabric or use a pretty napkin or place mat you inherited from grandmother.

Finished Size: 16" × 16"

Materials

Embroidered panel (pillow top), one 17" × 17"
Contrast A (back), one 17" × 17"
Contrast B (pillow form), one 34" × 17"
Bias binding, doublefold, 1½ yards
Pillow form, one 16"

Cutting Directions

1. Cut the pillow back from the contrast fabric, making it the same size as the embroidered panel.
2. Cut two 17" squares for the pillow-form cover.

Sewing Directions

1. All seam and hem allowances are ½".
2. Right sides together, join the top and back at the sides and bottom.
3. Make the ties. Zigzag (W,2-L,2) down the center of the bias strip. Cut the strip into six equal lengths.

4. Wrong sides up, position the bias strips ½" from the pillow top. Baste one pair in the center and the others about 2 inches from each end. (Illus. 100)

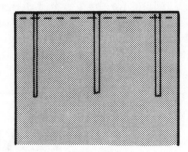

Illus. 100

5. Turn right side out.
6. Make a narrow hem at the top of the pillow, enclosing the raw edges of the ties.
7. Make the pillow-form cover and insert the form. To finish the open end, fold in ½" and machine stitch the folded edges together.
8. Insert the covered pillow form into the pillow and tie the ties.

SAMPLER PILLOW

This sampler pillow is a unique and fun gift to make if you want to explore the many decorative stitches on your sewing machine. The background for the pillow top is a striped fabric, which enables you to stitch straight without drawing lines.

My sampler was stitched on an Elna sewing machine with discs. If your machine doesn't have a lot of different stitches, vary the utility stitches by changing the stitch width and length.
Finished Size: 15″ × 15″

Materials

Remnant A (pillow top), one 16″ × 16″
Contrast (back), one 16″ × 16″
Stabilizer, one 16″ × 16″
Machine embroidery thread: red, orange, blue, yellow, green, purple.
Fibrefill
Fabric Notes: Use a striped fabric for the pillow top. I used pillow ticking for the top and denim for the back. Use several different thread colors or several shades of the same color. I used the rainbow colors.

Sewing Directions

1. All seam allowances are ½″.
2. Pin the stabilizer to the back of the pillow top.
3. Embroider the top with a variety of stitches and/or threads. Press.
4. Right sides together, join four sides, leaving a 4–5″ opening in the center of one side.
5. Turn right side out and press.
6. Fill with fibrefill and close the opening.

● ● ●

FLANGE PILLOW

Simple enough for a child to make, this lovely pillow will add a touch of elegance to any decor. This French pillow sham design is cut in one piece with seams at the top and bottom.
Finished Size: 18″ square

Materials

Fabric, ½ yard, 45″ wide
Pillow form, one 12″ square
Fabric Notes: Select an attractive, firmly woven fabric that blends with the room's furnishing. I used an upholstery material; slipcover (loose cover) and dress-weight fabrics are also suitable.

Cutting Directions

1. Cut one rectangle 45″ × 18″, leaving the selvage at one end to reduce bulk and prevent an unsightly ridge.
2. Mark the two fold lines with short clips on both long sides 13½″ from each end.

Sewing Directions

1. All seam allowances ½″.
2. Hem one short end. Fold under 1″ and topstitch ¾″ from the edge.
3. Right sides together, fold the hemmed end at the fold line; then fold the selvage end at the other fold line. Stitch.
4. Turn right side out.

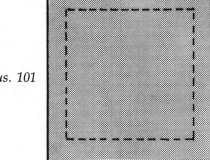

Illus. 101

5. Topstitch 2″ from all edges to make the flange. (Illus. 101)
6. Insert the pillow form.
Claire's Hint: To insert the pillow easily, turn the hemmed end wrong side out; insert the pillow; then return it to its finished position.

• • •

DECORATOR PILLOW

The simplicity of this elegant pillow makes it particularly versatile. A favorite of decorators, you can duplicate this easy-to-sew design for a fraction of the cost.

The pillow top and bottom have deep hems on all edges which are mitred at the corners. Then the two layers are assembled by topstitching through all layers 2″ from the edge.
Finished Size: 16″ square; pillow size, 12″ square

Materials

Fabric, ⅝ yard, 45″ wide
Fibrefill or 12″ pillow form
Fabric Notes: Choose a medium- or lightweight drapery or slipcover fabric, corduroy, velveteen, moiré, faille, and linen to complement the room's decor. I used a soft upholstery fabric.

Since fibrefill makes a softer pillow, I prefer it.

Cutting Directions

Cut two 21″ squares for each pillow.

Sewing Directions

1. All seam allowances are ½″; hem allowances are 2½″.
2. Fold the hem allowance under 2½″ on all four edges of both pillow sections.
3. Mitre and trim all 8 corners, making sure that the mitres are perfect before trimming.
4. Turn right side out and press. (Illus. 102a)

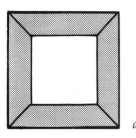 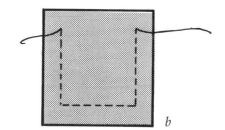 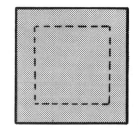

a *b* *c*

Illus. 102

5. Right side up, measure and mark the stitching line on one section 2″ from the edge.
Claire's Hint: Use a fadeaway pen or soap sliver for marking.
6. Wrong sides together, pin the sections together with the edges and corners aligned. Position the pins away from the marked line so you won't stitch over them and so they won't have to be removed until you've finished stitching.
7. Topstitch 2″ from the edge. Stitch on three sides of the pillow through all thicknesses. (Illus. 102b)
8. Insert the pillow form or fibrefill.
9. Close the opening. Change to a zipper foot and topstitch. (Illus. 102c)

• • •

THE CAT'S MEOW

For feline fanciers and pillow people alike, this eye-catching pillow is the cat's meow.
Finished Size: 12½″ circle

Materials

Fabric A (cat and pillow back), one 27″ × 13½″
Fabric B (pillow front), one 13½″ square
Zipper, one 12″
Fusible web, one 13½″ × 9″
Fusible interfacing, scrap
Machine embroidery thread: black and green
Round pillow insert, one 12″
Fibrefill
Fabric Notes: Choose firmly woven fabrics in a medium weight.

Cutting Directions

1. Enlarge the pattern for the cat. (Illus. 103)
2. From Fabric A, cut one 13¼″ circle for the pillow back and one 13¼″ square for the appliqué.
3. From Fabric B, cut one 13½″ circle.
4. Using a release sheet, fuse the fusible web to the wrong side of the Fabric A square. Cut out the cat.
5. From the fusible interfacing, cut out the eyes.

Sewing Directions

1. All seam allowances are ¼″.
2. Right sides up, fuse the cat to the pillow front. Fuse the eyes on the cat.
3. Satin-stitch (W,2) around the cat and eyes.

4. Using green embroidery thread, satin-stitch (W,4) the pupils of the eyes.
5. Set the zipper. Fold the back in half and cut on the fold line. Right sides together, stitch both sides of the zipper to the straight edges. Right side up, edgestitch close to the seam lines.
6. Open the zipper.
7. Right sides together, join the front and back. Press.
8. Turn right side out; insert the pillow form. Stuff bits of fibrefill around the edges to make it smooth.
9. Close the zipper.

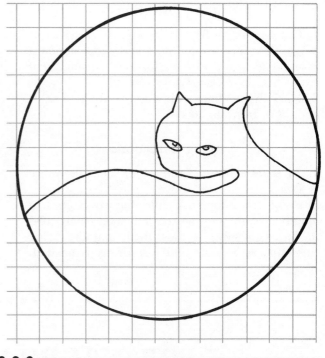

Illus. 103. ¼" = 1"

SEW-EASY PILLOWCASES

This basic pillowcase design can be made up in a variety of fabrics to suit any decor.
Finished Sizes: 31" × 21" for Standard pillows (26" × 20"); 35" × 21" for Queen-sized pillows (30" × 20"); 41" × 21" for King-sized pillows (36" × 20")

Materials

Fabric requirements are for one standard pillow; requirements for queen and king pillows are in parentheses. Double the fabric requirements to make a pair.
Fabric, 1 yard (1⅛ yards; 1¼ yards), 45" wide
Pillow, 1
Fabric Notes: Choose a firmly woven fabric. Sheets are particularly suitable as well as inexpensive. To calculate the number needed for the pillowcases you're making, use these measurements for standard flat sheets (before hemming): twin, 66" × 104"; full, 81" × 104"; queen, 90" × 110"; king, 108" × 110"

Cutting Directions

1. Cut one 43″ × 36″ (43″ × 40″; 43″ × 45″) rectangle. If you're using a twin sheet, cut standard cases 36″ wide and 43″ long; for fabric economy, cut two 22″ × 36″ rectangles for each pillow.
2. Mark the hemline with snips on the two short ends, 4½″ from the top.

Sewing Directions

1. All seam allowances are ½″; the hem allowance is 4½″.
2. Right sides together, fold the cover in half lengthwise and join the end and sides. (Illus. 104)
3. Turn right side out. Press the hem under, using the snips as a guide and measuring as needed.

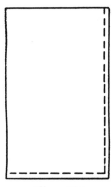

Illus. 104

Fold and pin the raw edge under; edgestitch. Press.
4. Insert the pillow.

● ● ●

FRENCH PILLOW SHAMS

Designed with a 2″ flange around the edges, French pillow shams are especially attractive with continental quilts. The sham design completely conceals the pillow and allows for easy removal. *Finished Size:* 30″ × 24″ (standard-size pillow)

Materials

Material requirements are for two pillow shams.
Fabric, 2¾ yard, 45″ wide
Pillows, 2

Cutting Directions

1. Cut two 30½″ × 24½″ pillow tops and four 20″ × 24½″ pillow backs.

Sewing Directions

1. Seam allowances are ¼″; hem allowances are 1½″.
2. Hem one long side of each back with a double ¾″ hem.
3. Right sides together, join the pillow top and two backs. (Illus. 105)
4. Turn right side out and press.
5. Topstitch around the pillow 2″ from the edge. (Illus. 106a)

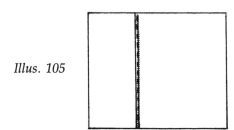

Illus. 105

Claire's Hint: For a fancy finish, satin stitch (W,4) with embroidery thread. For variety, begin and end the stitching at the edges. (Illus. 106b)
   Or stitch using one of the decorative stitches on your machine.
6. Insert the pillow.

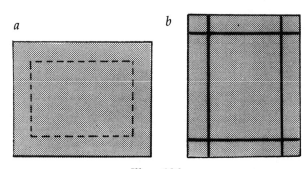

Illus. 106

QUICK-AND-EASY NECKROLL

This small, round neckroll fits a bolster 16" long and 5" in diameter. It has easy-to-make casings at both ends for the drawstrings.
Finished Size: Bolster 16" × 5" × 5".

Materials

Remnant, one 23" × 18"
Ribbon, 1½ yds, ¼"-wide
Bolster form, 1
  (If you don't have a bolster, use these directions to make a neckroll and stuff it with loose or rolled polyester fibrefill.)

Cutting Directions

1. Cut one 23" × 17" bolster.
2. Cut two 27" ribbon strips.

Sewing Directions

1. All seam allowances are ¼".
2. Right sides together, join the long sides to make a continuous loop. Start and end stitching 1" from the ends.
3. Press and turn the pillow right side out.
4. To make the casing at each end, fold ¾" to the wrong side; then fold the raw edge under ¼" and edgestitch close to the inside fold.
Claire's Hint: To secure the stitches, start at the seam, stitch around and overlap ½".
5. Thread the ribbon into the casings with a safety pin. Clip the ends of the ribbon diagonally to retard fraying or use a fray retardant.
6. Insert the bolster form. Pull up the ribbons and tie.

• • •

FRENCH FOLD COVERS

This ingenious design covers the pillow form completely and it's quick and easy to remove. It is particularly attractive when used with continental quilts.
Finished Size: 26" × 21"; fits a standard-size pillow 26" × 21"

Materials

Material requirements are for two pillow covers.
Fabric, 1⅝ yards, 45" wide
Pillows, 2

Cutting Directions

1. Cut two 22" × 58½" covers.

Sewing Directions

1. All seam allowances are ½"; hem allowances are 1½".
2. Make a double ¾" hem on both short ends.

3. Right sides together, make a fold 23½" from one end; then make a fold 8" from the other end. (Illus. 107)

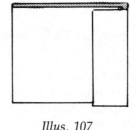

Illus. 107

4. Pin and stitch the top and bottom.
5. Turn right side out and press.
6. Insert the pillows.

HEIRLOOM SHAMS AND PILLOWCASES

A beautiful reminder of times past, these European-inspired shams and pillowcases are elegantly trimmed with eyelet embroidery. Perfect for summer or year-round bed dressing, they will be a lovely gift for romantics.

PILLOWCASES

These beautiful traditionally styled pillowcases belie the time and talent needed to make them.
Finished Size: Standard, 27″ × 21″; King, 39″ × 21″.

Materials

Material requirements are for two standard pillowcases; requirements for king-sized pillowcases are in parentheses.
Fabric, 1½ yards (2¼ yards), 45″ wide
Eyelet Edging, 2½ yards, 3½″–4″ wide
Beaded Insertion, 2½ yards, ⅝″–1″ wide
Ribbon, 2½″ yards, ¼″–⅜″ wide
Pillows, 2
Fabric Notes: Swiss cotton, handkerchief linen, and cotton/polyester blends are suitable fabrics. I used batiste, edgings, and insertions imported from Switzerland. These are available at specialty shops stocking smocking and French hand-sewing supplies.

Cutting Directions

1. Cut two pillowcases 43″ × 27″ (43″ × 45″)
2. Trim away the seam allowances on the beaded insertion.

Sewing Directions

1. All seam allowances are ½″.
2. Finish one long edge of each pillowcase and the long, unfinished edge of the eyelet edging. Fold the seam allowance under and zigzag (W,1-L,1) over the folded edge.
Claire's Hints: Trim close to the stitched line, using appliqué scissors to trim. Anchor the fabric under the presser foot to hold it taut while trimming.
3. Right sides up, butt the edges of the eyelet and insertion together, zigzag (W,2-L,2) to join. Repeat to join the insertion to the pillowcase. Trim the

edging and insertion even with the pillowcase. (Illus. 108)
Claire's Hint: If you have an occasional "holiday" (unstitched section), don't worry; it's easy to re-stitch it inconspicuously. If you have a lot of "holidays," zigzag with a wider (W,2.5) stitch.
4. Insert the ribbon into the eyelet beading. Cut off the ribbon tail.
5. French-seam the sides and end of the pillowcase.
6. Turn right side out. Press.

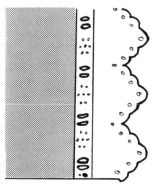

Illus. 108

PILLOW SHAMS

The soft eyelet flange on the four sides of these pillow shams gives them an elegant, tailored look. *Finished Size: 26″ square to fit 24″ square pillows.*

Materials

Material requirements are for two pillow shams.
Fabric, 3 yards, 45″ wide.
Eyelet Edging, 7¾ yards, 5½″–6″ wide
Pillows, two 24″ square

Cutting Directions

1. Cut two fronts 27″ square. Mark all edges with a snip 2½″ from each corner.
2. Cut four backs 17″ × 27″.

Sewing Directions

1. All seam allowances are ½″; hem allowances are 1″.
2. Make the eyelet flange. French-seam the ends of the edging to make a circle. Divide and mark the raw edge into quarters, placing the seam at one quarter mark. Make two short clips 5⅛″ on each side of the quarter marks.

    Place two gathering rows between the clipped points. Each section to be gathered will be 10¼″ with a long (22″) ungathered section between.
3. Join the flange to the pillow front. Right sides together, pin the flange and pillow front together, matching the snips and corner points. Pull up the gathering threads and adjust the gathers. Stitch the flange to the pillow front. (Illus. 109a)
Claire's Hint: For more attractive corners, trim the corners on the pillow top before joining the flange.

    Mark a point 4″ from each corner. Trim away ½″ at the corner, tapering to nothing at the marked point. (Illus. 109b)
4. Hem the pillow backs. Make a double ½″ hem on one long edge.
5. Assemble the pillow sham. Right sides together, pin one pillow back to the front; cover with remaining back, wrong sides up; repin. Stitch.

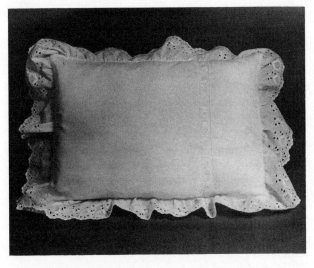

(Illus. 109c) Don't forget to trim the corners to correspond to the pillow top.
6. Trim the seam to ¼″ and round the corners.
7. Turn right sides out and insert the pillow.

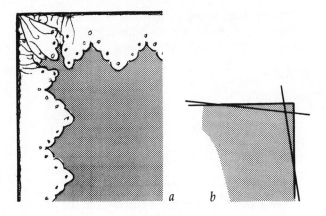

Illus. 109

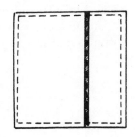

NECKROLL

Pretty as well as practical, this neckroll is especially appropriate with antique or period furnishings.

Finished Size: 5″ × 16″

Materials

Fabric, ⅜ yards, 45″ wide
Eyelet edging, 1½ yards, 3½″ or 4″ wide
Ribbon, 1 yard, ⅛″ or ¼″ wide

Cutting Directions

1. Cut one 17″ × 12″ pillow top and two 17″ × 5″ ends.
2. Cut the eyelet edging and ribbon in half.

Sewing Directions

1. All seam allowances are ½″; casing allowances are 1″.
2. Right sides together, join the short ends of the pillow top to make a circle. (Illus. 110) Repeat for the ends. Press the seams open.

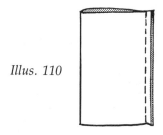

Illus. 110

3. Make one eyelet ruffle. French-seam the ends to make a circle; then divide and mark the raw edge into quarters. Place two gathering rows along the edge. Make the other ruffle.
4. Divide and mark the open ends of the pillow top into quarters.

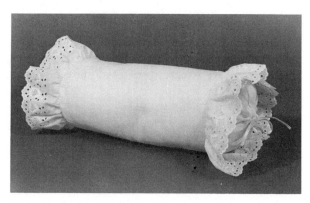

5. Join the ruffle and pillow top. Right sides together, pin, matching the marked points. Pull up the gathering threads and adjust the gathers evenly. Stitch.

Claire's Hint: It is easier to pin the ruffle in place with the pillow right side out; however, if you don't have an open-arm sewing machine, it is easier to stitch with it wrong side out.

6. Join the top and ends. Right sides together, pin the top and ends with the ruffle sandwiched between; stitch.
7. Make a ½″ double casing at each end.
8. Rip the seam about ½″ and thread the ribbon into the casing. (Illus. 111)

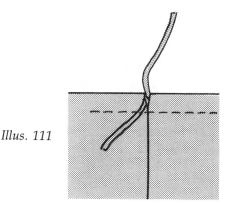

Illus. 111

• • •

BREAKFAST PILLOW

This breakfast or boudoir pillow is lavishly trimmed with a full ruffled border and should enhance any bedroom. It is particularly attractive in all white for a bride or a baby.

Finished Size: 12″ × 16″.

Materials

Fabric requirements are for one pillow.
Fabric, ⅜ yard, 45″ wide
Eyelet edging, 2 yards, 3½″ or 4″ wide
Beaded insertion, ⅜ yard, ⅝″ or 1″ wide
Ribbon, ⅜ yard, ¼″ or ⅜″ wide

Cutting Directions

1. Cut one large 12″ × 13″ front and one small 5″ × 13″ front.
2. Cut two 12″ × 13″ backs.
3. Trim away the seam allowances on the beaded insertion.

Sewing Directions

1. All seam allowances are ½″; hem allowances are 1″.
2. Make the pillow top. Finish one long edge on both the large and small pillow fronts. Right sides up, join them with the beaded insertion between. Thread the ribbon into the insertion.
3. Mark the midpoint on each side of the pillow top with a small snip.
4. Make the eyelet ruffle. French-seam the ends of the eyelet edging to make a circle; divide and mark the raw edge into quarters. Place two rows of gathering stitching along the edge. Break your threads at each quarter mark and start again so the rows will be easy to pull up.

5. Right sides together, pin the ruffle and front together, matching the marked points. Pull up the gathering threads and adjust the gathers evenly. Stitch the ruffle to the front. (Illus. 112) Move more gathers towards the corners if you want the ruffle to form a square border.

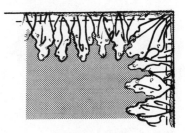

Illus. 112

6. Hem the pillow backs. Make a double ½″ hem on one long edge.
7. Assemble the pillow sham. Right sides together, pin and stitch the pillow backs to the front.
8. Trim the seam to ¼″ and round the corners.
9. Turn right sides out and insert the pillow.

● ● ●

QUILTED PILLOW COVERS

Made like pillow shams, these quilted pillow covers are lifesavers for expensive pillows. Although they are not inexpensive to make, similar quality covers—when and if you can find them—cost three to four times as much.
Finished Size: 20″ × 26″

Materials

Material requirements are for two pillow covers.
Fabric (quilted), 1⅝ yards, 45″ wide
Fabric Notes: Generally, white is the best color choice; however, I have used colors under sheer pillowcases to create an interesting effect.

Cutting Directions

Cut two 21″ × 57″ rectangles.

Sewing Directions

1. Fold under each short end ½″ and stitch ¼″ from the fold. To save time, I stitch all four ends without cutting the threads until I'm finished.
2. Mark the fold lines with small snips 5″ from one end and 25″ from the other end.
3. Right sides together, fold and pin the short end in place; then fold the long end over it. (Illus. 113)
4. Stitch the seams at the top and bottom.
5. Turn right side out.

Illus. 113

BOLSTER FORM

Finding the perfect size bolster form can be a challenge. Generally, I make the bolster forms so they can be custom sized. (Illus. 114)
Finished Size: 16″ × 5″ × 5″

Illus. 114

Materials

Remnant, one 18″ × 16″
Ties, two 18″
Bonded Batting, one 22½″ × 16″
Fabric Notes: Slippery fabrics are best for bolster forms, making them easy to slide into the cover. Any leftover ribbon, braid, hem tape, bias binding, or postal twine can be used for the ties.

You can substitute fibrefill for the bonded batting.

Sewing Directions

1. All seam allowances are ¼″; hem allowances are ¾″.
2. Make the casings on the two short ends. Fold under ¾″; then fold the raw edges under ¼″; edge-stitch.
3. Right sides together, join the long sides to make a continuous loop.
4. Clip 3 or 4 stitches in the seam to make an opening for the casing tie.
5. Cut the tie in half, and, using a small safety pin, thread the ties into the casings.
6. Stuff the bolster cover with loose fibrefill or make a roll of bonded batting. Loosely cross-stitch so it will hold its shape. Pull up the ties and knot.

• • •

KNIFE-EDGE PILLOW FORMS

Several gifts need pillow forms which you may wish to purchase. If you can't find the right size or shape, it's very easy to make your own.

Cutting Directions

SQUARE AND RECTANGULAR PILLOWS
1. Seam allowances are ½″.
2. Determine the finished pillow length and width. Add 1″ to each measurement.
3. Cut two. *Example:* 10″ × 12″ pillow form—cut two 11″ × 13″ sections.

ROUND PILLOWS
1. Seam allowances are ½″.
2. Determine the diameter of the finished pillow.
3. Cut two circles with a diameter 1″ larger than the finished pillow. *Example:* Round 12″ pillow—cut two 13″ circles.

UNUSUAL SHAPES
1. Draw the shape on your pattern paper and add ½″ seam allowances.
2. Pin pattern to fabric and cut out two sections.
3. If the shape is unusually intricate, mark the

stitching lines on one section. Occasionally, I draw the seam lines on the fabric, stitch, then cut out.

Sewing Directions

1. All seam allowances are ½″.
2. *Rectangle pillows:* Join the two sections on three sides.
Round pillows: Join the two sections, leaving approximately 6″ open.
Unusual pillows: Join the two sections, leaving approximately 6″ open along a straight or an almost-straight edge. (Illus. 115)

Illus. 115

3. Turn right side out.
4. Stuff with fibrefill. First, put a small amount in each corner, then lightly pad the seam lines, finish stuffing to the desired firmness.
5. Close the opening.
Claire's Hint: Fold in the seam allowances and edge-stitch the seam closed.

FOR THE EXECUTIVE

PADDED HANGERS

Padded hangers are a wonderful addition to any-body's closet. Practical and attractive, these hangers will keep garments wrinkle-free as well as preserve a garment's shape.

Materials

Remnant, one 24" × 6"
Fleece, one 18" × 7"
Ribbon, ⅝ yard, ⅜"–1" wide
Wooden hanger, 1
Optional: Stemmed buttons, two ¼"–⅜" diameter
Fabric Notes: Most fabrics, even muslin, are suitable for this gift, I try to avoid fabrics which crock or fade when exposed to steam. For your own closet, use the fabric scraps to make a hanger for each garment.

Cutting Directions

1. Cut two 3" × 9" bottoms and two 3" × 14" tops. Round one end on each of the four sections.
2. Cut the fleece into two 9" × 7" rectangles.

Sewing Directions

1. All seam allowances are ¼".
2. Place a row of gathers on each side of the long strips, using a heavy cord such as buttonhole twist and zigzagging (W,2-L,2) over it.
3. Pull up the gathers.
4. Make the cover for one end of the hanger. Right sides together, pin one long strip to one short strip. Zigzag (W,2-L,2) the sides and curved end.
5. Turn right side out. Try using a marking pen (with the cap on) to push the fabric through.
6. Make the cover for the other end.

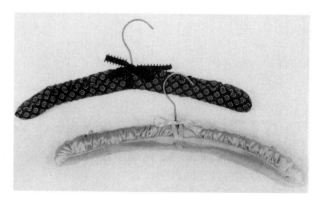

7. Wrap one piece of fleece around one end of the hanger. Fold the fleece end under about 2". Pull the cover over the padded end, centering the gathers on the top. Repeat on the other end.
Claire's Hint: Some covers are more difficult to pull on than others. Sewing expert Bobbie Carr taught me this trick to make them all easy.

Hold a piece of nylon panty hose, about 6" square, firmly over each end, then pull on the cover.

8. Sew the covers together at the center. This doesn't have to be too neat. I use a cross-stitch.

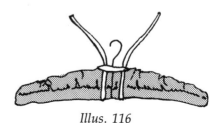

Illus. 116

9. Tie the ribbon around the hanger and tie a bow. (Illus. 116)
10. *Optional:* For ladies, sew the buttons on the top about 3" from each end.

THE EXECUTIVE PORTFOLIO

Precisely what every executive needs, this portfolio was designed by Marcy Tilton, owner of The Sewing Workshop (San Francisco). The possibilities for this gift are unlimited.
Finished Size: 14½" × 10".

Materials

Remnant A (portfolio), one 31" × 8¼"
Remnant B (lining and trim), one 45" × 11½"
Remnant C (cording), one 31" × 2½"
Fleece, 15" × 20", 1
Zipper, 14"
Cord, ⅞ yard, ¼"–⅜" diameter
Fabric Notes: Firmly woven fabrics such as canvas, duck, denim, velveteens and silk broadcloth are just a few of the suitable ones.

Cutting Directions

1. From Remnant A, cut two 15½" × 8¼" portfolio bottoms.
2. From Remnant B, cut two 15½" × 4" portfolio tops and two 15½" × 11¼" lining sections.
3. Use the pattern to cut four tabs. (Illus. 117)
4. From the fleece, cut two 15" × 11" rectangles.

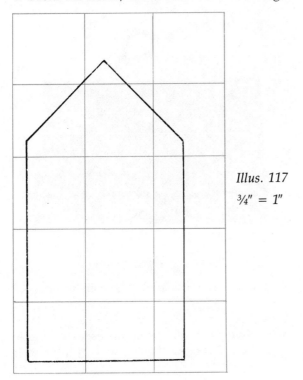

Illus. 117
¾" = 1"

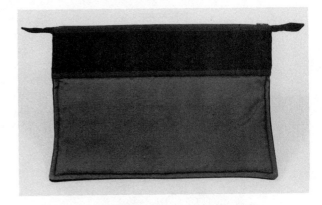

Sewing Directions

1. All seam allowances are ½".
2. Make the piped cording from Remnant C. Trim the seam allowances to ½".
3. Make the portfolio front and back. Right sides together, stitch the piping to the portfolio bottom. Right sides together, stitch the top and bottom together. Press.
4. Wrong side up, pin the fleece to the back and front. Stitch ⅜" from the edge.
5. Join the lining to the front and back. Right sides together, stitch all sides, leaving a 2"–4" opening at the bottom. For neater corners, take two diagonal stitches across each corner. (Illus. 118)

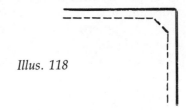

Illus. 118

6. Trim the corners; turn right side out; and press.
Claire's Hint: The completed portfolio back and front should look like two place mats.
7. Machine-quilt the top, spacing the rows ¼" apart. (Illus. 119) Using the all-purpose zigzag foot, stitch, using the outside edge as a gauge. Use a topstitching or larger needle than usual.

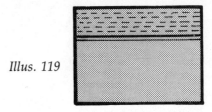

Illus. 119

8. Make the tabs. Right sides together, stitch. (Illus. 120) Turn right side out and press.

Illus. 120

9. Set the tabs to the zipper. Insert the ends of the zipper into the tabs. Topstitch in place. (Illus. 121)

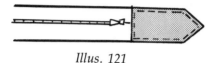

Illus. 121

10. Set the zipper. Right sides up, pin the zipper to the top of the portfolio front and back. Stitch at the edge of the zipper. (Illus. 122)

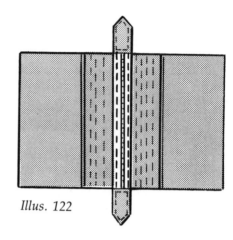

Illus. 122

11. Join the front and back. Topstitch the sides and bottom ¼″ from the edge.
Claire's Hint: To prevent skipped stitches when stitching over the cording, set your machine in low gear; stitch slowly, and use a needle lubricant.

• • •

COMPUTER BRIEFCASE

At last a briefcase specially sized to hold all those computer printouts; and, to make it even better, it's lightweight. All the computer-users on your gift list will want this useful gift.
Finished Size: 16″ × 14″.

Materials

Fabric, ½ yard, 45″ wide
Straight open-hex frame, one 18″
Optional: Cardboard, 16″ × 14″
Fabric Notes: Choose a firmly woven, light or medium fabric, synthetic suede or leather. I used a water-repellent rip-stop nylon.

Sewing Directions

1. All seam allowances are ½″; hem allowances are 2″.
2. Make the straps.
3. Make two ⅞″ buttonholes on each rectangle, placing them 2″ below the top and 2″ from each side. (Illus. 123)

Cutting Directions

1. Cut two 17″ × 15″ rectangles.
2. Cut two 4″ × 18″ straps.

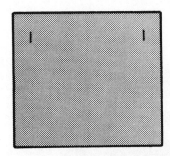

Illus. 123

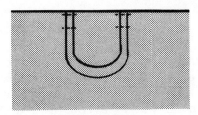

Illus. 124

4. Right sides together, center the straps with 5″ between at the top of each rectangle. Pin and stitch them to the hem allowance. (Illus. 124)
5. French-seam the sides and bottom.
6. Turn right side out.

7. Fold and pin the hem allowance to the inside of the briefcase. Pin the straps in place. Fold the raw edge under and edgestitch. Stitch again ¼″ from the top.
8. Insert the frame.
9. *Optional*: Insert the piece of cardboard.

• • •

EXECUTIVE NOTE PADS

Need a last-minute gift? Just want to say thanks or thinking of you? Executive note pads are ideal.

Materials

Remnant, one 22″ × 4″
Note pad, one 3″ × 5″
Fabric Notes: Select a fabric appropriate for the recipient. Silk, denim, Ultrasuede, wool, cottons, almost any fabric is suitable.

Cutting Directions

1. Cut one 22″ × 4″ cover. Mark the pocket fold lines 5″ from the ends.
2. To cover a different-size note pad, measure the pad in the closed position, beginning at the bottom of the front cover and ending at the bottom of the back cover. Measure the width. To determine the outside cover measurement, add ½″ ease to both measurements. To the outside cover measurement, add 10″ to the length for the two inside pockets.

Sewing Directions

1. All seam and hem allowances are ½″.

2. Hem the short ends of the cover. Fold the hem allowance under and topstitch ¼″ from the edge.
3. Right sides together, fold the cover at the marked points. Stitch the sides of the pockets. (Illus. 125)

Illus. 125

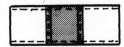

4. Press under the seam allowances in the unstitched section.
5. Turn right side out. Press.
6. Insert the note pad.

WOOLLEN SCARF

For meetings in the city, long hikes, active sports, or just plain cold weather, a new woollen scarf is a welcome addition to any person's wardrobe. And, if you shop as I do, you frequently have a piece of expensive wool, just the right size.
Finished Size: 54" × 12" or 60" × 12"

Materials

Remnant, 12" or ⅜ yard, 54"–60" wide
Fabric Notes: Soft, nonscratchy woollens such as flannels, cashmere, tartans, and lamb's wool are suitable.

Cutting Directions

Cut one rectangle across the width of the fabric 12" long.

Sewing Directions

1. On the short ends, zigzag (W,2-L,2) 2" from the edge.
Claire's Hint: Pull a thread 2" from the selvage and zigzag on the marked line.
2. Cut off the selvages and fringe the ends, cutting the fabric every 2"–3" inches to make it easy to fringe. (Illus. 126)

3. Zigzag (W,2-L,2) the remaining sides ¼" from the edge. Fringe the sides.
4. Voilà! You're finished.

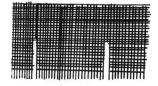

Illus. 126

THE ACCESSORY BOUTIQUE

MARCY'S BELT

Designed by Marcy Tilton, owner of The Sewing Workshop in San Francisco, this belt features a beautiful wide braid from Britex Fabrics.
Finished Size: 4" × 40"

Materials

Braid or ribbon, 1½ yards, 4" wide
Round cord, ⅝ yard

Sewing Directions

1. Make a loop at one end. Turn the end under ½". Then fold wrong sides together 9" from the end. Pin to the wrong side of the belt, as indicated by the broken line on the diagram. (Illus. 127a)

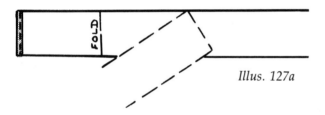

Illus. 127a

2. Stitch as shown. (Illus. 127b)

Illus. 127b

3. Finish the other end. Fold under 1". Accordion-pleat the fold to make it as small as possible. Wrap the cord around the end. (Illus. 127c)

Illus. 127c

Claire's Hint: Hide one end of the cord in the folds before beginning. Wrap about 1"; then thread the cord into a yarn needle and sew it under the wrap.

• • •

COLLAGE BELT

This handsome belt looks more difficult to make than it actually is.
Finished Size: 46" × 4"

Materials

Fabric A (Lamaire—brown) ⅛ yard, 54" wide
Contrast B (multi-colored fabric), ⅜ yard, 45" wide
Remnant C (Ultrasuede—blue), one 6" × 4"
Remnant D (Ultrasuede—gold), one 8" × 3"
Remnant E (Ultrasuede—purple), one 7" × 1½"
Crisp fusible interfacing, ⅜ yard
Fusible web, ¼ yard
Fabric Notes: For the belt back (Fabric A), choose a nonwoven material such as leather or suede (real or synthetic). For the belt front and appliqués, choose woven, knit, and nonwoven material in complementary colors.

Cutting Directions

1. Enlarge the belt pattern. Add a strip 13" long at the dotted line. (Illus. 128a)
2. Trace the appliqués. (Illus. 128b)
3. From Fabric A, cut one belt back 46" long and one Appliqué A.

Fuse the interfacing to the wrong side of Contrast B. Then cut the interfaced fabric into 4" wide bias strips; join them to make one long strip. Using the enlarged pattern, cut one belt front.

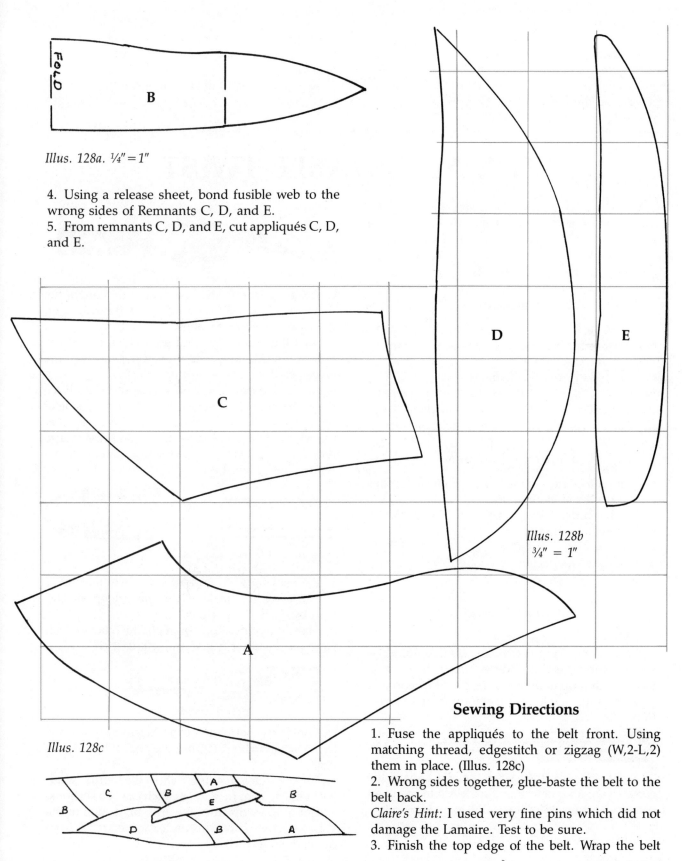

Illus. 128a. ¼" = 1"

4. Using a release sheet, bond fusible web to the wrong sides of Remnants C, D, and E.
5. From remnants C, D, and E, cut appliqués C, D, and E.

Illus. 128b
¾" = 1"

Illus. 128c

Sewing Directions

1. Fuse the appliqués to the belt front. Using matching thread, edgestitch or zigzag (W,2-L,2) them in place. (Illus. 128c)
2. Wrong sides together, glue-baste the belt to the belt back.
Claire's Hint: I used very fine pins which did not damage the Lamaire. Test to be sure.
3. Finish the top edge of the belt. Wrap the belt

back over the top of the front. Edgestitch. Trim the back close to the stitched line.

Claire's Hint: To ensure even stitching on Lamaire or leather, dab a little needle lubricant or talcum powder on the right side of the material.

To prevent skipped stitches on Ultrasuede, Facile, or suede, use a new needle and needle lubricant.

4. Repeat to finish the bottom of the belt.

• • •

THE ADJUSTABLE TWIST

You'll get raves with this wardrobe accessory. The design features corded bias tubing tied in a permanent knot between the two belt sections and adjustable Velcro fasteners at the back.

Finished Size: Fits 24"–33" waists.

Materials

Fabric, ¼ yard (½ yard for bias-cut belt), 45" wide
Nonwoven, fusible interfacing, ⅛ yard
Velcro fastening tape, 6"
Cording, 3½ yards, ⅜" diameter
Fabric Notes: Silks, polyesters, lightweight cottons, and polyester/cotton blends are good choices.

I prefer Style-A-Shade for my fusible interfacing.

Cutting Directions

1. From the fabric, cut four 14" × 2¾" belt sections on the bias or straight grain.
2. For the corded loops, cut enough 2" wide bias to make four 18" strips.
3. Cut one 1½" × 5" belt loop.
4. From the interfacing, cut four 13¼" × 2" rectangles.

Sewing Directions

1. All seam allowances are ⅜".
2. Make the corded bias tubings. Place each bias strip on the table right side up. Place the cord on top of each strip, letting one cord end extend 20". Machine-stitch the long end of the cord to the bias. (Illus. 129)

Illus. 129

3. Right sides together, wrap the bias around the cord. Using a zipper foot, stitch close to the cord; trim the seam to ⅛". (Illus. 130)

Illus. 130

Claire's Hint: Don't stitch too close to the cord or the finished tubing will be lumpy and the ridges on the cord will show through.

Hold the end of the cord securely and turn the tube right side out over the cord. Cut away the excess cord.

4. Make two belt and two facing sections. Place the interfacing fusible side up on the wrong side of the sections. Fold the fabric seam allowances over the edges of the interfacing. Carefully press to fuse them in place. Do not allow the iron point to touch the fusible. (Illus. 131)

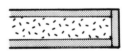 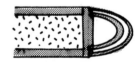

Illus. 131   *Illus. 132*

5. Pin both ends of two corded loops to the end of one belt section, making the inner loop shorter than the outer loop. (Illus. 132)
6. Make the center knot; then pin the other ends in place on the other belt section. (Illus 133)

Illus. 133

7. Center the soft side of the Velcro strip on one facing section about 1" from the end. Edgestitch in place.
8. Fusible sides together with the cords sandwiched between, fuse. Edgestitch the belt sections.
9. Cut a 2½" strip from the stiff, hook side of the Velcro. Center it on the underlap about ½" from the end; edgestitch in place.

10. Make the loop for the end of the overlap. Wrong sides together, press in half lengthwise. Fold the raw edges to the fold line; align the folds; and edgestitch both sides of the strip.

11. Stitch the strip to the end of the overlap.
12. Tack the ends together on the underside to make the loop.

• • •

CUMMERBUND VARIATION

The cummerbund is an easy-to-make variation of the adjustable twist belt. (Illus. 134)

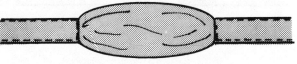

Illus. 134

Materials

Fabric, ¼ yard, 45" wide
Nonwoven fusible interfacing, ⅛ yard
Velcro, 6"

Cutting Directions

1. Cut one 13" × 9" cummerbund, four 14" × 2¾" belt sections, and one 2" × 5" loop.
Claire's Hint: This variation is particularly attractive cut from a diagonally striped fabric or on the bias. Purchase ½ yard for a bias-cut design.
2. From the interfacing, cut four 13¼" × 2" rectangles.

Sewing Directions

1. All seam and hem allowances are ⅜".
2. Make a machine-rolled hem on each of the long sides of the cummerbund.
Claire's Hint: To make a machine-rolled hem, begin

right sides up. Fold under ¼" and edgestitch. Trim closely. Wrong side up, fold again and edgestitch.

The secrets of a very narrow hem are to stitch very close to the edge and to trim very close to the stitched line.
3. Make the belt sections, following the directions above.
4. Gather each of the short ends of the cummerbund to fit the ends of the belts (2"). Baste. (Illus. 135)
5. Complete the belt following the directions above.

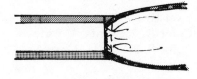

Illus. 135

• • •

RIBBON BELT

This popular belt design has been used by beltmakers and designers in all price ranges. Since one size fits many waistlines, it is perfect for gifts.

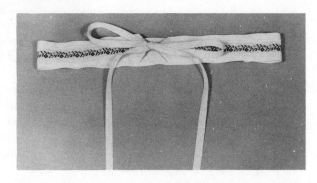

Materials

Ribbon A, one ¾ yard (small/medium); ⅞ yard (medium/large), ¾" wide
Ribbon B, same yardage as Ribbon A, 1" wide
Ribbon C, 1½ yards, ¼" wide

Sewing Directions

1. Make the belt. Center Ribbon B on Ribbon A, edgestitch together.
2. Cut the narrow ribbon in half to make the ties. Right sides up, center on the belt at each end; pin. (Illus. 136a)

3. Right sides together, fold the belt in half lengthwise. (Illus. 136b)
4. Turn right side out. (Illus. 137)

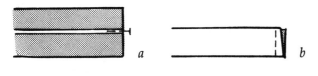

a

b

Illus. 136

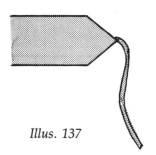

Illus. 137

• • •

EASY DESIGNER BELT

Inspired by a very expensive Nina Ricci design, this belt takes less than a half hour to sew.

Long enough to wrap around the waist twice and tie at the front, it's made of a decorative braid and two coordinating ribbons.
Finished Size: 3" × 88"

Materials

Braid, 2½ yards, 1"–1½" wide
Ribbon, Color A, 2½ yards, 1" wide
Ribbon, Color B, 2½ yards, 1" wide

Sewing Directions

1. Seam allowances are ¼".
2. Join the braid and ribbons. Right sides up, center the braid between the ribbons, butt the edges, and zigzag (W,2-L,2).

3. Finish the ends. Right sides together, fold the belt in half lengthwise. Stitch a straight seam across the ends.
4. Turn right side out. Press.

• • •

EASY FASHION BELT

A little bit of Ultrasuede, Facile, real leather, suede, or Lamaire, a pair of D-rings and less than an hour are the only requirements for this elegant belt.
Finished Sizes: Small (24"–26" waist), 32"; Medium (28"–32" waist), 37"; Large (34"–38" waist), 43"

Materials

Fabric requirements are for small-size belts; requirements for other sizes are in parentheses.
Fabric, ⅛ yard, 45" wide
Fusible web, 34" (40"; 45"), 2" wide
D-rings, two 1½"
Fabric Notes: Select a nonwoven material for the belt.

Cutting Directions

1. Cut one 32" × 4½" (37", 43") belt.
2. Cut two 1" × 4½" strips to cover the D-rings.

Sewing Directions

1. Make the covers for the D-rings. Wrong sides together, stitch a skimpy ¼" from the raw edges. Carefully trim close to the stitched line. (To get a close trim without zigs and zags, use very sharp scissors, such as appliqué scissors.)
2. Cover the D-rings. Using pliers, open the D-rings enough to slip the covers over them. Close.
3. Wrong sides together, fold the belt in half lengthwise. Slip the fusible web between the layers and fuse.

Claire's Hint: Generally, leather, suede, Ultrasuede, Facile, and Lamaire can be fused without problems. To be sure, always test on a scrap before fusing the belt.

4. Trim away a triangle at the corner to make an attractive end, beginning the point of the triangle at the folded edge. (Illus. 138) If you prefer, however,

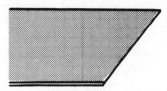

Illus. 138

leave the end straight like many of the purchased belts. This is a particularly good idea if you are a little short of fabric or making an extra large belt.
5. Topstitch the belt. Topstitch ¹⁄₁₆" from the fold line and shaped end; topstitch the other side ¼" from the edge. Trim close to the stitched line.
Claire's Hint: For smooth, skip-free stitching, use a needle lubricant.
6. Thread the straight end into the D-rings; fold the end over 1½", and stitch, using a zipper foot to stitch close to the D-rings.

• • •

CLASSIC OBI

The classic obi tie is a flattering belt for most figures. And it's easy to make in suede or leather (real or synthetic) for yourself and your friends.
Finished Size: Small, 3½" × 72"; Medium, 3½" × 80"; Large, 3½" × 92"

Materials

Fabric, 12 inches, 36" wide
Fusible Web, ¼ yard
Fabric Notes: I used Ultrasuede; however, real suedes, leathers, and Lamaire would also be attractive. If your fabric is 48" wide or wider, purchase ¼ yard for small-size belts.

Cutting Directions

Directions are for a small belt; directions for medium and large belts are in parentheses.

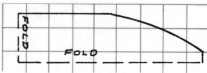

1. Enlarge the pattern (Illus. 139)
2. Cut two 21" × 4" belt sections and two 26" (30", 36") × 2" ties.

Illus. 139.
¼" = 1"

3. From the fusible web, cut one 21″ × 4″ belt and two 26″ (30″, 36″) × 2″ ties.

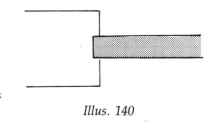

Illus. 140

Sewing Directions

1. Make the ties. Wrong sides together and the fusible web sandwiched between, fold each tie in half lengthwise and fuse. Edgestitch ¹⁄₁₆″ from the tie foldline. Topstitch ⅛″ from the raw edges. Trim the raw edges close to the topstitching.
2. Wrong sides up, glue-baste the ties to the ends of the belt, centering them. (Illus. 140)
3. Fold the belt in half lengthwise to determine the centers. Use small clips to mark.

4. Fuse the belt. Right sides out with the fusible web and ties sandwiched between. Fuse the belt sections together.
5. Using the obi pattern, draw the belt on the material, using a sliver of soap or a fadeaway marking pen.
6. Topstitch ¼″ from the raw edges and trim.

• • •

QUICK-AND-EASY TIE

Some belts are for special occasions; others to wear every day. This versatile belt fits both categories. Make them for all your friends in a variety of fabrics and colors.
Finished Size: Small–Medium: 44″ × 3½″; Large: 53″ × 3½″

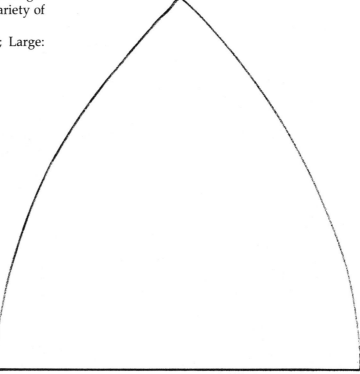

Illus. 141

Materials

Material requirements are for small/medium; requirements for a large belt are in parentheses.
Fabric A, ¼ yard (54" wide, ¼ yard), 45" wide
Optional: Crisp fusible interfacing, ½" yard (⅝ yard)
Fabric Notes: Fabrics like raw silk, linen, Ultrasuede, and Lamaire make very attractive belts.

Cutting Directions

1. Trace the pattern. (Illus. 141)
2. Cut two 4" wide strips the width of the fabric. Using the pattern, shape the ends.
Claire's Hint: This belt is more attractive when it isn't pieced. For a longer belt, cut it on the straight grain.
3. For a stiffer belt, fuse the interfacing to the wrong side of Fabric A before cutting. Piece the interfacing as needed.

Sewing Directions

1. All seam allowances are ¼".
2. Right sides together, stitch the tie, leaving a 4"–5" opening at the center.
3. Trim the corners at each end.
4. Turn right side out; press.
5. Pin the opening closed. Edgestitch the tie.
6. If the tie isn't interfaced, quilt it so it won't "wilt." (Illus. 142)

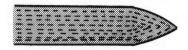

Illus. 142

Claire's Hint: Use the edge of the presser foot as a gauge for spacing the quilting rows.

• • •

CORDUROY TOTE BAG

Everyone can use another tote bag, especially an attractive, roomy one. Personalized or plain, it will delight the recipient. This is a lovely gift to keep on hand.
Finished Size: 12½" × 11½" × 6"

Materials

Fabric A (the bag), ½ yard, 45" wide
Fabric B (lining), ½ yard, 45" wide
Nonwoven fusible interfacing, ½ yard
Stabilizer, 5" square
Embroidery thread
Fabric Notes: For the tote, select a firmly woven, sturdy material such as corduroy, canvas, denim, duck, leather, Lamaire, synthetic suedes and leathers. I used a pinwale corduroy and lined it with a contrasting plaid.

For the interfacing, select a good quality, nonwoven fusible. The extra stiffness of body makes the bag very durable.

Cutting Directions

1. Enlarge the pattern for the tote body. (Illus. 143)

2. From Fabric A, use the pattern to cut two tote bodies, two 3" × 15" handles, and two 20" × 3" facings.

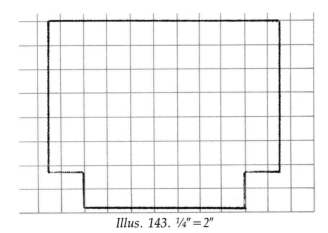

Illus. 143. ¼″ = 2″

3. From Fabric B, use the pattern to cut two tote bodies and one 10″ × 9″ pocket.

4. From the interfacing, cut two tote bodies.

Sewing Directions

1. All seam allowances are ½″.

2. Machine-embroider the monogram on one bag section.

Claire's Hint: The monogram can be placed anywhere you choose. Mine is in one corner 6″ from both the side and bottom. With a fadeaway marker, draw three parallel lines, spacing them ¾″ apart; then draw the monogram.

3. Fuse the interfacing to the wrong side of the lining sections.

4. Make the lining pocket. Make a ½″ hem on one long edge. On the remaining three edges, press under the seam allowances. Right sides up, center and stitch the pocket 3″ below the top of one lining section.

5. Right sides together, stitch the lining corners. Repeat for the bag.

6. Right sides together, stitch the side/bottom seam on the lining, matching the corners. Repeat for the bag. (Illus. 144)

Illus. 144

7. Turn the bag right side out. Wrong sides together, place the lining in the bag. Pin the bag and lining together at the top and trim the lining if needed.

8. Make the handles. Press the long edges under ¼″. Wrong sides together, fold the straps in half lengthwise and edgestitch both sides.

Claire's Hint: Since this bag can also be used to carry books, topstitch again ¼″ from the edges for additional strength.

9. Sew the straps to the bag. Right sides together, center the straps with a 5″ space between; pin. Machine-stitch around the top of the bag ⅜″ from edge. (Illus. 145) Stitch back and forth over each strap 2 or 3 times for additional strength.

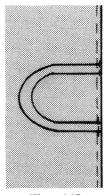

Illus. 145

10. Make the facing. Right sides together, join the short ends of the facing strips to make a circle.

11. Join the facing and bag. Right sides together, stitch the facing to the top of the bag. Understitch.

12. Fold the facing to the inside of the bag. Turn the raw edge under and machine-stitch in place.

Claire's Hint: Turn the facing under until the cut edge meets the seam line so the top of the bag will hold its shape.

HOBO BAG

Designed to hold everything from cosmetics to a favorite paperback, the hobo bag is the perfect gift for an on-the-go friend.
Finished Size: Approximately 18″ × 12″

Materials

Fabric A (bag), ⅝ yard, 45″ wide
Fabric B (lining), ⅝ yard, 45″ wide
Zipper, one 18″
Ribbon, ⅛ yard, ⅛″ wide
Fabric Notes: I used a novelty velveteen in a beautiful shade of cream for this bag. Other suitable materials include corduroy, canvas, denim, leather, suede, synthetic suedes, and Lamaire (synthetic leather).

Cutting Directions

1. Enlarge the bag pattern. (Illus 146)
2. From Fabric A, use the pattern to cut two bag sections and one 26″ × 6″ handle.
Claire's Hint: For fabric economy, cut the strap on the cross grain. If this is unflattering for your fabric, use a leather or ribbon strap.
3. From Fabric B, use the pattern to cut two lining sections.

Sewing Directions

1. All seam allowances are ¼″ except as noted.
2. Using short stitches, reinforce the corners on the bag and lining sections. Clip to *but not through* the stitched line. (Illus. 147)
3. Right sides together, stitch the darts on the bag and lining.
4. Set the zipper. Right sides together, stitch the zipper to the long straight edge of the two bag sections.
5. Join the lining sections to the top of the bag. Right sides together, stitch with the zipper sandwiched between the bag and lining.
6. Press. Pull the bag and lining away from the zipper and press, wrong sides together.
7. Topstitch. Stitch through all layers ¼″ from the zipper.
8. Join the bag bottoms. Right sides together, match and pin the darts on the curved edges of the bag; stitch. (Illus. 148)

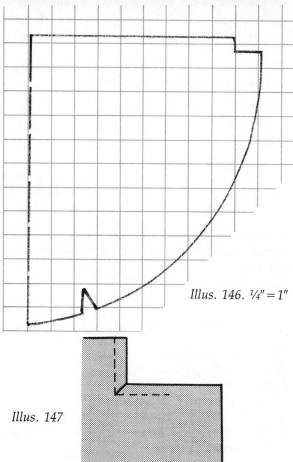

Illus. 146. ¼″ = 1″

Illus. 147

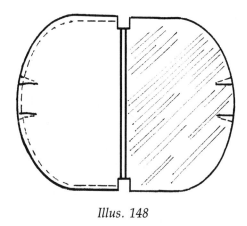

Illus. 148

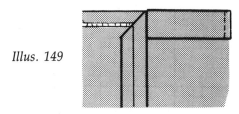

Illus. 149

9. Repeat on the lining, leaving a 6″-long opening at the bottom.

10. Make the strap. Right sides together, fold the strap in half lengthwise; stitch a 1″ wide seam. Press the seam open. Turn the strap right side out, centering the seam on the underside. Press again. Topstitch each side of the strap ¼″ from the edge.

11. Right sides up, baste the ends of the strap to the top of the bag. The strap should fit perfectly at the ends of the zipper between the reinforced corners. (Illus. 149)

Claire's Hint: Machine-stitch back and forth several times to reinforce the strap seam.

12. Right sides together, fold the bag at the reinforced corner; repeat with lining. Stitch through all layers. (Illus. 150)

13. Turn right side out.

14. Close the opening in the lining. Fold the seam allowances to the inside and edgestitch the folds together.

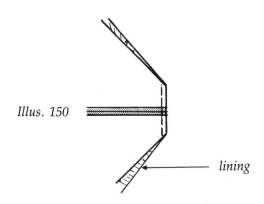

Illus. 150

lining

• • •

CLUTCH BAG

Softly shirred onto a spring-action frame, this roomy clutch will be a great addition to any wardrobe.

Finished Size: 10″ × 7″ × 1″

Materials

Remnant A (bag), one 21¾″ × 18″
Remnant B (lining), one 40″ × 8″
Fusible interfacing, one 20″ × 18″
Straight open-hex frame, one 10″

Fabric Notes: Ultrasuede, Lamaire, Facile, real leather and suede, corduroy, velveteen, satin, and pretty novelty fabrics are just a few of the many choices for this attractive clutch.

Cutting Directions

1. From Fabric A, cut one handbag body 20″ × 18″ and one fabric tie 1¾″ × 6″.

2. From the lining fabric, cut two 20″ × 7¾″ rectangles.

3. From the interfacing, cut one 20″ × 18″ rectangle.

Sewing Directions

1. All seam allowances are ¼″.
2. Fuse the interfacing to the wrong side of the fabric following the manufacturer's directions.
3. Make four ⅝″ buttonholes, placing them ½″ from the top and ¾″ from each side. (Illus. 151a)
Claire's Hint: Use a very sharp seam ripper to open the buttonholes.
4. Right sides together, join the long sides of the handbag body to the lining sections.
5. Right sides together, stitch the side seams. (Illus. 151b)
6. Stitch the boxing at the bottom of the bag. Match the side seams with the fold line at the bottom. Mark a point on the fold lines 1½″ from the corner. Draw a line to connect them. Stitch on the marked line. (Illus. 151c)
7. Turn right side out. Close the open seam at the bottom of the lining by folding the seam allowances to the wrong side and edgestitching.
8. Push the lining into the bag and pin in place so the top of the lining is 1″ below the top of the bag. All buttonholes should be on the inside of the bag. Topstitch 1″ from the top.
9. Insert the handbag frame into the buttonholes.
10. Make the tie. Wrong sides together, fold in half lengthwise; fold the raw edges to the fold line; and edgestitch the folded edges together.
Claire's Hint: If the edgestitching is conspicuous, the bag will be more attractive if you edgestitch again along the fold line.

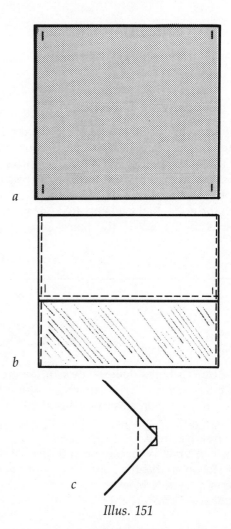

a

b

c

Illus. 151

11. Tie a knot and trim the ends diagonally. Right sides together, center the tie about ½″ below the top. Hand-stitch in place.

• • •

LACE SCARF

Smart fashion accessories make any occasion special. This lace scarf is surprisingly easy to make and lovely to wear.
Finished Size: 10″ × 45″

Materials

Lace, ¼ yard, 45″ wide
Lace trim, 2¾ yards, ½″ wide

Cutting Directions

Cut one 45" × 9" rectangle. Shape the ends to make a point.

Sewing Directions

1. Right sides up, begin at one end with the lace trim extending 1". Lap and pin the trim over the edge of the scarf ¼". Zigzag (W,2-L,2) in place.
2. Break your threads and cut the trim, leaving a 1" tail. Repeat on the other side of the scarf.
3. Finish the ends. Right side up, fold one lace end under, making a mitre to the point; pin. Zigzag

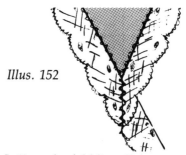

Illus. 152

(W,1-L,1) on the fold line. Repeat on the other end. (Illus. 152)
4. Turn the scarf over. Trim all seams close to the stitching line.

• • •

FANCY COMB

Transform crocheted doilies—new or antique—into attractive combs. If you don't have one the right size in your own stash of collectibles, scout thrift shops and yard sales; or pick up one in a Chinese novelty shop.

For the conservative dresser on your gift list, use a longer ribbon so that the bow can be worn at the neckline of a favorite blouse.
Finished Size: Approximately 6" × 2"

Materials

Fancy doily, one 5½" or 6" diameter
Ribbon, ⅛ yard (⅝ yard for necktie), ¼" wide
Comb, one 2½"–3"

Sewing Directions

1. Place a gathering thread through the doily center. Pull it up; wrap the ends around the gathered row several times; tie securely together.
2. Tie the ribbon around the doily, covering the gathered row.
Claire's Hint: When making a necktie, center the bow on the ribbon.
3. Hand-sew the doily to the comb.
Claire's Hint: When I make these for myself, I use double-stick tape to attach them to the combs.

FRANKLY FANCY

CAMISOLE

This exquisite camisole will make any lady—young or old—feel special. Lavishly trimmed with lace and tucks, the camisole will fit sizes 6–14.
Finished Size: 39½" × 12½"

Materials

Fabric, ⅞ yard, 45" wide
Lace insertion, ⅞ yard, ⅝" wide
Entredeux, 7 yards
Eyelet insertion, ⅞ yard, 1" wide
Galloon beading for ⅛" wide ribbon, 3¼ yards
Ribbon, 3⅞ yards, ⅛" wide
Buttons, three ⅜"
Fabric Notes: I prefer Swiss batiste, linen, lawn, and silk; but they do require ironing. If this gift is for a non-ironer, select a good quality polyester/cotton blend.

Cutting Directions

1. From the batiste, cut one 35" × 14" camisole body, one 4" × 30½" tucking strip, and one 4" × 30½" placket strip.
2. Cut a paper pattern 1¼" × 15¼".
3. From the galloon beading and ribbon, cut two shoulder straps 16" long.

Sewing Directions

1. Make the placket. Wrong sides together, press in half lengthwise; fold the raw edges so they meet at the center. Press again, making the pressed strip four thicknesses of fabric with the folded edges aligned. Zigzag (W,1-L,2) the folded edges together.
2. Complete the tucking strip. Mark the three tuck fold lines, spacing them 1" apart and centering them in the middle of the tucking strip.
   Stitch three rows of scalloped tucks. Set the machine for a hemming stitch (W,3-L,1); then, with the bulk of the fabric to the right of the needle, stitch the tucks so that the needle swings off the edge of the fabric to form a small scallop. Press.
Claire's Hint: Although it takes a little longer, stitch and press each tuck before beginning the next one.
3. Pull threads to mark the stitching lines on each side of the tucked strip so the finished width is 1¼" and the tucks are centered.

Claire's Hint: Use the paper pattern as a guide.
4. Finish the edges of the tucked strip by folding the seam allowance under and zigzagging (W,1-L,1) over the edge. Trim away the seam allowances. Press.
5. Finish the short ends of the camisole body.
6. Trim the fabric from one side of the entredeux and zigzag (W,2-L,2) to the camisole.
Claire's Hint: To avoid being caught short, stitch, then trim the entredeux even with the camisole.
7. Complete the camisole. Working towards the center front on one side, join the embroidered insertion, a row of entredeux, the tucked strip (tucks pressed towards the side), entredeux, lace insertion, entredeux and placket strip.
   Trim each row even with the camisole body and stitch the other side.
8. Hem the galloon. Measure the top of the camisole; add 1", and cut two strips of galloon beading this length to trim the top and waistline. Make a tiny hem at each end of the beading by hand or machine. Cut two pieces of ribbon 20" longer and thread them into the beading.
Claire's Hint: Very small beading is difficult to thread with ribbon. Sew buttonhole twist to one

end of the ribbon with a tapestry needle; using the needle, pull the ribbon through.

9. Finish the top edge. Wrong sides together with the edges aligned, pin one strip of the threaded galloon at the top of the camisole. Stitch ⅝" from the edge. Trim the camisole close to the stitched line.

10. Press the galloon to the right side of the garment; and stitch again just below the ribbon, approximately ⅝" from the top.

11. Finish the waistline. Mark the waistline 5" from the bottom. Center and pin the galloon beading over the marked line. Right side up, pin and stitch the galloon to the camisole above and below the ribbon.

12. Finish the camisole bottom with a narrow machine hem.

13. Wrong side up, mark the strap locations at the top of the camisole 4½" from the center back and 5" from the center front.

14. Set the straps. Thread the ribbon into the shoulder straps. Center, pin, and stitch the straps to the wrong side of the garment.

Claire's Hint: It's hard to guess the exact strap length when you're sewing for a friend. Add a small tuck on the back straps which can be ripped out as needed. Right sides together, machine-baste a ½" tuck just above the camisole body.

15. Make the buttonholes. Mark the locations in the center of the right placket strip, spacing them 2½" apart with the top buttonhole 1⅛" below the ribbon. Stitch them vertically.

16. Sew on the buttons.

• • •

CLOSET LUXURIES

That special woman friend or relative deserves a set of ultrafeminine closet accessories to treasure for years to come. Practical, as well as pretty, luxurious hangers, shoe stuffers, garment covers, and a lingerie keeper will protect and preserve a wardrobe.

LUXURY HANGER

Finished Size: 25" × 13"

Materials

Remnant, one 15" square
Lace trim, 2½ yards, 1" to 1½" wide
Ribbon, ⅜ yard, ¼" or ⅜" wide
Bonded polyester batting, one 24" × 9"
Wooden hanger, 1
Fabric Notes: Select a pretty, firmly woven fabric to cover the hanger. I used moiré taffeta in a dusty blue and Poly-Fil Extra-Loft batting, which has a thick, bonded surface.

This is also a wonderful hanger for a man to use to hold overcoats. Select an appropriate print or color in a firmly woven fabric and trim with rickrack, plain ribbon or a simple braid.

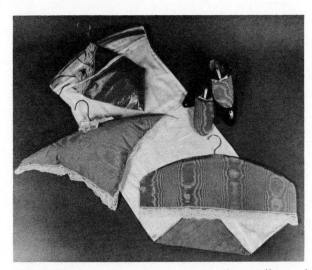

Photo shows hangers, garment covers, shoe stuffers and lingerie keeper.

Cutting Notes

1. From the remnant, cut one 15" square.
2. From the batting, cut a 15" square and a 9" square.
3. Make a 1" long buttonhole in the center of the fabric square. (Illus. 152)

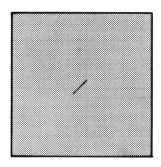

Illus. 152

Claire's Hint: To prevent tunnelling, pin a piece of nonwoven stabilizer under the buttonhole area before stitching.

6. Finish all edges if the fabric frays badly. Right side up, fold the raw edge under ¼"; and edgestitch.

7. Right sides up, stitch the lace to the square, overlapping the edges ¼". Leave a 1½" tail at the beginning and end at each corner.

Claire's Hint: To shape the square, stretch the lace when stitching.

8. Mitre the lace at the corners. Fold one tail under.

Zigzag (W,2-L,2) over the folded edge. Trim away the excess from the underside.

9. Make a hole in the center of the batting squares.

10. Slip the small batting square on the hanger, and slip the large one over it. Cover both with the cover. Align the points and pin the layers together. (Illus. 153)

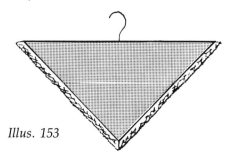

Illus. 153

11. Topstitch the edges through all layers.

12. Gather the remaining lace into a circle. Fasten the threads securely and slip the circle over the hanger. Tack in place.

13. Tie the bow around the hanger.

● ● ●

GARMENT COVERS

Finished Size: 22" × 9"

Materials

Fabric, ¼ yard, 45" wide
Lace edging, 1¼ yards, 1"–1½" wide

Cutting Directions

1. Enlarge the pattern. (Illus. 154)
2. Using the pattern, cut two covers.

Sewing Directions

1. All seam and hem allowances are ½".
2. Finish the opening for the hanger. On the front and back cover, clip to the seam line 1" from the center. Fold the hem allowance under and edgestitch. (Illus. 155)
3. Finish the long straight edges. Fold under ¼"; edgestitch.
4. Right sides together, join the front and back. Stitch the curved edges together.

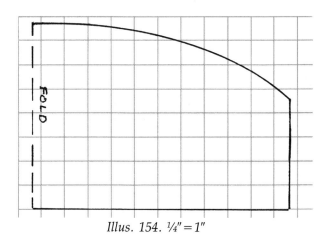

Illus. 154. ¼" = 1"

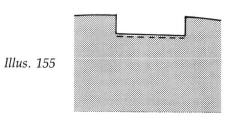

Illus. 155

5. Right sides up, stitch the lace to the bottom, overlapping the ends ½".

LINGERIE KEEPER

This hanging lingerie keeper makes a wonderful addition to any closet and it's ideal for short trips. *Finished Size: 17″ × 35″*

Materials

Remnant A (bag), one 36″ × 36″
Remnant B (lining), one 18″ × 36″
Plastic, one 18″ × 37″
Zippers, three 16″
Cording, 4¼ yards
Fabric Notes: Since the lining will be next to the garments, choose something soft and silky. I used a polyester satin.

For the inner bag, I prefer soft plastic so that the contents are easy to see; however, plastic is a little more difficult to sew than most fabrics.

Cutting Directions

1. Enlarge the pattern. (Illus. 156)
2. From Remnant A, cut one 17″ × 36″ outer bag and four 2″ × 36″ strips for the corded piping. Use the enlarged pattern to shape the top of the outer bag.

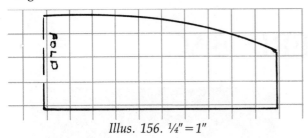

Illus. 156. ¼″ = 1″

3. From Remnant B, cut one 17″ × 36″ lining, using the pattern to shape the top.
4. On the lining, mark the opening for the hanger ½″ from each side of the center by clipping to the seam line.
5. From the plastic, cut pockets, one 17″ × 4″, two 17″ × 19″, and one 17″ × 13″.

Sewing Directions

1. All seam allowances are ¼″.
2. Make the corded piping.
3. Right sides together, align the edges and stitch the corded piping to the outer bag.
Claire's Hint: Stitch carefully to prevent the underlayer creeping. Begin and end at one of the lower corners for an inconspicuous join.
4. Set the zippers to the plastic pockets. Open the zippers. Right sides up and the zipper on top, align the zipper coil and plastic edge. Topstitch at the edge of the zipper and again ¼″ from the edge; repeat on the other side. (Illus. 157)

Illus. 157

Claire's Hint: Trim the plastic so it won't catch in the zippers.
5. Right sides up, smooth the plastic layer over the lining. Pin the edges together; any excess plastic can be trimmed away after stitching. Stitch, beginning and ending at the hanger opening.
6. Trim away the excess plastic. At the hanger opening, clip to the seam line and fold the plastic seam allowance into the opening.
7. Make the pockets. Stitch through all layers just above the zippers.
8. Join the bag and lining. Right sides together, pin and stitch the edges, leaving the bottom open.
9. Turn right side out.
10. Close the bottom. Fold the seam allowances in and machine-stitch.
Claire's Hint: To make an inconspicuous closing, use a zipper foot.
11. Insert a hanger between the plastic and lining.

SHOE STUFFERS

Fill the shoe stuffers with potpourri to make them extra-special.
Finished Size: 4″ × 6″

Materials

Remnant, one 19″ × 7″
Ribbon, ⅜ yard, ¼″–⅜″ wide
Fibrefill
Optional: Potpourri

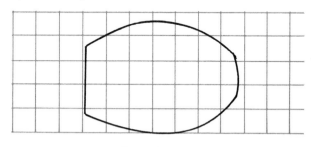

Illus. 158. ¼″ = 1″

Cutting Directions

1. Enlarge the pattern; cut four sections. (Illus. 158)
2. Fold one short length of ribbon in half crosswise to make a loop. Right sides up, align the edges and baste in place. (Illus. 159)

Illus. 159

3. Right sides together, stitch the curved edge.
Claire's Hint: Using pinking shears, trim the seam.
4. Turn right side out. Fill with fibrefill and a little potpourri.
5. Close the opening.
6. Make a bow and hand-stitch at the base of the loop.
7. Repeat to make a pair.

• • •

LACY LINGERIE BAG

Even the finest underthings can go into the washing machine when they're in this lacy lingerie bag.
Finished Size: 17½″ square

Materials

Lace remnant for bag, one 36″ × 18″
Padded hanger, 1 (Page 82)
Ribbon, 2 yards, ⅜″–1″ wide
Stemmed buttons, two ¼″–⅜″ diameter
Fabric Notes: Although the lace makes a beautiful bag, many open-weave fabrics, eyelet and sheer nylon tricot are appropriate. I used a satin-covered hanger.

Cutting Directions

1. Cut two bag sections 18″ square. On each square, round the two bottom corners.
2. Cut the ribbon into two equal-length strips.

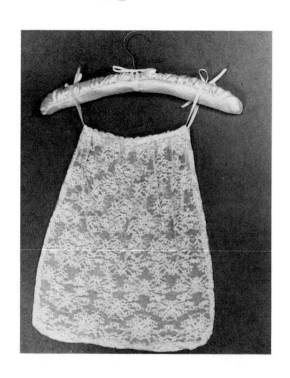

Sewing Directions

1. All seam allowances are ½″; the hem allowance is 1″.
2. At the top of each bag section, fold under the seam allowance for 2″ on each side and edgestitch. Backstitch and clip to the end of the stitched line. (Illus. 160)

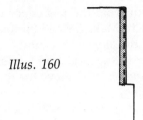

Illus. 160

3. Right sides together, stitch the sides and bottom.
Claire's Hint: Stitch in low gear or slowly to prevent puckering.
4. Turn right side out.
5. Make the casing. Fold the hem allowance to the wrong side and stitch ¾″ from the folded edge. Press.
6. Insert the ribbons into the casing and make a bow on each side.
7. Sew two stemmed buttons to the padded hanger about 3″ from each end.
8. Hang the bag on the padded hanger with the ribbon ties hooked over the buttons.

• • •

JEWELRY ROLL

Designed for travellers, this jewelry bag is practical as well as pretty. It features three zippered compartments, a strap for rings, and a large pouch for necklaces.
Finished Size: Open, 9″ × 12½″; Rolled, 9″ × 3″

Materials

Remnant A (bag), one 30″ × 13½″
Remnant B (lining), one 19″ × 13″
Interfacing (lightweight, nonwoven, fusible), one 9″ × 4½″
Zippers, three 7″
Ball button, one ¼″
Corded piping or lip braid, 1¼ yards
Cotton
Fabric Notes: Choose a light- to medium-weight, firmly woven fabric for the bag and a lightweight lining fabric for the bag lining. I used moiré taffeta and piped it with a purchased gold piping.

Cutting Directions

1. From Remnant A, cut one 9½″ × 13″ cover, one inside (9½″ × 12″) section, and one (9½″ × 2″) facing. Cut one 2″ × 7″ bias ring-strap and two 1″ × 13″ bias ties. (Illus. 161)

2. From Remnant B, cut one 9½″ × 13″ cover lining and one (9½″ × 12″) pocket lining.
3. From the interfacing, cut three 1½″ × 9″ strips.

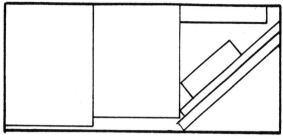

Illus. 161

Sewing Directions

1. All seam allowances are ¼".
2. Mark the location for each zipper opening on the wrong side of the inside bag section, positioning the top and bottom zippers approximately 2" from the ends with the middle zipper about 5" below the top one. (Illus. 162)

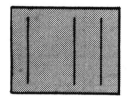

Illus. 162

Claire's Hint: Use a sliver of soap to draw a line 7" long.

3. Using the interfacing strips, face the zipper openings. Right sides together (fusible side up), stitch a rectangle around each location line. Slash through the centers and clip to all corners. (Illus. 163)

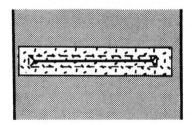

Illus. 163

4. To avoid clipping too far, use scissors that cut all the way to the ends of the points. Position the points exactly where you want the clip to be. Clip.
5. Fold the interfacing to the wrong side and press. During pressing, the fusible will bond to the wrong side of the bag section.

6. Set the zippers. Right sides up, pin the zippers behind the faced windows; topstitch in place. Press.
Claire's Hint: Use a washable gluestick or water-soluble basting tape to baste the zippers into the windows.
7. Make the ring-strap. Fold the wide bias strip in half lengthwise, right sides together; stitch. Turn the strap right side out. Fold the raw edges in on one end and edgestitch. Make a small buttonhole ¼" from the end. Fill the strip with cotton.
8. Sew the ring-strap to the bag. Right sides together, position the ring-strap 1" above the middle zipper; stitch. (Illus. 164)

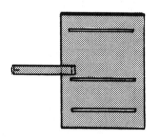

Illus. 164

9. Sew on the button for the ring-strap. Fold the ring-strap into place and mark the location.
10. Join the zippered bag section and small lining. Right sides together, stitch one short end together. Turn right side out; and edgestitch.
11. Stitch the pockets on the zippered bag section. Wrong sides together, pin the lining to the bag. Divide the bag into pockets by stitching through all layers at the tops of the middle and bottom zipper. Set the zippered bag section aside.
12. Make the cover lining. Right sides together, pin and stitch the fabric facing to one end of the lining. Press the seam allowances towards the lining and edgestitch. Set aside. (Illus. 165)

Illus. 165

13. Right sides up, pin and stitch the piping to the cover.

14. Make the ties. Fold the strips in half lengthwise, right sides together; stitch and turn right side out. Knot one end of each tie.

Claire's Hints: Stretch as you stitch to avoid breaking the stitches when the strips are turned right side out.

To turn the ties right side out, use a tapestry needle and a short length of buttonhole twist. Fasten the thread at one end of the ties; and insert the needle into the tube, turning as you go.

15. Right sides up, center the ties at the top of the cover; baste in place. (Illus. 166)

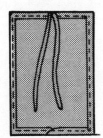

Illus. 166

16. Assemble the bag. Right sides together, align and pin the raw edges of the cover and zippered pocket section so the finished edge of the top is approximately 1″ below the cover. Stitch the sides and bottom together. (Illus. 167)

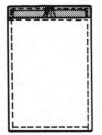

Illus. 167

17. Attach the cover lining. Right sides together and the zippered pocket in between, pin the lining to the bag. Join the edges, leaving a 3″–4″ opening at the bottom.

18. Turn the bag right side out. Close the opening with a slipstitch.

19. Press.

BEDSIDE CADDY

Although this is a practical gift for anyone who likes to read in bed, it is a particularly nice one for an elderly or handicapped friend.

The easy-to-make bedside caddy tucks between the mattress and springs. It has six pockets for organizing reading materials, glasses, and other bedside needs.

Finished Size: 14″ wide × 18″ long

Materials

Fabric A, ½ yard, 45″ wide
Style-A-Shade fusible interfacing, one 28″ × 17″
Gathered lace edging, 1 yard, ⅝″ wide
Flat lace trim, 1 yard, ⅝″ wide
Cardboard, one 14″ × 7″

Fabric Notes: Choose a fabric color and design to coordinate with the bedroom. Almost any fabric will make up attractively. Satin, gingham, eyelet, denim, chintz, and moiré taffeta are just a few suggestions.

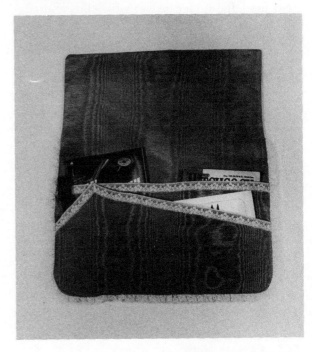

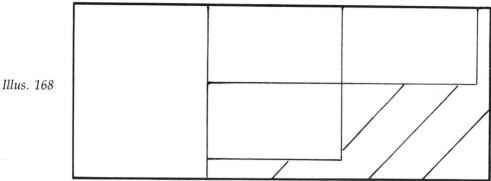

Illus. 168

Cutting Directions

1. From the fabric, cut one 14½" × 18" caddy body and three 14½" × 8" pockets. (Illus. 168)
2. Mark Pocket A on one long edge 3" from one end. Mark the short sides 3½" from the top. Mark the long sides of the caddy body 7" from one end. *Claire's Hint:* Use short clips to mark.
3. From the fusible interfacing, cut one 14½" × 17" rectangle and two 13½" × 7" rectangles.

Sewing Directions

1. All hem and seam allowances are ¼".
2. Center the interfacing on the wrong side of the caddy body and Pockets A and B; fuse.
3. Hem the pockets. On Pockets B and C, fold one long edge under ¼" and edgestitch. On Pocket A, fold the edge under between the clips and edgestitch. (Illus. 169)

Illus. 169

4. Right sides up, place the flat lace edging on Pockets A and B, matching the straight edge of the lace to the hemmed edge of the pocket. Edgestitch. Mitre the lace as needed. (Illus. 170)

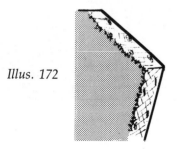

Illus. 172

5. On Pocket A, round the corners at the bottom.
6. Right sides up, stack Pocket A on Pocket B. Machine-stitch from the point to the bottom. (Illus. 171)

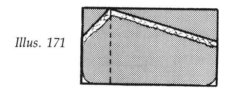

Illus. 171

7. Right sides up, pin the pocket stack to the unnotched end of the caddy body. Fold Pocket A out of the way and machine-stitch through the center of Pocket B. (Illus. 172)

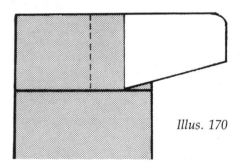

Illus. 170

8. Machine-baste the pockets to the caddy around the sides and bottom. Trim Pocket B and the caddy body to match Pocket A.
9. Right sides together, stitch the gathered lace trim to caddy, beginning and ending at the notches.
10. Right sides together, join Pocket C to the other end of the caddy. Turn Pocket C to the underside of the caddy.
11. Fold the seam under at the bottom and sides of the caddy and zigzag (W,2-L,2) through all layers.
12. Insert the cardboard into Pocket C.

STATIONERY CADDY

Even the plainest stationery will look fancy in this eyelet stationery folder. Although all the ladies on your gift list will want one, this is a particularly thoughtful gift for a shut-in. And, if she's a close friend or relative, add stamps.

Finished Size: Open, 17½" × 11"; Closed, 8½" × 11"

Materials

Fabric A, ½ yard, 45" wide
Fleece, ⅝ yard
Cord, 1⅝ yard; or purchased piped cording, 1⅝ yard
Lace trim, ½ yard, 1" wide
Ribbon, ½ yard, ¼" wide
Lace motif, new or antique

Fabric Notes: Choose a fabric design and color that will complement the stationery inside. I used a cream-colored eyelet; however, satin, gingham, denim, chintz and muslin will be equally attractive.

To trim the cover, I used a small crocheted coaster which I purchased in a Chinese shop. You may prefer a doily from your collection of odds and ends. If not, there are many new, beautiful lace motifs.

Cutting Directions

1. From Fabric A, cut two 18" × 11½" body sections. Cut one 18" × 6" pocket, and one 8½" × 4" pocket. For the cording, cut enough 1" wide strips on the cross grain to make 1⅝ yards.
2. From the fleece, cut two 18" × 11½" rectangles.

Sewing Directions

1. All seam allowances are ¼".
2. Finish the opening of the small pocket. Make a narrow hem on one long edge.
3. Finish the opening of the large pocket. Wrong side up, zigzag (W,2-L,2) the lace trim to one long edge, overlapping the pocket ¼".

Fold the lace to the right side of the pocket and zigzag ¼" below the fold to enclose the raw edge. (Illus. 173)

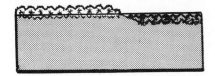

Illus. 173

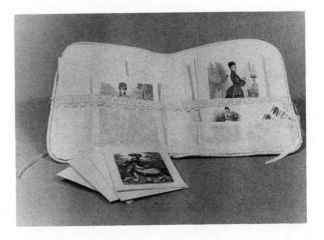

4. Make the pocket stack. Right sides up, align the edges at the lower right corner; pin.

Fold the left end of the small pocket under ½"; edgestitch to the large pocket. Set the stack aside. (Illus. 174)

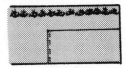

Illus. 174

5. Pin the fleece to the wrong sides of the two body sections. Machine-baste ¼" from the raw edges.
6. Set the pockets to the inside of the caddy. Right sides up, pin the pocket stack to one fabric/fleece section, aligning them at the bottom. Press.
7. Stitch a 1½" wide pocket in the center for pens. (Illus. 175)

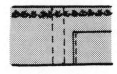

Illus. 175

8. Make the cover. Right side up, center the ribbons on the short ends of the remaining fabric/fleece section; stitch.
9. Make the corded piping and trim the seam allowances on it to ¼".
10. Right sides up, stitch the piping to the cover.

11. Right sides up, pin the lace motif in the center of the caddy front. Hand- or machine-stitch in place.
Claire's Hint: Close the caddy to be sure the motif is centered before stitching.

12. Right sides together, join the two fabric/fleece sections, leaving 4–5″ opening at the bottom. Trim as needed and turn right side out. Press.
13. Close the opening with a slipstitch.
14. Fill the caddy with stationery, and tie.

• • •

BRIDAL HANDKERCHIEF AND GARTER

The perfect bridal gift in traditional white. This beautiful handkerchief and garter will become a family heirloom and the bride will never guess how easy they were to sew.
Finished Sizes: Handkerchief, approximately 12″ square; Garter, small, 13″ (large, 20″)

HANDKERCHIEF

Materials

Fabric, one 9″ square
Lace insertion, 1¼ yards, ½″–⅝″ wide
Lace edging, 1⅜ yards, ¾″–1″ wide
Fabric Notes: Select a fine linen or cotton for the handkerchief. I used Swiss batiste and imported laces. The laces do not have to match; and, if desired, several insertions can be used instead of one.

Sewing Directions

1. All seam allowances are ¼″.
2. Fold under ½″ and zigzag (W,1-L,1) over the edges. Trim.
3. Right sides up, join the lace insertion to the handkerchief. Allowing a ¾″ tail at the beginning and end of each side, butt the edges together and zigzag (W,2-L,2).
Claire's Hint: Do not stitch past the corner of the handkerchief so that the tails remain free.
4. Join the lace edging to the handkerchief, allowing a 1¼″ tail at the beginning and end of the insertion. Press. (Illus. 176a)
5. Mitre the corners. Place the handkerchief on a table right side up. At each corner, fold under one

set of tails at a 45° angle; pin. Check to be sure the corners are flat. (Illus 176b)

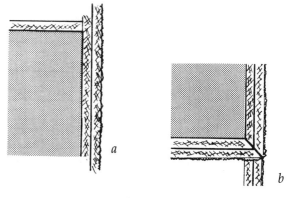

Illus. 176

6. Zigzag (W,1-L,1) from the fabric corner to the edge of the handkerchief; zigzag back to the fabric for security. Trim the mitred seam close to the seam line. Press.

GARTER

Materials

Material requirements are for a small-to-medium garter; requirements for a large one are in parentheses.

Satin ribbon, 1 yard (1½ yards), 1″ wide
Satin ribbon, 1¼ yards (1¾ yards), ⅝″ wide
Lace edging, 1 yard (1½ yards), ⅜″–½″ wide
Lace edging, 1 yard (1½ yards), ¾″–1″ wide
Elastic, ⅜ yard (⅝ yard), ¼″ wide

Directions

1. All seam allowances are ¼″.
2. Join the laces to the wide ribbon. Right sides up, zigzag (W,2-L,2) the narrow edging to one side of the wide ribbon; zigzag (W,2-L,2) the wide edging to the other side.
3. Wrong sides together, center the narrow ribbon on the wide ribbon. Starting and stopping 2″ from each end, edgestitch.
4. Right sides together, join the ends of the wide ribbon; repeat for the narrow ribbon.
5. Thread the elastic into the garter and join the ends. To reduce bulk, overlap the elastic ends.
6. Edgestitch the unstitched section of the casing.
7. Make a small bow with the remaining ribbon and tack to garter.

Claire's Hint: Drop the feed dogs and zigzag (W,2-L,0) through all layers to secure the bow.

POTPOURRI LINER

Do you have a friend who has everything? Well, almost everything? If so, make her a potpourri liner. Even if she already has one or several, she can always use another.

The liners look like lace place mats. Filled with potpourri, they are guaranteed to fill her drawers with wonderful fragrance.

Finished Size: 18″ × 13″

Materials

Remnant A (liner top), one 18″ × 13″
Contrast B, one 36″ × 13″
Lace edging, 1¾ yards, 1″–2″ wide
Potpourri, ½ cup

Fabric Notes: Choose a pretty lace for the top and sheer nylon tricot for the bottom. The tricot is tightly knitted and will hold the potpourri securely.

Cutting Directions

1. Even the edges of the lace remnant to make a perfect rectangle.
2. From Contrast B, cut two 18″ × 13″ rectangles.

Sewing Directions

1. All seam allowances are ¼″.
2. Right sides up, stitch one Contrast rectangle to the lace.

Claire's Hint: To prevent puckering, set the machine speed to slow or stitch slowly.

3. Join the top and bottom. Wrong sides together, stitch (L,2), leaving 4″–5″ open on one side.
4. Put the potpourri into the liner and stitch the opening closed. Don't worry about the potpourri being lumpy. It can be smoothed out when the liner is put into a drawer.
5. Trim all edges close to the stitched line.
6. Right sides up, center the lace edging over the raw edges. Mitre and pin the corners. Zigzag (W,2-L,2).

Claire's Hint: Zigzag close to the center of the lace.

SACHETS

SACHET POUFS

Here's a lovely way to say you care, just add a note and give to one of your special friends.
Finished Size: 2½" diameter

Materials

Lace remnant, one 7" circle
Lining remnant, one 7" circle
Lace, ⅜ yard, 1½"–2" wide
Ribbon, ½ yard, ¼" wide
Potpourri, ¼ cup
Buttonhole twist
Fabric Notes: Use sheer nylon tricot or chiffon to line the lace so the potpourri won't fall out.

Sewing Directions

1. Wrong sides together, stitch the two circles together around the edge.
2. Right sides up, position the lace trim, overlapping the raw edge ¼"; zigzag (W,2-L,2).

3. Lining side up, put about ¼ cup potpourri on the lace circle.
4. Gather the lace around the potpourri and tie securely with buttonhole twist.
5. Tie the ribbon around the sachet and make a bow.

• • •

RIBBON AND LACE PILLOWS

Don't know what to do with little pieces of lace left from French hand- and machine-stitched designs? These beautiful potpourri pillows are the perfect answer and no one need know they were made from scraps.
Finished Size: 3" × 3¾"

Materials

Lace, ½ yard, 1½" wide or lace, ¼ yard, 3" wide
Remnant, one 2½" × 9"
Ribbon, ¼ yard, 1" wide
Ribbon, ⅜ yard, ⅛"–¼" wide
Optional: Rosette, 1
Potpourri, 3–4 tablespoons
Fabric Notes: Use sheer nylon tricot, organza, or chiffon for Remnant A, if the holes between the lace motifs are large enough for the potpourri to filter out.

Any combination of lace widths can be used to make 3" pillows.

Sewing Directions

1. Cut the lace in half. Right sides up, butt the straight edges together and zigzag (W,2-L,2).
2. Pin the sheer fabric to the wrong side of the lace.
Claire's Hint: Place the pins on the lace side near the edges so you can complete the next step without removing the pins.
3. Right sides up, center and edgestitch the ribbon to the lace.
4. Make the pillow. Wrong sides together, fold the strip in half crosswise. Stitch the sides of the pillow.
5. Fill with potpourri.
6. Fold the raw edges in at the top and edgestitch.
7. Cut the narrow ribbon into two pieces—4" and 9½" long. Make a bow with the longer length and a loop with the shorter one.
8. Sew the ribbons to the top of the pillow.
9. *Optional:* Glue or sew the rosette in place.

SATIN AND LACE SACHET

Make any occasion special with this beautiful satin and lace sachet.
Finished Size: Approximately 4¾″ × 2″

Materials

Fabric, ⅛ yard, 36″ wide
Lace edging, ½ yard, 2″ wide
Small cording such as postal twine, ½ yard
Covered button forms, two ¾″
Fibrefill
Potpourri, 2 tablespoons

Cutting Directions

1. Cut one 16″ × 3″ top, one 16″ × 4½″ side/bottom, one 16″ × 1″ piping strip, and two 2″ circles. *Note:* For fabric economy, the piping strip is cut on the cross grain. Since it will be sewn into a straight seam, it will have no adverse effect on the finished appearance.

Sewing Directions

1. All seam allowances are ¼″.
2. Make the corded piping. Place the cord on the wrong side of the piping strip. Wrap the strip around the cord; stitch, using a zipper foot, close to the cord. Trim the seam allowances to ¼″.

3. Right sides together, stitch the corded piping to one edge of the top.
4. Right sides up, position the lace strip, on the top. Stitch ¼″ from the raw edge. (Illus. 177)

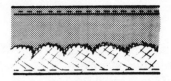

Illus. 177

5. Right sides together, join the top and side/bottom sections.
6. Right sides together, join the ends to make a circle.
7. Cover the button forms with fabric.
Claire's Hint: Dampen the fabric to stretch and shape easily.
8. Fold in the seam allowance at the top and hand-gather the edge. Pull up the threads to make a very small hole. Tie and knot the threads securely. Sew the button in the center to cover the gathers.
Claire's Hint: Use buttonhole twist for gathering so the thread won't break when pulled.
9. Fill the sachet loosely with fibrefill and 2 tablespoons potpourri.
10. Gather the remaining edge and cover with a button.

● ● ●

LACE AND ROSES SACHET

Whole rosebuds are trapped in a delicate lace cage to perfume lingerie. The subtle beauty of this gift will delight every lady on your list.
Finished Size: 5½″ × 5½″

Materials

Lace remnant, one 6″ square
Satin remnants, two 6″ square
Fibrefill
Mr. Lord's Potpourri, 3 tablespoons
Note: Mr. Lord's Potpourri is one of the few with whole rosebuds. It is available from Caswell-Massey, Co., Ltd.

Sewing Directions

1. All seam allowances are ¼″.
2. Right sides up, stitch the lace to one satin square, leaving one side open. Insert the rosebuds and stitch across the opening.
3. Right sides together, stitch the lace to the other square, leaving a 3″ opening on one side.
4. Turn right side out and fill with fibrefill.
5. Close the opening.
Claire's Hint: To close the opening inconspicuously, use a short slipstitch, making it look like a perfect ladder—no slanted steps.

TEDDY BEAR SACHET

Teddy bears are so sweet, especially when they're sachets.
Finished Size: Approximately 4″ × 5″

Materials

Lace remnant, one 6″ square
Nylon tricot, two 6″ square
Stabilizer, one 6″ square
Ribbon, ½ yard, ⅛″ wide
Potpourri, 6 tablespoons
Fabric Notes: Use a sheer nylon tricot so you can see the potpourri.

Sewing Directions

1. Trace the teddy bear pattern (page 159) onto the stabilizer.

Claire's Hint: The heart design (page 43) also makes attractive sachets.

2. Stack from the bottom up: nylon tricot square, lace square, nylon tricot square and stabilizer.

3. Shorten the stitch length (24 spi or 1mm) and stitch around the teddy bear, leaving about 1″ unstitched between the ears.

4. Remove the stabilizer and trim the seam allowances to ⅛″.

Claire's Hint: Clip to the stitching line at each angle for a smooth turn.

5. Turn right side out and fill with potpourri.

Claire's Hint: Use a small funnel to fill the teddy bear.

6. Using a short slipstitch, close the opening inconspicuously.

7. Tie the ribbon around the bear's neck.

TRAVEL WORLD

TRAVEL ENSEMBLE

Just right for a weekend in the country or an overnight business trip, this travel ensemble includes a hanging garment bag, weekend duffel and cosmetic case.

HANGING GARMENT BAG

The hanging garment bag features a roomy gusset and easy-to-carry handles. Make it long for dresses or short for suits.
Finished Sizes: Long, 24" × 52" × 3"; Short, 24" × 39" × 3"

Materials

Material requirements are for the long bag; requirements for the short bag are in parentheses.
Fabric, 3⅜ yards (2⅝ yards), 36" or 45" wide
Ribbon, ⅛ yard, ⅛" or ¼" wide
Corded piping, 14 yards (12¾ yards)
Zipper, one 50" (37")
Heavy-duty thread or buttonhole twist
Fabric Notes: Select a firmly woven fabric. Many slipcover and lightweight upholstery fabrics are suitable. A border print is particularly attractive.

Use a heavy-duty upholstery zipper. These are often available from local upholstery shops.

Cutting Directions

1. Enlarge the pattern. Slash the pattern on the broken line and add a strip 45" (32") long. (Illus. 178)
2. Using the pattern, cut two fronts.

3. Using the pattern, cut one back with a fold in the center.
4. Cut two gussets 3½" × 119" (3½" × 93").
5. Cut two straps 5" × 12" (5" × 12").
6. Cut one zipper extender 1" × 9" (1" × 6").

Sewing Directions

1. All seam allowances are ¼"; hem allowances are 1".
2. Wrong sides together, fold the zipper extender in half crosswise. Right sides up, place at the bottom of the zipper so that the folded edge overlaps the zipper teeth 1". Machine-stitch both sides of the extender to the zipper tape. (Illus. 179)

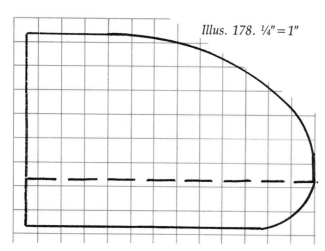

Illus. 178. ¼" = 1"

Illus. 179

Claire's Hint: The zipper extender eliminates stitching over the metal zipper teeth at the bottom.

3. Set the zipper. Right sides together, stitch the front sections to the zipper. Press. Right sides up, edgestitch both sides of the zipper through all layers.

4. Trim the zipper extender even with the front if it is too long. Make a small dart at the bottom of the zipper extender so that the front edges meet. (Illus. 180)

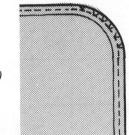

Illus. 180

5. Pin the corded piping to the front, beginning at the bottom. Using a zipper foot, stitch it in place. Repeat for the back.

Claire's Hints: For a smooth fit do not stretch the piping. Clip the piping seam allowances around the curves. Finish the ends by overlapping about ½″.

6. Make the straps.

7. Right sides up, center the end of one strap at the

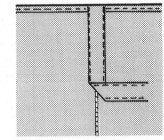

Illus. 181

top of the zipper. Stitch. Repeat with the other strap at the bottom of the bag. (Illus. 181)

8. Right sides together, join the gussets to make one long strip.

9. Hem the ends of the gusset with a double ½″ hem.

10. Right sides together, pin the gusset to the garment bag front so that the seam matches the dart at the bottom of the zipper. Using a zipper foot, stitch, using heavy-duty thread.

11. Right sides up, pin and stitch the straps to the raw edge of the gusset so they will be centered at the top and bottom of the bag.

12. Open the zipper about 6″.

13. Right sides together, pin and stitch the back to the bag.

14. Zigzag (W,4-L,3) all raw edges for neatness and security.

15. Turn the bag right side out and press.

16. Tie the short piece of ribbon in the zipper tab.

• • •

WEEKEND DUFFEL

This oversized duffel is great for shoes, hair dryer, and all the bulky stuff needed for a short trip.

Finished Size: 17″ × 10½″ × 10″

Materials

Fabric, 1¾ yards, 45″ wide
Optional: Style-A-Shade, one 27″ × 46″
Zipper (heavy-duty), one 18″
D-rings, four ¾″
Swivel spring hooks, two 2½″
Fabric Notes: Select a firmly woven fabric. If your fabric doesn't have enough body or stiffness, back it with a heavy nonwoven, fusible interfacing; I like one called Style-A-Shade.

Cutting Directions

1. From the fabric, cut two 18″ × 17½″ side/bottoms, two 18″ × 5¾″ tops, 11″ × 11½″ ends, two 5″ × 60″ straps, one 5″ × 36″ shoulder strap, two 5″ × 3″ tabs, and two 1″ × 2″ zipper extenders. (Illus. 182)

2. From the fusible interfacing, cut two 17½″ × 17″ side/bottoms, two 17½″ × 5¼″ tops; and 10½″ × 11″ ends. (For easy fusing, the interfacing is cut slightly smaller than the sections to be stiffened.)

Sewing Directions

1. All seam allowances are ½″.

2. Fuse the interfacing to the backs of the tops, side/bottoms, and ends.

3. Make the straps.

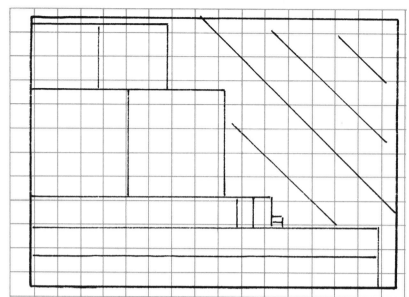

4. Wrong sides together, fold the zipper extenders in half crosswise and stitch to the ends of the zipper.

5. Set the zipper and topstitch through all layers.

6. On the side/bottom sections, mark the strap locations 5½" from each side.

Claire's Hint: Make two snips on the long sides. Connect them with a fadeaway marking pen.

7. Right sides together, join the top and side/bottom sections.

Claire's Hints: Begin and end ½" from the raw edges. Later, when you join the ends to the bag, this will make it easier and neater. (Illus. 183)

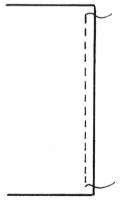

Illus. 183

Be sure to backtack at both ends.

8. Set the straps on the side/bottom sections. Pin so that the outside edges are on the marked lines and the raw edges align at the bottom.

Edgestitch both sides of the straps, stopping at the seam line.

Claire's Hint: Stitch a cross in a rectangle at the top of each strap.

9. Right sides together, join the side/bottom sections. Press open and topstitch the seam on both sides.

10. On the side/bottom sections, mark the bottom corners 5" from the seam line.

Claire's Hint: Using a fadeaway marking pen, make the mark ½" long—all the way to the seam line. Using short stitches, stitch a "V" for reinforcement; then clip to the end of the "V." (Illus. 184)

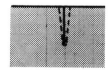

Illus. 184

11. Make the tabs. Thread one tab into a D-rings. Fold in half and stitch the raw edges together. Repeat to make the other tab.

12. With the duffel top right side up, match the raw edges and pin the tabs to each end of the zipper.

13. Open the zipper.

14. Right sides together, pin and stitch the ends to the bag, matching the clips at the bottom corners and the seams at the top. Press.

15. Finish the raw edges with a zigzag (W,4-L,3) and turn the bag right side out.

16. Finish the shoulder strap. Using pliers, open the D-ring and thread it into the swivel spring hook; close the D-ring.

Thread the end of the shoulder strap into the D-ring and fold 2″ from the end. Turn under the raw edge and stitch securely with a cross in a rectangle. Finish the other end of the strap.

17. Hook the shoulder strap onto the bag.

COSMETIC CASE

This elegant cosmetic case is the perfect travel companion and it's roomy enough to hold all of one's cosmetics.

Finished Size: 10½″ × 8″ × 3″

Materials

Remnant, one 19″ × 13½″
Style-A-Shade fusible interfacing, one 19″ × 13½″
Ribbon, 2⅜ yards, ⅝″ wide
Zipper, one 10″
Fabric Notes: The leftover material from either the hanging garment bag or the weekend duffel will be ample to make the cosmetic case.

Cutting Directions

1. Fuse the Style-A-Shade to the wrong side of the fabric.
2. Cut two 8″ × 10½″ for the front and back, two 1½″ × 10½″ tops, and two 13⅝″ × 3″ side/bottoms. (For fabric economy, the side/bottom has been cut in two pieces. If you prefer, cut one 26¾″ × 3″.)

Sewing Directions

1. All seam allowances are ¼″.
2. Press the ribbon in half lengthwise.
3. Set the zipper and topstitch through all layers.
4. Make the ribbon tabs. Cut off 4½″ of ribbon and zigzag (W,2-L,2) down the center. Cut into two equal strips.
5. With the top right side up, fold the ribbon loops in half crosswise and stitch at each end of the zipper.

6. Right sides together, join the tops and side/bottom sections to make a gusset.
7. On the gusset, mark the locations of the bottom corners 5⅛″ from the bottom seam. Reinforce and clip.
8. Wrong sides together, pin and stitch the front to the gusset, matching the clips to the bottom corners and the seam to the top corners.
9. Wrong sides together, join the back to the bag.
Claire's Hint: To ensure accuracy, pin all corners first.
10. Bind all edges with ribbon. Slip the raw edges between the ribbon folds. Baste and zigzag (W,2-L,2).
Claire's Hints: Begin binding at the bottom. For a neat finish, fold the ribbon end under and overlap ½″.

To save time, baste with water-soluble basting tape.

TRAVELLING BAG

This traditional travelling bag will hold one or two suits and can easily be carried onto a plane. The bottom loop slips over garment hangers for compact travelling.
Finished Size: 23″ × 39″; folded 23″ × 19″

Materials

Fabric A, 1⅛″ yards, 54″ wide or 2¼ yards, 45″ wide
Interfacing scrap, one 1″ × 5″
Zipper, one 38″ or two zippers, 20″
Fabric Notes: I like fabric-backed vinyl because it's lightweight, waterproof, and durable. Many other fabrics such as corduroy, rip-stop nylon, canvas, denim, nylon polyester, and twill-weave synthetics would also be suitable.

Extra-long zippers are hard to find; however, many upholstery shops will sell you zipper-by-the-inch. And, in a pinch, you can use two shorter zippers positioned so that the pull tabs meet in the center.

Cutting Directions

1. Enlarge the pattern. (Illus. 185)
2. Using the pattern, cut two bag fronts.

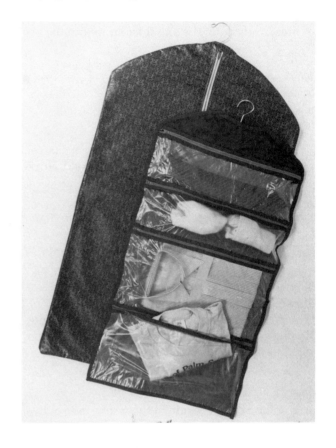

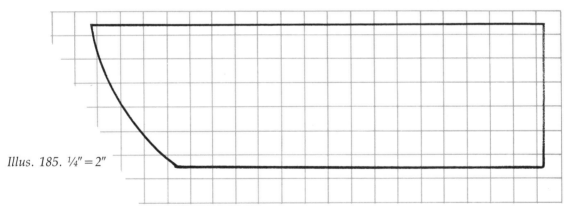

Illus. 185. ¼″ = 2″

3. Cut one 25″ × 39½″ rectangle for the bag back. Do not shape the top at this time.
4. Cut one 2″ × 6″ loop and two 1¼″ × 3″ zipper extenders.
5. Cut enough strips 1″ wide to make 3½ yards of piping. Seam as needed.

Sewing Directions

1. All seam allowances are ¼″.
2. Set the zipper extenders to the zipper ends. Close the zipper. Wrong sides together, fold one extender in half crosswise. Center over the zipper with the folded edge just covering the zipper stop; stitch the extender to the zipper tape. (Illus. 186)

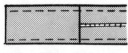

Illus. 186

Illus. 187

Stitch the other extender to the top of the zipper. *Claire's Hint:* This is an easy way to make a zipper 2"–4" longer; and, if you're using zipper-by-the-inch, it eliminates the problem of stitching over the teeth at the zipper bottom and the top.

3. Set the zipper. Right sides together, pin and stitch the zipper to the long edge of the bag front. Then, right sides up, edgestitch through all layers.

4. Close the zipper and place the bag front on the back rectangle. Trim the back to match the front. *Claire's Hint:* Since zipper tape widths vary, the zipper is set to the front before cutting out the back to ensure that both sections will be the same width.

5. Make the piping. Fold the 1" strip, wrong sides together, in half lengthwise and stitch ¼" from the fold.

Claire's Hint: If you wish, cord the piping; however, I prefer it flat.

6. Set the piping to the front. Right sides together, stitch the piping, beginning at one of the bottom corners and clipping the seam allowances of the piping at the curves and other corner so the piping will fit smoothly.

7. On the bag back, make a 3" long buttonhole. Center it about 1¼" from the top. (Illus. 187) *Claire's Hint:* To reinforce the buttonhole, glue a scrap of interfacing on the wrong side of the bag.

Use a seam ripper to open the buttonhole. Beginning at each end, slash to the center.

8. Make the bottom loop. Fold the strip in half, wrong sides together; then fold the raw edges to the fold line; zigzag (W,2-L,2) down the center of the strip.

9. Join the loop to the bag front. Right sides up, mark the loop position with small clips 2" from the center. Right sides up, stitch the loop, aligning the ends with the snips. Stitch in place. (Illus. 188)

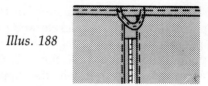

Illus. 188

10. Open the zipper.

11. Join the bag front and back. Stitch right sides together.

Claire's Hint: Use paper clips to baste when sewing on vinyl.

12. Turn right side out.

• • •

TRAVEL ORGANIZER

If the traveller on your gift list likes to be organized, he (or she) will appreciate this gift. Ready to be used without unpacking, it has four see-through pockets on one side and two roomy hampers on the other.

Finished Size: 19" × 36"

Materials

Fabric A, ⅝ yard, 45" wide
Soft plastic, one 38" × 36"
Zippers, six 18"
Wide bias binding or ribbon, 10 yards, 1" wide

Fabric Notes: I like plastic for the front pockets so that the contents are visible, and I prefer plastic for the inside divider so the clean garments remain fresh. However, plastic is much more difficult to work with and I sometimes cheat, especially on the divider.

On the back, I use nylon taffeta or any other firmly woven fabric.

Cutting Directions

1. Enlarge the pattern. (Illus. 189)
2. From Fabric A, cut two 20" × 15½" pockets.

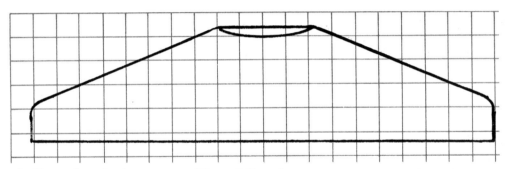

Illus. 189. ¼" = 1"

3. From the plastic, cut two 19" × 6½" pockets, two 19" × 10" pockets, and one 19" × 36" rectangle center divider.

4. Using the pattern, cut a top back and top front.

5. Scoop out the top front as indicated and mark the notches on the front.

Sewing Directions

1. All seam allowances are ¼".

2. Assemble the front from top to bottom in this order: the top, two narrow plastic pockets, and two wide plastic pockets.

3. Set a zipper between each section of the organizer. Wrong sides together, join the zipper and long edge of one pocket. Bind the edges with tape or folded ribbon.

Claire's Hints: To avoid pinholes that show, place the pins within the ¼" seam allowance.

Check as you go to be sure the the pockets stay in line.

4. Assemble the back with the top above the large pockets. Set the zippers using the directions above.

5. Right sides up, place the front on top of the divider. Pin the tops of three zippers to the divider; stitch just above each zipper to make the bottom of the pocket above. (Illus. 190)

6. Stitch the pockets on the back. Wrong sides together, place the front/divider section on top of the back, matching the two zippers at the top. Pin the bottom zipper to the divider without pinning into the front section. Stitch just above the zipper.

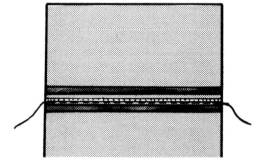

Illus. 190

Claire's Hint: This is tricky. Fold the front out of the way so that it won't get caught in the stitching line.

7. Finish the last pocket on the front. Front side up, fold the back out of the way, and stitch, just above the bottom zipper.

8. Stitch the divider and front together at the top. Trim away the excess plastic.

9. Bind the top between the notches.

10. Lay the organizer out flat. Smooth and pin the edges together.

Claire's Hint: If the edges don't match at the bottom, trim the longer of the two. Use a ruler to mark a straight line on each side. Pin the layers together on the marked line.

11. Machine-baste ¼" from the edge on the marked line. Trim as needed.

12. Bind the edges.

13. Press the bias binding or ribbon in half. Bind the bottom first. Finish by binding the sides and top, turning under ½" at the beginning and end.

● ● ●

JOGGER'S TRAVELLING COMPANION

The jogger's travelling companion was designed for my husband who always takes his running gear when we travel. Many times his clothes are damp when it's time to pack, and I cannot put them in next to the fresh clothes.

Equipped with its own handle and two water-proof compartments, the jogging bag is great to carry for overnight trips.
Finished Size: 18½" × 17"

Materials

Fabric A (bag), ½ yard, 45" wide
Fabric B (lining), ¾ yard, 45" wide
Zippers, two 18"
Fabric Notes: I used a fabric-backed vinyl for the bag and soft plastic for the inside compartments. Canvas, denim, corduroy, and nylon taffeta would also be appropriate for the bag. I particularly like the plastic lining because it doesn't absorb the dirty clothes odor.

Cutting Directions

1. From Fabric A, cut one 19" × 18" bag back, one 19" × 15" bag front, and one 4" × 12" strap.
2. From Fabric B, cut two 19" × 11" rectangles to line Pocket A. Cut one 19" × 15½" rectangle and one 19" × 13" rectangle to line Pocket B.

Illus. 191

Sewing Directions

1. All seam allowances are ¼".
2. Mark the fold line on the large bag section 1½" from the top.
3. Using small clips, mark both ends.
4. Make the strap.
5. Position the strap, centering it on the fold line of the large bag section. Fold under the ends ½". Stitch them in place with a cross in a rectangle. (Illus. 191)
Claire's Hint: To avoid making pinholes in the vinyl, use tape, transparent or drafting, to "baste" the strap in place.
6. Right sides together, stitch the bag sections to the zippers.

7. Make the pockets. Pocket A is at the bottom of the bag and Pocket B is at the top just below the handle.
   Right sides together, with the zipper sandwiched between, stitch.
8. Pull the bag and pockets away from the zipper teeth; edgestitch through all layers.
9. Close the zippers. Right side up, stitch across the zipper tape about ¼" above the tab.
Claire's Hint: Stitch carefully to avoid stitching through the bag or pockets.
10. Open the zippers. Right sides together, stitch

the bottom of Pocket A. Then stitch the sides of the pocket and bag, stopping when you reach the top zipper. (Illus. 192)

Claire's Hint: To avoid pinholes, use paper clips or straight pins only in the seam allowance to baste.

12. Right sides together, stitch the bottom and sides of Pocket B, stopping when you reach the zipper.

13. Continuing with the right sides together, fold the top of the bag at the fold line. Pin or clip the edges together from the fold line to the zipper. Then smooth and match the raw edges of Pocket B to the bag below the zipper. Stitch through all layers, stopping 1"–2" below the zipper. (Illus. 193)

14. Turn right side out.

15. Close the bottom of Pocket B.

16. Arrange the pockets in the bag.

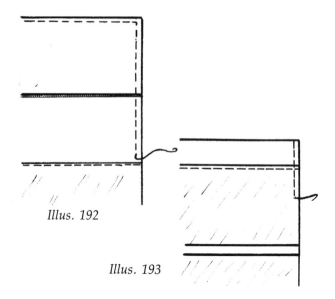

Illus. 192

Illus. 193

• • •

JEWELRY MINI-ROLL

Easy to make and fun to give, this jewelry mini-roll is the perfect gift for short-trip travellers.

Finished Size: 4¾" × 6¾"

Materials

Suede (real or synthetic), one 15" × 7"
Fusible interfacing, one 4½" × 6½"
Fusible web, 1½" × 4½"
Fibrefill
Snaps, 3
Zipper, one 4" or 7"
Fabric Notes: I used Ultrasuede.

Cutting Directions

Cut two 5" × 7" rectangles, two 1½" × 4½" earring-straps, and one 2" × 4½" ring-strap.

Sewing Directions

1. All seam allowances are ¼".

2. Make the earring-strap. Wrong sides together with the fusible web in between, bond the two earring-straps together. Shape them using the pattern. (Illus. 194)

Stitch around the strap ¼" from the edges; trim the seam to ⅛". Set the snap ball at the small end.

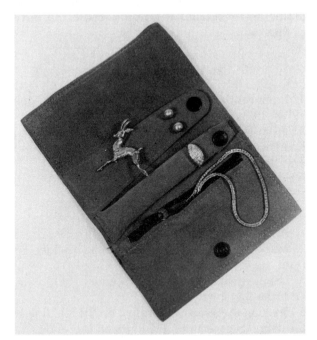

3. Make the ring-strap. Wrong sides together, stitch the ring-strap, tapering it at one end. Trim the seam to ⅛". (Illus. 195)

Stuff with fibrefill and set the snap ball at the tapered end, centering the seam on the underneath.

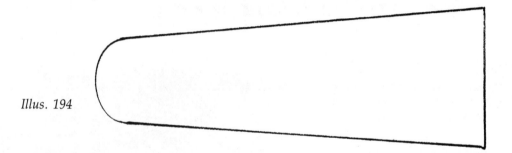

Illus. 194

4. Cut a 3½″ × ¼″ window for the zipper, centering it 2¼″ from the bottom of one rectangle.
Claire's Hint: Use a single-edged razor blade or mat knife to cut the window smoothly.
5. If you're using a 7″ zipper, shorten it. Make a bar tack 4½″ from the top stops; cut off the excess zipper below the bar tack. (Illus. 196)
6. Set the zipper. Right sides up, stitch the zipper under the window. (Illus. 197)
Claire's Hints: Use water-soluble basting tape or a gluestick to baste the zipper in place.
7. Pin the earring- and ring-straps in place; then set the corresponding socket snaps. (Illus. 198)
8. Center the interfacing on the wrong side of the other rectangle; fuse in place.
9. Sew one socket snap to the right side of the interfaced section, centering it ⅝″ from the top.
10. Assemble the roll. Wrong sides together, topstitch ¼″ from all edges. Trim away ⅛″.
Claire's Hint: Use a zipper foot to avoid hitting the snaps.
11. Set the remaining socket snap through all layers at the bottom of the mini-roll, centering it ½″ from the edge.

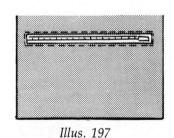

Illus. 195

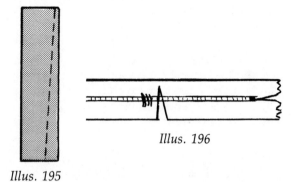

Illus. 196

Illus. 197

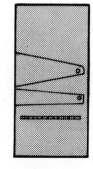

Illus. 198

TRAVEL MESH BAGS

Give your favorite traveller a set of mesh bags to keep things organized and see the contents. And, since they're completely washable, they're perfect for socks and small items in the washing machine.
Finished Sizes: Small, 9" × 13"; Large, 11" × 17½"

Materials

Fabric requirements are for two small bags; requirements for two large bags are in parentheses.
Fabric, ⅜ yard (½ yard), 45" wide
Zippers, two 12" (18")
Fabric Notes: Choose a washable knit or woven fabric with an open weave. These were made in a beautiful beige and black cotton/silk/linen blend for our son who had accused the dryer of eating his socks. I knew it would shrink so I purchased an extra ⅛ yard and preshrank the fabric before cutting.

Cutting Directions

Cut two 18" × 12½" (22½" × 18") bags.

Sewing Directions

1. All seam allowances are ¼".
2. Set the zipper to the short ends of the bag.

Right sides together, pin and stitch. Press and top-stitch close to the seam line.
3. Wrong sides together, fold the back of the bag over the zipper tape, positioning the zipper about ⅜" below the fold line. Mark the ends of the fold line with ⅛" clips.
4. Right sides together, fold at the clips; stitch the end with the zipper tab.
5. Open the zipper and stitch the other end.
6. Topstitch around the bag ¼" from the edge. Press.

• • •

TIE CADDY

A tie caddy is a marvellous gift for any man who travels. Inspired by a very expensive leather accessory, this one is guaranteed to keep ties pressed and wrinkle-free.
Finished Size: Closed, 7" × 17"; Open, 14½" × 17"

Materials

Fabric Remnant A (tie case cover), one 14" × 17"
Fabric Remnant B (lining) one 14" × 17"
Fleece, one 16" × 26"
Cardboard, crescent board or matboard (pasteboard), one 11½" × 15½"
Wide bias binding or 1" wide ribbon, 2½ yards

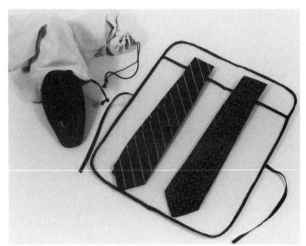

Photo also shows shoe bags.

Fabric Notes: I used fabric-backed vinyl for the outside of the case and cotton flannel for the lining. Firmly woven fabrics and stable knits are also suitable. The flannel lining holds the ties in place so that they won't slide and wrinkle.

Crescent board or matboard is available at art suppliers. If the board isn't available, use two layers of cardboard from a large detergent box.

Cutting Directions

1. From Remnant A, cut one 14″ × 17″ case cover.
2. From Remnant B, cut one 14″ × 17″ case cover.
3. From the fleece, cut two 13″ × 16″ rectangles.
4. From the cardboard, cut two 5¾″ × 15½″ rectangles. Round two corners on one side of each section. (Illus. 199)
5. Using the cardboard as a guide, round the corners on the case, lining, and fleece.

Sewing Directions

1. All seam allowances are ¼″.
2. Glue-baste the fleece to the wrong side of the lining and cover.
3. Join the case and lining. Wrong sides together, baste and stitch, leaving the bottom open 8″–10″.
4. Insert the cardboard between the fleece layers. Mark the stitching line in the center of the case between the cardboard sections. Stitch. (Illus. 200) *Claire's Hint:* I stitched from the outside of the case because the vinyl had a pattern which could be used as a stitching guide. To prevent the presser foot from sticking to the vinyl, use a needle lubricant.

When stitching from the lining side, use a fadeaway pen to indicate the stitching line. Use a piece of stabilizer or paper between the fabric and feed dogs to protect the vinyl.
5. Stitch the opening closed. Trim-stitch the raw edges around the case close to the stitched line.
6. Fold 1 yard of the bias binding in half length-

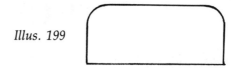

Illus. 199

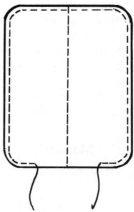

Illus. 200

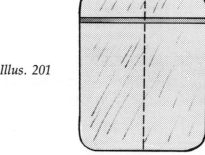

Illus. 201

wise, and zigzag (W,2-L,2) down the center of the strip. Cut the strip into three pieces—one 14″ and two 11″.
7. Center and pin the two short strips on the outside of the case. Pin the long strip to the lining side about 3″ from the top. (Illus. 201)
8. Bind the edges.

● ● ●

SHOE BAGS

Shoe bags are great for those occasions when you need a "little gift"; they're even great for wrapping gifts of money or checks. This is a particularly thoughtful gift for travellers; and, if the recipient has never used shoe bags before, he'll wonder how he ever managed without them.

These bags are roomy enough to hold one man's shoe or two lady's shoes. Last, but not least, they take only 10 minutes to make and can be made from a variety of materials.

Finished Size: Large: 8″ × 16½″

Materials

Remnant, one 34″ × 18″
Cord, 1¼ yards
Fabric Notes: Any soft fabric is suitable. I prefer cotton flannel.

Cutting Directions

1. Cut two 17″ × 18″ rectangles.
2. Cut the cord into two equal lengths.

Sewing Directions

1. All seam allowances are ¼″; hem allowance is 1″.
2. Fold under ¼″ on one short edge and edge-stitch.

3. Right sides together, fold the bag in half lengthwise and round the lower corners. Stitch the bottom and sides, stopping 1¼″ from the top. (Illus. 202)
4. To finish the unstitched section of the seam, fold under each seam allowance. Stitch it in place. (Illus. 203)
Claire's Hint: Use a washable gluestick to baste.
5. Turn right side out.
6. Make the casing. Fold under the hem allowance. Stitch ¾″ from the edge.
7. Thread the cord into the casing, and knot the ends.

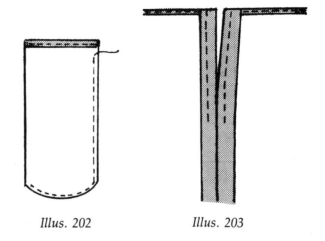

Illus. 202   *Illus. 203*

- - - ● ● ● - - -

CAR ORGANIZER

The car owner on your gift list will want this handy car organizer. It has a large zipped pocket for maps or important papers, a small zipper pocket for small change and insurance card, a small pocket for a pen and a large one for sunglasses. Elastic straps on the back hold it on the visor.

Finished Size: 12½″ × 6″

Materials

Remnant A, one 31″ × 6″
Zipper, one 12″
Zipper, one 5″ or 7″
Elastic, ½ yard, ½″ or ⅝″ wide

Wide bias binding, 1¼ yards
Fabric Notes: Select a medium-weight, firmly woven fabric. I used striped denim.

Cutting Directions

1. Cut one 12″ × 6″ back, one 12″ × 5½″ front, one 5½″ × 2″ pocket section A, one 5½″ × 4″ pocket section B, and one 6″ × 6″ pocket. (Illus. 204)
2. Cut the elastic into three 6″ strips.

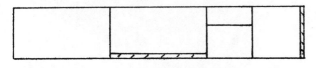

Illus. 204

Sewing Directions

1. All seam allowances are ¼″.
2. Right sides together, set the short zipper between pocket sections A and B. Press and edgestitch.
Claire's Hint: When using a 7″ zipper, stitch across both ends before trimming to avoid cutting off the tab.
3. Bind one end of the pocket.
4. Join the two pockets. Right sides together, match one end of the zipper pocket with the bottom—the side opposite the binding—of the pocket C, and stitch. Press.

Claire's Hint: Since zipper tapes vary in width, the bottom of the pockets may be uneven. Don't worry; but don't trim at that time.
5. Right sides up, stack the pockets on top of the front. Stitch-in-the-ditch along the vertical seam line. Divide and stitch the pocket into two smaller pockets, 4″ and 2″ wide. (Illus. 205)

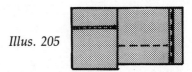

Illus. 205

6. Right sides together, pin and stitch the 12″ zipper to the top of the front; press and topstitch close to the seam line.
7. Wrong sides together, pin and stitch the top of the zipper to the back.
8. Turn the organizer over. Pin and stitch the elastic strips in the center and about 1″ from each end. (Illus. 206)

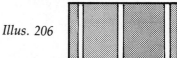

Illus. 206

9. Bind the edges.
Claire's Hints: Press the binding in half before beginning. Bind the top and bottom first, then the ends.

For a neat finish on the ends, allow a ½″ tail and fold it over the top (bottom) before folding it in half lengthwise around the end.

• • •

TIRE-GAUGE CASE

Packaged in an attractive ribbon pouch, this easy-to-find tire gauge is a must for everyone with a car. If you're giving it to a new car owner, show him or her how to use it.

Materials

Ribbon, ⅜ yard 1″ or 1½″ wide
Tire gauge, 1

Sewing Directions

1. Press under ½″ on one end of the ribbon and 2¼″ on the other.

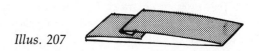

Illus. 207

2. Wrong sides together, fold crosswise 6″ from the top. (Illus. 207)
3. Edgestitch both sides of the ribbon.
4. Insert the tire gauge.

MAP CASE

This handy map case is a perfect adjunct for organized travelling. Designed to fit most glove compartments, it has four pockets large enough to hold several maps.

Finished Size: Folded, 5¾" × 22"; Open, 22" × 11"

Materials

Remnant, one 22" × 17"
Narrow bias binding, 2½ yards
Fabric Notes: Choose a fabric that is attractive on both sides such as drill, canvas, awning material, broadcloth, Ultrasuede, Lamaire, and see-through plastic. Or make your own double-faced fabric using two fabrics, bonded wrong sides together with fusible web. I used a printed vinyl with a cotton twill backing.

Cutting Directions

1. Cut one 22" × 11" rectangle and one 22" × 6" rectangle.
Claire's Hint: If your fabric doesn't have a one-way design, cut one 22" × 17" rectangle and eliminate the seam at the bottom.

Sewing Directions

1. All seam allowances are ¼".
2. Bind the top of the pocket with bias binding.
3. Wrong sides together, join the pocket and case at the bottom and sides.
4. Divide the pocket into four equal sections 5¼"

wide, and mark the stitching lines with a sliver of soap; and topstitch through all layers. (Illus. 208)
5. Round the upper corners of the case.
6. Bind the lower edge; then bind the sides and top.

Illus. 208

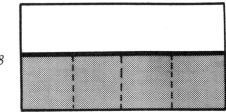

TRAVELLER'S WALLET

Safe and convenient, this traveller's wallet is perfect for a passport and extra cash. The loop on the wallet slips over the belt, allowing it to be worn on either the inside or outside of the trousers.

Finished Size: 9" × 4½"

Materials

Remnant, one 11" × 9"
Zipper, one 11"
Fabric Notes: Lamaire, Ultrasuede, and Facile are excellent choices; however, any firmly woven fabric is suitable.

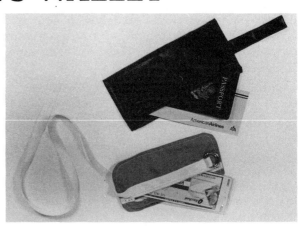

Cutting Directions

Cut one 9" square wallet and one 2" × 9" strap.

Sewing Directions

1. All seam allowances are ¼".
2. Make the strap. Wrong sides together, fold the strap in half lengthwise. Topstitch ¼" from the raw edge and edgestitch the fold line. Trim the raw edges close to the stitched line. (Illus. 209)
   Set the strap aside.

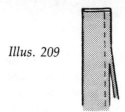

Illus. 209

3. Set the zipper. Right sides together, stitch the zipper to the ends of the wallet. Right sides out, topstitch through all layers close to the seam line. *Claire's Hint:* To stitch Lamaire smoothly, rub the material with needle lubricant.
4. Sew the strap to the wallet. Fold the strap in half crosswise; stitch 2" from the fold. Right sides together, pin the strap to the wallet. Stitch. (Illus. 210)

Illus. 210

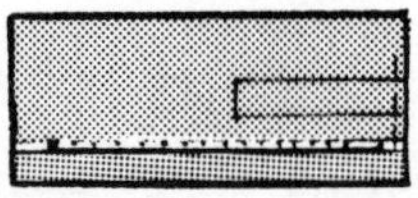

5. Wrong sides together, fold with the zipper about ½" below the fold line. Mark the ends of the fold line with short clips.
6. Open the zipper. Right sides together, stitch the ends of the wallet.
7. Turn right side out and topstitch ¼" from the edge.

• • •

MONEY BELT

A great gift for travellers, hikers, bikers, and runners, this money belt is perfect for stashing cash, traveller's cheques, and important documents.
Finished Size: 8¼" × 4"

Materials

Remnant A, one 18" × 5"
Zipper, one 7"
D-rings, 1 pair ½"
Ribbon, 1 yard, ¾" wide
Fabric Notes: Use a lightweight, firmly woven fabric with a water-repellent finish. Or, treat the fabric with a fabric protector to avoid wet money.

Cutting Directions

1. Cut one 8¾" × 4½" back, one 8¾" × 1½" front, and one 8¾" × 3¼" front.
2. Round the corners on the back section.

Sewing Directions

1. All seam allowances are ¼".
2. Right sides together, stitch the two front sections to the zipper. Right sides up, topstitch each side of the zipper through all layers.
3. Thread the ribbon into the two D-rings. Fold the end under 1" and stitch.
4. Right sides together, pin the ribbon to the front just below the zipper; stitch. (Illus. 211)

Illus. 211

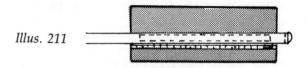

5. Open the zipper.
6. Right sides together, join the front and back. Trim away the corners on the front.
7. Turn the money belt right side out. Topstitch ¼" from the edge.

• • •

WRAPAROUND WRIST WALLET

For the runners on your list, this ingenious wraparound wrist wallet will solve a very familiar problem—where to stash a little cash, driver's license, bank card, or even the hotel room key.
Finished Size: Child, 3″ × 8″; Ladies, 3″ × 9″; Men, 3″ × 10″

Materials

Material requirements are for a child's wallet.
Requirements for the larger sizes are in parentheses.
Remnant A (wallet), 3½″ × 8½″ (3½″ × 9½″; 3½″ × 10½″).
Contrast B (wallet lining), 3½″ × 8½″ (3½″ × 9½″; 3½″ × 10½″).
Zipper, one 7″
Velcro, 3″ of 1½″ wide
Fabric Notes: Select firmly woven, lightweight fabrics such as poplin, canvas, and denim for the wallet and an absorbent material like cotton terry or cotton knit for the lining.

Sewing Directions

1. All seam allowances are ¼″.
2. Close the zipper and stitch the tape ends together just above the pull tab.
3. Using a fadeaway marking pen, draw the zipper location on the wallet 1″ below one long edge. Stitch a rectangle around the marked line.
Claire's Hint: Use the edge of the zigzag foot as a guide and stitch ¼″ from each side of the marked line. Shorten the stitches at the end for reinforcement.
4. Slash on the marked line and clip to, but not through, the corners. (Illus. 212)

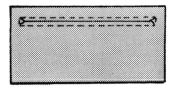

Illus. 212

Claire's Hint: Using scissors that cut to the ends of the points, position the scissors points exactly where you want the clip to be; then clip.
5. Using the stitched rectangle as a guide, fold and press the raw edges around the opening to the wrong side.
6. Right sides up, position the opening over the zipper; baste then topstitch around the opening to secure it.
Claire's Hint: Use a washable gluestick or water-soluble basting tape to baste.
7. Open the zipper.
8. Right sides together, pin and stitch the lining to the wallet. Trim the corners and turn right side out.
9. Right sides up, baste the soft side of the Velcro to one end of the wallet. (Illus. 213)

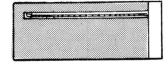

Illus. 213

10. Lining side up, baste the firm or hook side to the other end.
11. Topstitch around the wallet ¼″ from the edges. Each piece of Velcro remains unstitched on one side. Stitch in place.

THE STITCHERY

NEEDLE BOOK

Everyone—novices and experts—will enjoy a needle book. Decorated with scraps of lace, this gift is as pretty as it is practical.

The needle book is lined with felt and has four felt pages for storing machine as well as hand needles.

Finished Size: Closed, 4″ square; Open, 8″ × 4″

Materials

Remnant A, one 9″ × 4½″
Contrast B, one 4½″ square
Felt, wool or rayon, one 9″ × 12″
Lace insertion, ¼ yard, ½″ or ⅝″ wide
Entredeux, ¼ yard
Eyelet insertion, ⅛ yard, ¾″ or 1″ wide
Double-faced satin ribbon, ½ yard, ⅛″ or ¼″ wide
Fabric Notes: This is an excellent opportunity to use small scraps of pretty cottons or silks which you have accumulated. The contrast fabric for Remnant B will highlight the insertions.

Polyester felt is not suitable; needles will rust when pinned to it for several weeks. If wool or rayon felt is unavailable, use cotton flannel.

Cutting Directions

1. From Remnant A, cut one 1¼″ × 4½″ rectangle and one 7½″ × 4½″ rectangle for the cover.
2. From the felt, cut one 9″ × 4½″ cover lining, and two 7″ × 3½″ pages.
3. Cut two 4½″ strips of lace insertion.
4. Cut two 4½″ strips of entredeux. Trim away the seam allowances.
5. Cut the ribbon in half.

Sewing Directions

1. All seam allowances are ¼″.
2. Make the case cover. Finish one short end on each cover section. Right sides up, join (W,2-L,2) the entredeux and lace insertion to each section; then join both sections to the wide eyelet insertion. Press. (Illus. 214)
3. Place the contrast fabric under the insertions and zigzag (W,2-L,1) again where the entredeux joins the cover. Wrong side up, trim away the excess contrast.
4. Measure the case cover. If it is longer than 9″, cut off enough so the insertions will be centered on the cover front.

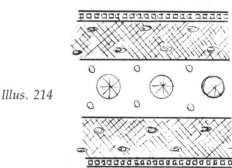

Illus. 214

5. Right side up, center and pin the ribbons at each end.
6. Right sides together, join the cover and cover lining. Leave a small opening at the bottom of the back cover.
7. Trim the corners and turn the cover right side out. Press.
8. Close the opening by hand.
9. Lining side up, center and pin the felt pages in place. Machine-stitch through the center of all layers from the top to the bottom. (Illus. 215)
Claire's Hint: For accuracy, use a fadeaway marking pen to indicate the stitching line.

Illus. 215

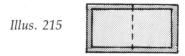

SEWING CADDY

If your stitcher friends are like mine, this handy sewing caddy will be a special treat. My friends who enjoy embroidery and handwork hate machine-sewing and some don't even have a machine. The friends who enjoy machine work never have time to make a gift for themselves.
Finished Size: 7" × 18"

Materials

Remnant (double-faced quilted), one 18" square
Bias binding, 1⅞ yards
Cotton cording, ½ yard, 1" diameter
Fabric Notes: If the fabric you select isn't double-faced, back the caddy with a firmly woven nonslip fabric like corduroy or velveteen.

Cutting Directions

1. Cut one 7" × 18" caddy, two 7" × 6" pockets, and one 4" × 12" strip.
2. Round the corners of the caddy and two pockets.
3. Separate the fabric and batting layers of the strip. Select the fabric layer you prefer and discard the remainder.

Sewing Directions

1. Bind the straight edge of each pocket.
2. Join the pockets and caddy. Right sides up, pin and stitch the pockets to the ends.
3. Divide and stitch one pocket into two sections.
4. Make the pincushion. Right side up, place the center of the cord on one end of the fabric strip. Baste together at the cord center. (Illus. 216)
   Right sides together, wrap the strip around the cord. Using a zipper foot, stitch close to the cord. Trim the seam to ⅛".

Holding the end of the cord, turn right side out. Cut off the excess cord.

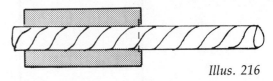

Illus. 216

5. Join the pincushion and caddy. Center the pincushion on the caddy. Baste at both ends.
Claire's Hint: For a neater finish, trim both ends of the pincushion cord so that it will be shorter than the tubing and won't be sewn into the seam.
6. Bind the edges.
7. Press.

IRONING BOARD COVER

Wouldn't it be nice if your ironing board had grainlines marked on it? This gingham cover is the perfect solution, and once you've used it, you'll wonder how you ever sewed without it. Treat yourself and a friend to this timesaver.

Finished Size: 19" × 56"

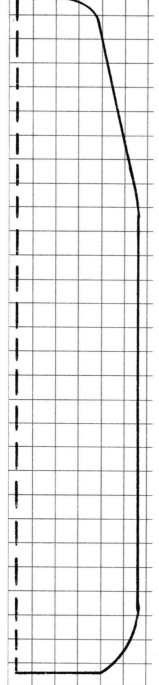

Illus. 217. ¼" = 2"

Photo also shows pressing cloth and wrist pincushion

Materials

Material requirements are for two covers.
Fabric, 1⅝ yards (for one cover, a 21" × 58½" remnant), 45" wide
Postal twine
Fabric Notes: Use 1" checked colorfast gingham.

Cutting Directions

1. Enlarge the pattern. (Illus. 217)
2. Using the pattern, cut two covers from the gingham.
Claire's Hint: To eliminate finishing the raw edge of the casing, use pinking shears to cut out. This is one of the few exceptions to a *Never, Never* rule.
3. To make a pattern for a sleeve board, trace the padded board and add 3" to all edges.

Sewing Directions

1. The casing allowance is 1".
2. Make two ½" buttonholes at the large end ½" from the raw edge. (Illus. 218)

Illus. 218

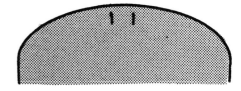

3. Fold the casing to the wrong side and topstitch ¾" from the edge. Press.
Claire's Hint: Make small pleats in the casing to remove excess fullness on the curves.
4. Insert the twine.

PRESSING CLOTH

Of course you can buy pressing cloths, but not like this one. It's really two cloths in one: a wool pressing cloth for top-pressing woollen garments and a muslin cloth for general pressing.
Finished Size: 24" × 16"

Materials

Muslin remnant (prewashed), one 24" × 16"
Wool remnant, one 24" × 16"
Fabric Notes: Select a firmly woven, light-colored wool for all colored fabrics. I used a cream-colored flannel. Wash the muslin 5 or 6 times to remove all the sizing.

Sewing Directions

1. Using pinking shears, trim all edges evenly.
2. Right sides out, join the two cloths at one end with a ¼" seam.
Claire's Hint: If you don't have pinking shears, join the cloths with a French seam and topstitch around each cloth ⅛" from the edge.

• • •

WRIST PINCUSHION

Every home-sewer can use another pincushion. I have several so I can keep different kinds of pins sorted.
Finished Size: Approximately 2" × 4"

Materials

Remnant, one 6" square
Elastic, 7" piece, ½" or ⅝" wide
Stuffing: sawdust, wool yarn or scraps, birdseed, 100% cotton
Fabric Notes: Choose a firmly woven wool or cotton scrap. I like fabrics that are easy to stick with pins. Some such as Ultrasuede would cause an ulcer with one wearing.

Do not use polyester fibrefill for the stuffing; it will rust your pins.

Cutting Directions

1. Trace the pattern. (Illus. 219)
2. Using the pattern, cut two. Trim one ⅜" on all edges.
3. Mark the centers at the sides and ends with tiny clips.
4. Cut one 2½" × 2" strap.

Sewing Directions

1. All seam allowances are ¼".
2. Fold the long sides of the strap under and edge-stitch. Set aside.

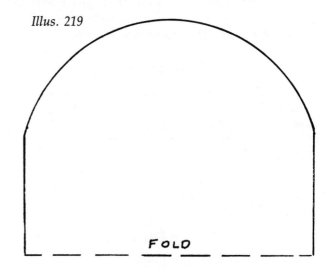

Illus. 219

FOLD

3. Right sides up, center the strap on the pincushion bottom; stitch. (Illus. 220)

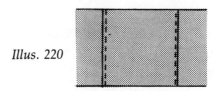

Illus. 220

4. On the top, place a row of gathering thread *almost but not quite* ¼" from the edge.
Claire's Hint: Start and stop at the center of each side. Loosen the upper tension and stitch with a

heavy thread such as buttonhole twist in the bobbin.

5. Join the top and bottom. Right sides together, match and pin the centers. Pull up the gathering thread, and stitch, leaving a small opening on one side.

6. Turn right side out. Stuff and close the opening by hand.

7. Thread the elastic into the strap and join the ends.

Claire's Hint: Use a longer elastic strip so that the pincushion will fit over the sewing-machine top. This is a fantastic timesaver and you'll quickly learn to stick the pins in without shifting your eyes from your stitching.

- - -

PRESSING AIDS

HAM

A pressing ham is essential for professional results and they are so expensive these days. However, it only takes about an hour to make one from a couple of remnants. This is a wonderful gift to make for yourself or a friend who sews.

Materials

Remnant A (foundation cover), one 18″ × 14″
Remnant B (outer cover), two 12″ square
Sawdust, 2 gallon cans full

Most lumberyards are delighted to give you sawdust.

Fabric Notes: Use muslin or a firmly woven cotton or cotton blend for the foundation cover; use wool for the outer cover.

Cutting Directions

1. Enlarge the pattern. (Illus. 221)
2. Using the pattern, cut two muslin covers on the straight grain.
3. Using the pattern, cut two wool outer covers on the bias.

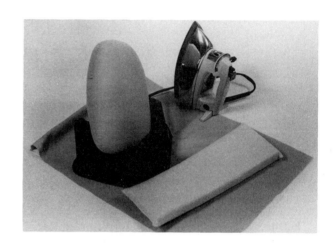

Sewing Directions

1. All seam allowances are ⅜″.
2. Right sides together, stitch the muslin covers, leaving a 3″–4″ opening at the large end. Trim the seam allowances and turn right side out.

Claire's Hint: Use pinking shears to trim the curved seam.

3. Turn right side out.
4. Remove large particles from the dried sawdust and pack the ham *very firmly*. Close the opening by hand.
5. Place a row of ease-basting at the large end of each wool cover. (Illus. 222)

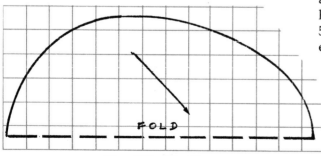

FOLD

Illus. 221. ¼″=1″

Illus. 222

Claire's Hint: To ease-baste, zigzag (W,2-L,2) over a strong cord such as buttonhole twist.

6. Right sides together, stitch around the wool cover, leaving the large end open. Trim the seam.

7. Turn right side out and insert the ham foundation.

8. Steam the wool cover and, while it is damp, pull it over the muslin-covered ham.

9. Pin one of the covers in place and pull up the ease-basting. Lap the other cover over it; pin, and close the opening by hand.

10. Steam and press the seams as needed to flatten them.

● ● ●

SEAM ROLL

To avoid seam impressions on the right side of the garment, always use a seam roll when pressing. (Illus. 223)

Illus. 223

Materials

Remnant A (foundation cover), one 18″ × 10″
Remnant B (outer cover), one 22″ × 15″
Sawdust, 2 gallon cans
Fabric Notes: Use muslin or a firmly woven cotton or cotton blend for the foundation and wool for the outer cover.

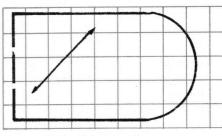

Illus. 224. ¼″ = 1″

Cutting Directions

1. Enlarge the pattern. (Illus. 224)
2. Using the pattern, cut two muslin covers on grain.
3. Using the pattern, cut two wool covers on the bias.

Sewing Directions

Assemble the seam roll, using the directions for the ham.

● ● ●

PRESSING PADS

This pressing pad is a fantastic aid for pressing sleeves perfectly without creases. And, if you have a friend with an Elnapress, she'll be particularly pleased to have one.
Finished Size: 5″ × 13″

Materials

Remnant, one 16″ × 13″
1″-thick foam, 5″ × 13″; or ½″-thick foam, 9″ × 13″
Fabric Notes: Muslin is always a good choice; however, any firmly woven, colorfast fabric is suitable.

Foam can be purchased from military surplus suppliers or salvaged when it's used as a packing material. If your foam is a different size, change the size of the cover or cut the foam to fit these directions.

Cutting Directions

To make a different size cover, measure the width (W) and length (L) of the foam. Cut the cover 2(W) + 2″ × 2(L) + 2″.

Sewing Directions

1. All seam allowances are ½″.
2. Right sides together, fold the fabric in half lengthwise and stitch the bottom and side.
3. Trim the corner and turn right side out.
4. Insert the piece of foam.
5. Close the opening. Fold the raw edges in; pin and edgestitch, using a zipper foot.

SEWING MACHINE COVER

Most of us like to leave our machines up, ready to sew. This attractive cover is the perfect answer for keeping it dust-free. The large pocket can be used for storing the instruction book and frequently used sewing aids.

Finished Size: Large to fit a Bernina 930, 22″ × 12½″ × 9″; Small to fit most other machines, 17″ × 10½″ × 7″

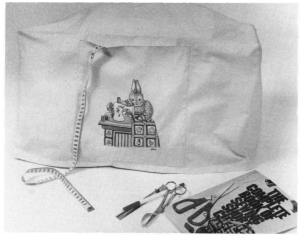

Materials

Fabric requirements are for the large size cover; requirements for the smaller size are in parentheses.

Fabric, 1⅜ yard (1⅛ yard), 45″ wide
Silk-screened panel, one 10½″ × 11″
Fleece, one 8″ square

Fabric Notes: Any firmly woven fabric is suitable. I used muslin with a permanent-press finish to match the background of the silk-screened panel. This silk-screened panel is particularly nice for a sewing room. If the cover will be used in the family room or bedroom, coordinate the cover and pocket with the room's decor.

Cutting Directions

1. Cut two 13¾″ × 22½″ (11¾″ × 17½″) rectangles for the front and back.
2. Cut one 9½″ × 49″ (7½″ × 37″) side/top panel.
3. Cut one 10½″ × 11″ (10½″ × 9½″) pocket lining.

Sewing Directions

1. All seam allowances are ¼″; the hem allowance is 1″.
2. Quilt the silk-screened panel. Center the fleece under the design and straight-stitch over all or part of the design lines.
3. Make the pocket. Right sides together, join the panel and pocket lining on all sides, leaving a 3″–4″ opening at the bottom. Trim the corners and turn right side out. Press.
Claire's Hint: If you press the unstitched seam allowances carefully, they can be closed when the pocket is stitched to the cover.
4. Center the pocket on the cover front 1¼″ above the bottom. Pin and edgestitch the pocket in place.
Claire's Hint: To eliminate removing the pins when stitching, position the pins with the heads towards the center and the points near *but not at* the pocket edge.
5. Using a fadeaway marking pen, mark both sides of the side/top panel 13½″ (11½″) from both ends. Machine-stitch to the seam line and back to the raw edge at the marked points. Clip to the seam line. (Illus. 225)

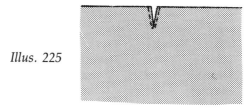

Illus. 225

6. Right sides together, match the corners on the cover front to the clips on the side/top panel. (Illus. 226)

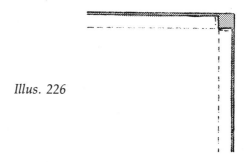

Illus. 226

Pin and stitch. Repeat for the back. Finish the edges with a zigzag (W,4-L,2). Press.
Claire's Hint: To prevent rolling when zigzagging, stitch with strips of Ziploc bags underneath. Tear the plastic away when finished.
7. Make a double hem at the bottom. Press.

BABY BAZAAR

BIB AND BURP

This is the ideal baby shower gift—a burping cloth to protect mom's (or dad's) shoulder and a bib for baby. For variety, appliqué teddy bears, gingerbread men, or hearts on them.

Materials

Remnant A (bib and burping cloth), one 18″ × 22½″
Remnant B (sails—white), two 4″ × 6″
Remnant C (boat—red), two 4″ × 4″
Remnant D (sun—yellow), two 5″ × 4″
Fusible web, one 16″ × 8″
Narrow bias binding, 3 yards
Small button, 1
Embroidery thread: red, white, yellow
Fabric Notes: Terry and quilted fabrics are particularly nice for this unlined design. When using firmly woven cottons or polyester/cotton blends, cut two; fuse them together; and treat as one layer.

Cutting Directions

1. Enlarge the bib pattern. (Illus. 227)
2. Fold the pattern paper into quarters and enlarge the burping cloth pattern. (Illus. 228)
3. Trace the appliqué patterns. (Illus. 229)
4. From Remnant A, cut one bib and one burp.
5. Using a release sheet, bond the fusible web to the wrong sides of Remnants B, C, and D.
6. Cut out the appliqués.

Sewing Directions

1. Fuse and appliqué the sailboats and sun to the bib and burping cloth.
2. Bind all edges with bias binding.
3. Make a small buttonhole on the bib back.
4. Sew the button in place.

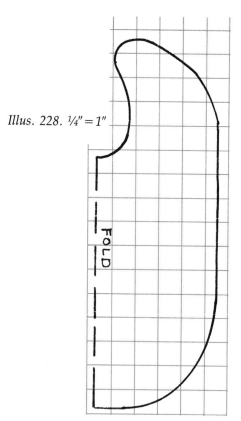

Illus. 228. ¼″ = 1″

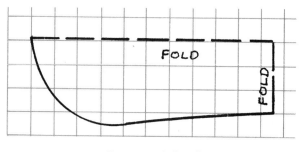

Illus. 227. ¼″ = 1″

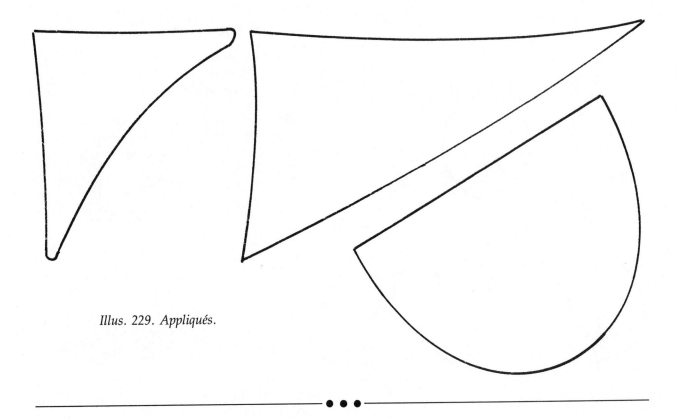

Illus. 229. Appliqués.

• • •

TEDDY BEAR BIB

This irresistible teddy bear bib will surely be a favorite. Keep several on hand for unexpected young guests.

Materials

Fabric A, quilted (bib), one 10½″ × 15″
Contrast B (bib lining), one 10½″ × 15″
Remnant C (teddy bear—brown), one 5″ × 7″
Scraps: red and brown
Decorative snap, 1
Machine embroidery thread: red, black, brown
Fabric Notes: Use a napped fabric such as terry velour, corduroy, flannel, suede cloth or velveteen for the teddy bear. Firmly woven prints and solids are also suitable but they lack that tactile quality.

Cutting Directions

1. Enlarge the bib pattern on page 144.
2. Trace the teddy bear appliqué. (Illus. 230)
3. Cut one bib from Contrast B. Do not cut the bib from Fabric A at this time.

Sewing Directions

1. All seam allowances are ¼".
2. Appliqué the teddy bear to the quilted rectangle, positioning it about 1" from the side and 2" from the bottom.
3. Right sides together, pin the lining to the bib rectangle. Stitch around the bib, using the lining edge as a guide. Leave one side open 4"–5" for turning.

Claire's Hint: This technique is easier and more accurate than the traditional method of cutting out both bib sections and matching the raw edges.

4. Trim away the excess fabric and turn the bib right side out.
5. Fold in the raw edges at the opening and pin. Edgestitch around the bib.
6. Set the snaps at the back corners.

Illus. 230

QUILTED BIB

Who would believe this clever bib could be so easy to sew? Designed to keep baby busy as well as clean, the quilted bib has a soft toy—football, heart, or teddy bear—just waiting to play.
Finished Size: 11″ × 14½″

Materials

Remnant A, quilted (bib), one 11″ × 21″
Remnant B (pocket and football), one 15″ × 7″
(heart, 15″ × 7″; teddy bear, 10″ × 7″)
Bias binding, 2½ yards
Machine embroidery thread: brown or red
Fibrefill

Cutting Directions

1. Enlarge the pattern. (Illus. 231)
2. Trace the toy pattern. (Illus. 232)

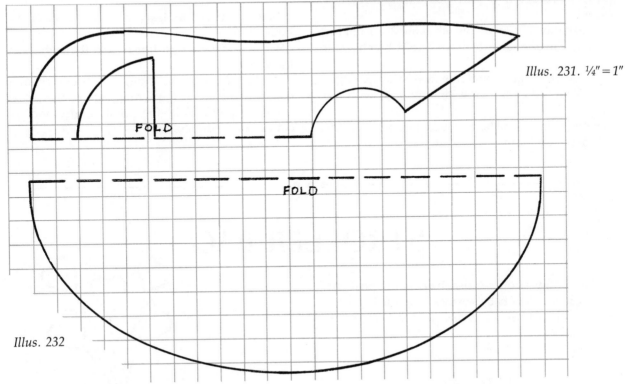

FOLD

FOLD

Illus. 231. ¼″ = 1″

Illus. 232

3. From Remnant A, cut one bib.
4. From Remnant B, cut one pocket and two footballs.
5. For the heart, cut two 4″ squares (pattern on p. 43). For the teddy bear (pattern on p. 158), cut two 5″ × 7″ rectangles.

Sewing Directions

1. All seam allowances are ¼" unless indicated otherwise.
2. Make the football. Right sides together, stitch around the football, leaving 1"–2" open for turning. (Illus. 233)

Illus. 233

Trim the seam with pinking shears and turn right side out. Stuff with fibrefill and close the opening with a slipstitch.

Heart and teddy bear: Seam allowances have not been allowed. Trace the design onto the wrong side of one fabric section. Right sides together, stitch the two sections together on the marked line, leaving 1"–2" open for turning. Trim, turn right side out and close the opening by hand.

3. Make the pocket. Right sides together, stitch the curve, leaving 1"–2" open for turning. Trim and turn the pocket right side out. Pin the opening closed.
4. Center the pocket on the bib about 2½" from the bottom. Pin and edgestitch to the bib. Stitch again ¼" away.
5. Bind the edges. Bind the two straight edges first. Trim the ends of the binding even with the bib.

Bind the sides and bottom, leaving a ½" tail at the beginning and end.

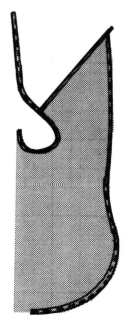

Illus. 234

Bind the neckline, leaving 12" ties at each end. (Illus. 234)

Claire's Hint: For a neat finish, fold the ends in ¼"; then stitch.

6. Make the armhole. Using a fadeaway marker, measure and mark the wrong side of the bib 12" from the point. Fold the points under and machine-tack to the marks.
7. Press.

• • •

STROLLER BAG

This roomy stroller (pushchair) bag is just the right size for all of baby's extras. Trim the bag with a football helmet or make a heart bouquet. (Illus. 235)

Finished Size: 15" × 17½"

Materials

Fabric A (bag), quilted, ⅜ yard, 45" wide
Fabric B (lining and appliqué), ½ yard 45" wide
Buttons, two ⅞"
Machine embroidery thread: brown, red and black

Illus. 235

Cutting Directions

1. Enlarge the football helmet pattern. (Illus. 236a) Or trace the heart design. (Illus. 236b)
2. From Fabric A, cut two 16" × 19½" bag sections and two 4" × 8" straps.
3. From Fabric B, cut two 16" × 17½" linings and one 12" square appliqué.

Sewing Directions

1. All seam allowances are ½"; the hem allowance is 1½".
2. Appliqué the design to the bag front. Complete the heart bouquet with machine embroidery for the cords and bow.
3. Right sides together, join the sides and bottom of the bag. Trim the corners.
4. Right sides together, join the sides and bottom of the lining, leaving a 10" opening at the bottom.
5. Make the straps. Right sides together, fold the straps in half lengthwise; stitch. Press the seams open. Center the seam and stitch across the ends. (Illus. 237) Trim and turn the strap right side out.

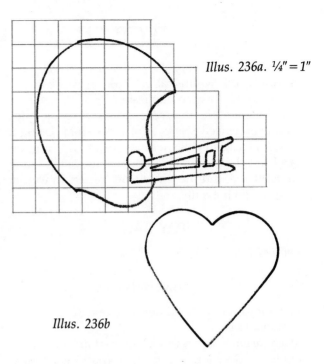

Illus. 236a. ¼" = 1"

Illus. 236b

Illus. 237

6. Make the buttonholes on the straps, centering them 1" from the ends.
7. Press the bag, lining, and straps. Turn the bag right side out.
8. Right sides together, align the raw edges and baste the straps to the top of the bag back 2" from the side seams.
Claire's Hint: Machine-baste, stitching back and forth several times for security.

9. Using a fadeaway marker, mark the hemline on the bag 1½" from the raw edge.
10. Right sides together, join the tops of the bag and lining.
11. Turn the lining right side out.
12. Close the opening.
Claire's Hint: To close the opening, push the seam allowances to the wrong side. Fold on the seam line with the seam allowances together. Edgestitch the opening closed.
13. Position the lining in the bag and fold the hem into place, using the marked line as a guide.
Claire's Hint: To make topstitching easier, position the pins on the outside of the bag about ½" below the fold line.
14. Topstitch around the top of the bag close to the edge and again ⅝" away, catching the straps in the stitching.
15. Sew the buttons on 1" below the top of the bag.
Claire's Hint: Use a gluestick to "baste" the buttons in place. Make a thread shank by zigzagging over a toothpick.

● ● ●

TOY BAG AND PILLOW

Inspired by a very expensive line of baby accessories, the whimsical artwork on this toy bag and pillow is easy to duplicate.

These gifts are an excellent learning project for an inexperienced seamster or older child. Using a simple zigzag stitch to outline the design, she or he can learn the mechanics of how to move the fabric smoothly around the curves and corners as well as how to stitch evenly.

TOY BAG

Finished Size: 24" × 20"

Materials

Remnant (double-faced quilted), one 31" × 44"
Buttons, two ⅞"
Machine embroidery thread: blue (cloud and eyes); orange and yellow (sun); green (hill); red (house and person)

Cutting Directions

1. Cut two 22" × 24½" bag sections and two 12" × 6" straps.

Sewing Directions

1. All seam allowances are ¼" except as indicated; the hem allowance is 1¾".
2. Mark the hemline fold 1¾" below the top of the two bag sections.

Claire's Hint: I use a fadeaway marker, if I'm planning to finish the bag that day; otherwise, I use a water-soluble marking pen.

3. Draw the design on the front of the bag. (Illus. 238) Be original and create your own illustration. Don't draw in the hem allowance.
4. Using an embroidery foot, outline the design with a zigzag (W,2 ½-L,5) stitch. This is not a satin stitch.

Claire's Hints: To stitch the eyes and doorknob, widen the stitch width as you approach the center and narrow it when you stitch away from it. I started with a 1.5 width, widened to 4, and returned to 1.5.

Illus. 238

To avoid an uneven stitch length, allow the fabric to feed evenly without pulling it in front or behind the embroidery foot.

5. Finish the edges at the tops of the bag sections. Rip the layers apart for ½"; and trim away the batting. Fold the raw edges in ¼"; edgestitch the folds together.

6. Right sides together, join the sides and bottom. *Claire's Hint:* To avoid a lumpy corner, shorten the stitch length 1" before reaching the corner; take three diagonal stitches across the corner. Trim. (Illus. 239)

7. Make the straps. Right sides together, fold in half lengthwise; stitch a 1" wide seam. Press open; center the seam; and stitch across the end. (Illus. 240) Turn right side out. Finish the raw edges with a zigzag (W,4-L,3).
Claire's Hint: Use a screwdriver or knitting needle to straighten the corners.

8. Right sides together, stitch the ends of the straps to the top of the back of the bag 3" from the side seams.

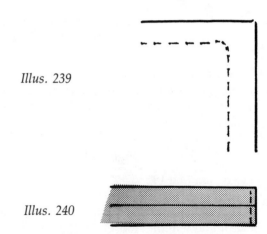

Illus. 239

Illus. 240

9. Fold the hem to the inside of the bag; pin; and topstitch close to the edge and again 1" from the fold.

10. Press.

11. Turn right side out.
Claire's Hint: To remove water-soluble pen marks, spray the bag with a plant mister.

12. Sew the buttons ½" below the top of the bag.

• • •

BABY PILLOW

This colorful pillow is just the right size to tuck behind baby in the stroller.
Finished Size: 15" square

Materials

Remnant (quilted), one 40" × 16"
Pillow form, 14"
Machine embroidery thread: blue (cloud and eyes)
orange and yellow (sun)
green (hill)
red (house and person)

Cutting Directions

1. Cut one 40" × 16" rectangle.

2. To mark the fold lines, make small clips on the two long edges 12½" from each end.

Sewing Directions

1. All seam and hem allowances are ½".
2. Draw the design between the two fold lines.
3. Embroider the design. Press.
4. Make a narrow machine hem on the two short ends.
5. Complete the seams at the top and bottom. Right sides together, fold one end at the snips; repeat with the other end, overlapping the ends at the center; pin and stitch. Press.
6. Turn right side out and insert the pillow form.
Claire's Hint: To insert the pillow easily, turn one end right side out; insert the pillow; then, turn the other end right side out.

• • •

CHRISTENING PILLOW

This dainty pillow makes a lovely baby or christening gift. Made from an embroidered place mat, you'll be amazed how easy and quick it is to finish.
Finished Size: 19" × 12"

Materials

Place mat, one 19" × 12"
Remnant A, one 30" × 13"
For a different-size pillow top, measure the width and length. Add 11" to the width and 1" to the length.
Fabric Notes: Napkins, linen hand towels, and embroidered pillow tops also make beautiful pillows.

Cutting Directions

Fold Remnant A in half and cut two 15" × 13" backs.

Sewing Directions

1. All seam and hem allowances are ½".
2. On each back section, hem one short side with a narrow machine hem.
3. Press the seam allowances to the wrong side and mitre the corners.

4. Wrong sides together, align the folded edges on one back with the finished end and sides of the pillow top; baste together. Align the remaining back with the other end of the top so that the backs overlap at the center; baste.
Claire's Hint: Use a gluestick or water-soluble basting tape to baste.
5. Edgestitch around the pillow.
Claire's Hint: To edgestitch evenly, use the inside of the presser foot as a guide.
6. Make a pillow form (p. 180) and insert it.

• • •

HOODED BATH TOWEL AND WASH MITT

This soft, hooded towel and its accompanying mitt will delight any new parent. Designed from soft, absorbent fabrics, it is perfect for cuddling and drying the little one.
Finished Size: Towel, 36" square; Mitt, 6" × 8½"

Materials

Fabric A (towel), 1 yard, 45" wide
Contrast (hood and binding), ⅝ yard, 45" wide
Fabric Notes: For the towel, select a soft, absorbent fabric like cotton terry, knit, flannel, or velour. I used an imported cotton in a children's design for

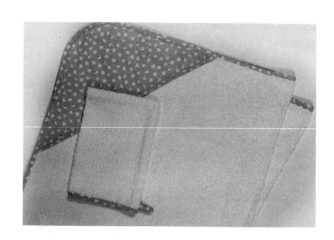

the contrast trim and hood. Seersuckers, ginghams, and cotton/polyester blends are also suitable.

Cutting Directions

1. From Fabric A, cut one 36″ square for the towel and one 9″ × 13″ rectangle for the mitt.
2. From the contrast, cut one 12″ × 12″ × 17″ triangle for the hood, one 1½″ × 4″ bias for the loop, and enough 1½″-wide bias to make 4½ yards.

Sewing Directions

TOWEL

1. Right sides together, piece the bias strips as needed to make 4½ yards.
2. Bind the long edge of the hood with bias and round the remaining corner.
Claire's Hint: I used an 8″ plate to establish the corner curve.

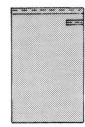
Illus. 241

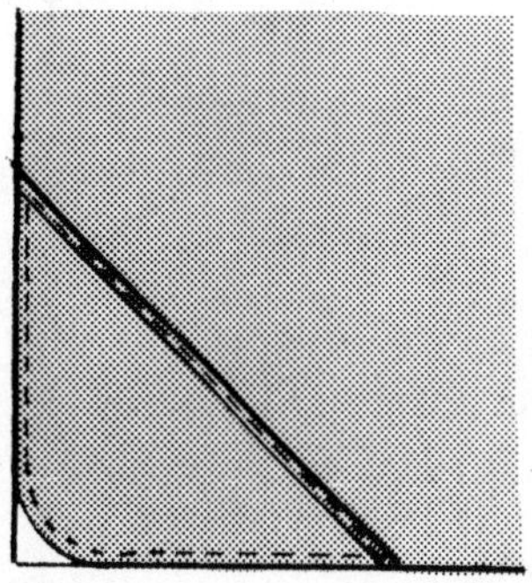

3. Right sides up, place the hood on one towel corner. Pin and stitch ¼″ from the raw edge. (Illus. 241)
4. Round the towel corners to match the hood.
Claire's Hint: Fold the towel into quarters and trim the corners to match the hood.
5. Bind the edge of the towel with the remaining bias. Wrong sides up, stitch the bias to the towel ¼″ from the edge. Wrap the bias around the edge. Press. Turn under the raw edge; baste; and stitch.

• • •

WASH MITT

1. All seam allowances are ½″.
2. Bind one long edge with bias.
3. Make the bias loop.
4. Fold the strip in half crosswise. Pin the loop to the right side of the mitt about 1″ below the bound edge (Illus. 242)
5. Complete the mitt using French seams.

Illus. 242

• • •

BABY BONNET

Reminiscent of another era, this easy-to-make heirloom is the perfect accessory for a beautiful christening gown, a special photograph, or just an afternoon in the park. This cap will fit a newborn to three months.

Materials

Embroidered batiste, ½ yard, 5½" or 6" wide
Double-faced white satin ribbon, ⅝ yard, ¼" wide
Double-faced white satin ribbon, 1 yard, ⅝" wide
Fabric Notes: I used a beautiful, imported Swiss batiste to make a "special occasion" bonnet; however, an easy-care cotton/polyester blend is a good choice for everyday wear.

Pattern and Cutting Out

The scalloped edge will be the bonnet front and the long unfinished edge the back.
1. Measure and mark 1" from each end on the scalloped edge. Using a fadeaway marking pen, draw a line on each end from the marked line to back corner. Cut on the two lines. (Illus. 243)

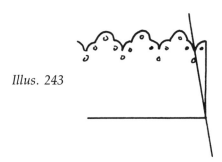

Illus. 243

2. Trim the long, unfinished edge so it is on the grain.

Sewing Directions

1. The hem allowance is ½".
2. Right side up, make a machine-rolled hem at each end. Fold ⅜" under; edgestitch. Trim away the hem allowance. Wrong side up, fold the hem over again and stitch.
Claire's Hints: The secrets for making a very tiny hem are to stitch as close to the fold line as possible and to trim as close to the stitched line as possible.

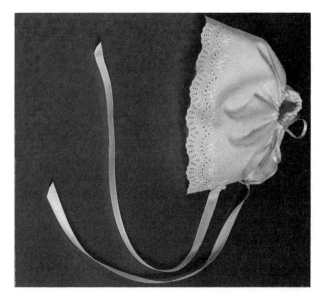

For a very close trim, use appliqué scissors.
The second stitched line will be very inconspicuous if you stitch on top of the first one.
3. Make the casing. Press the long unfinished edge under ⅝". Fold the raw edge under ¼"; pin and stitch.
4. Mark the locations for the ribbon ties 1" from the scalloped edge and ¼" from the ends. Make a double loop and secure the ties in the center with a zigzag (W,3-L,0). (Illus. 244)

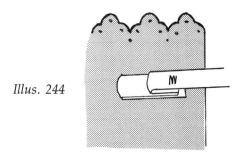

Illus. 244

5. To finish the cap, thread the narrow ribbon into the casing. Draw it tight and make a bow.
Claire's Hint: To prevent the tie from pulling out, machine-stitch (W,4-L,0) through all layers at the center.
6. Trim the ends of all ribbons on the diagonal and dab a small amount of fray retardant on them.

PRAM COVERLET

Pram coverlets are a real luxury for most babies today. Fortunately, they're very easy to make and they'll make any baby feel special.
Finished Size: 31" square

Materials

Remnant A (coverlet), one 31½" square
Remnant B (lining), two 31½" square
Lace edging, 3⅝ yards, ¼"–½" wide
Fabric Notes: Inspired by a very expensive import, I used a beautiful imported cotton with baby hearts on it for the coverlet (Fabric A) and a shiny white Swiss batiste for the lining. And, even though the pram coverlet was not inexpensive, it was only a fraction of the cost of the import.

For economy and/or easy care, select two firmly woven fabrics in a polyester/cotton blend.

Sewing Directions

1. All seam allowances are ¼".
2. Right sides together, join all edges, leaving a 6" opening on one side.
3. Trim the corners and turn right side out.
Claire's Hint: Use a manicurist's orange stick to straighten the corners.
4. To close the opening, push the seam allowances to the inside and stitch the folds together. Press.
Claire's Hint: The lace will cover the stitching line; however, for a very inconspicuous finish, zigzag (W,1.5-L,2), letting the needle swing off the edge to the right.
5. Right sides up, begin at one corner, leaving a ½" lace tail. Butt the edges of the lace and coverlet together; zigzag (W,2-L,2).
Claire's Hint: If you want the lace to lie flat at the corners, fold a small mitre. To do this easily, stop

about 2" from the corner. Mitre the lace, pin or baste it in place. Zigzag and continue so that the lace will lie flat.
6. To finish the last corner, fold the end of the lace under on the diagonal. Zigzag (W,1-L,1) along the fold to the edge corner; zigzag back to the coverlet. Trim the lace neatly. (Illus. 245)

Illus. 245

7. Inspect your coverlet. If you have some "holidays" (holes), restitch.

RECEIVING BLANKETS

The first-time mother needs at least six receiving blankets and it's nice to have them in a variety of sizes.

When our older son was born, my grandmother crocheted the edges of the receiving blankets she made for him. They were not only prettier, they were larger, lasted longer, and didn't pill like the purchased ones.

I still haven't learned to crochet very well, but I can make some beautiful decorative stitches with my machine.

Finished Sizes: 44" square, 35" square, 26" × 35", or 26" × 39"

Materials

Machine embroidery thread
One 44" square blanket
  Fabric, 1¼ yards, 45" wide
One 35" square blanket
  Fabric, 1 yard, 36" wide
Two 26" × 35" blankets
  Fabric, 1 yard, 54" wide
Two 26" × 39" blankets
  Fabric, 1⅛ yards, 54" wide
Fabric Notes: Choose soft cotton flannels, cotton knits, and cotton/polyester blends. I do not like synthetics or blends with a high synthetic content because they are not absorbent, don't breathe, and may cause skin irritations.

Cutting Directions

1. Cut the blanket 1" longer and wider than the desired finished size.

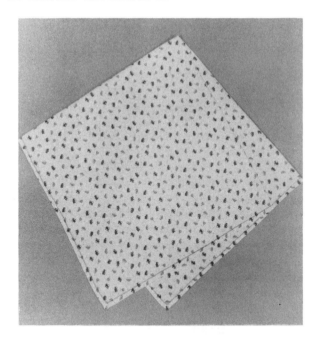

Sewing Directions

1. Fold under the edges ½". Using machine embroidery thread and a decorative stitch, stitch around the blanket ⅜" from the edge.
Claire's Hints: I spent about 15 minutes trying different stitches before I decided on the feather stitch (Elna-disc-107). And, since this fabric had a four-color print, I experimented with different colored threads.

To prevent puckering, use strips of a stabilizer between the fabric and feed dogs. You can use one of the tear-away types, a water-soluble stabilizer, Ziploc bags or tissue paper.

CHILDREN'S WORLD

TEDDY BEAR ENSEMBLE

Everyone loves teddy bears and this teddy ensemble will delight young and old alike.

TEDDY APPLIQUÉ

Materials

Material requirements are for one teddy appliqué.
Remnant A (teddy bear), 6″ × 7″
Remnant B (teddy's nose), 2″ square
Fusible web, scrap
Stabilizer
Machine embroidery thread: brown
Fabric Notes: Since I like the tactile quality of naps, I used corduroy for the teddy bear.

Appliqué Instructions

1. Trace the pattern. (Illus. 246)
2. Using a release sheet, bond the fusible web to the back of Fabric B. Then cut a 1¼″ circle for teddy's nose.
3. Right side up, trace the bear onto the Fabric A.
Claire's Hint: To trace the design, I used a piece of white dressmaker's carbon and a dry ballpoint pen.
4. Fuse the nose in place; pin a piece of stabilizer under the head; and satin-stitch (W,2) the nose.
5. Embroider the eyes. Outline them first; then, fill them in.
6. Right sides up, position the bear rectangle as indicated in the individual instructions. Then, using a short stitch, outline the bear. Trim close to the stitched line.
Claire's Hint: To avoid puckering, pin a piece of stabilizer to the wrong side of the quilted fabric.

    To get a very close trim, use appliqué scissors.
7. Satin-stitch (W,2.5) around the bear.

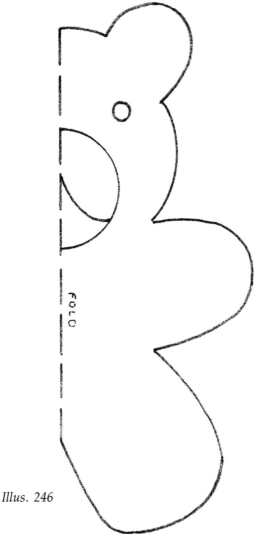

Illus. 246

TEDDY'S BRIEFCASE

Finished Size: 15" × 10½"

Materials

Remnant A, double-faced quilted (briefcase), one 31" × 12"
Zipper, one 14"
Appliqué (see Teddy Appliqué), one
Fabric Notes: If your fabric isn't double-faced, purchase an equal amount of contrast fabric to line the briefcase.

Cutting Directions

Cut one 15½" × 10½" briefcase front and one 15½" × 11¾" briefcase back.

Sewing Directions

1. All seam allowances are ¼".
2. Using the directions for the Teddy Appliqué, make the teddy bear. Position it on the briefcase front 1¾" from the bottom and 2¾" from the side. Appliqué in place.
3. Finish the top of the briefcase front and back. Rip the two layers apart for ½". Trim out the batting. Fold the raw edges in; then edgestitch the folds together.
4. Set the zipper. Right sides up and zipper on top, pin the open zipper to the top of the front, aligning

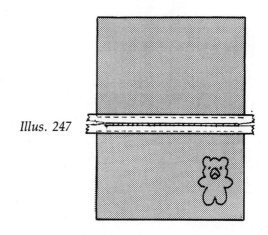

Illus. 247

the coil and the finished edge. Stitch close to the edge of the zipper tape. Repeat for the back. (Illus. 247)
5. Open the zipper.
6. Right sides together, zigzag (W,2-L,1) the sides and bottom together. Trim all edges close to the seam line.
7. Turn the briefcase right side out.
8. Topstitch the sides and bottom ¼" from the edge.

• • •

TEDDY'S PHOTO ALBUM COVER

Designed to fit a 10½" × 11" photo album, this cover also fits most notebooks.
Finished Size: Closed, 10" × 12½" × 2"; Open, 21½" × 12½"

Materials

Remnant A, double-faced quilted (album cover), ⅜ yard, 45" wide
Appliqué (see Teddy Appliqué)

Cutting Directions

1. Cut one 39½" × 13½" rectangle.

2. On both long edges, make short snips to mark the fold line 9¼" from each end.

Sewing Directions

1. All seam allowances are ¼".
2. Using the directions for the Teddy Appliqué, make the teddy bear. Position it on the front of the album cover 2½" from the bottom and 1½" from the right side. Appliqué in place.
3. Hem the two short ends by folding 1" to the wrong side. Topstitch ¾" from the fold.
4. Right sides together, fold both ends at the snips; stitch the top and bottom. (Illus. 248)
5. Turn right side out.

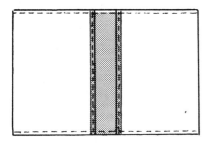

Illus. 248

6. Finish the raw edges between the two pockets. Rip the two layers apart for ½". Trim away the batting and inside fabric for ½". Fold the raw edge of the outer fabric to meet the trimmed edges; fold again, and edgestitch.
7. Insert the photo album or notebook.

• • •

TEDDY'S DUFFEL

Teddy's duffel is the perfect travelmate for overnight or trips to the skating rink.
Finished Size: 17" × 8" × 6½"

Materials

Remnant A, double-faced quilted (duffel), ⅝ yard, 45" wide
Zipper, one 16"
Corded piping, 1½ yards
Optional: Cardboard bottom, one 6" × 16½"
Appliqué (see Teddy's Appliqué)

Cutting Directions

1. Enlarge the pattern for the duffel ends. (Illus. 249)

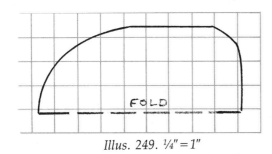

Illus. 249. ¼" = 1"

2. Cut two 18" × 11½" side/bottom sections, two 18" × 3½" tops, two 22" × 4" straps, and two duffel ends.
3. Using short snips, mark the center of the duffel ends at the top and bottom.

Sewing Directions

1. Seam allowances are ¼" and ½" as indicated.
2. Using the directions for the Teddy Appliqué, make the teddy bear. Position it on one side/bottom section centering it 1½" from the top. Appliqué in place.
3. Finish the one long edge of each top section. Rip the two layers apart for ½". Trim out the batting; then fold the raw edges in; edgestitch the folds together.
4. Set the zipper. Right sides up and the zipper on top, pin the open zipper to the finished edges, aligning the coil and edge. Stitch in place close to the edge of the zipper tape.
5. Make the straps.
6. Right sides together, pin in the straps to the top edge of the side/bottom sections 2½" from each end. Machine-stitch the straps in place.
Claire's Hint: Stitch first ½" from the edge; then stitch back and forth several times in the seam allowance for strength. (Illus. 250)

Illus. 250

7. Right sides together, join the top and side/bottom sections with a ½" seam. Press the seams down and topstitch through all layers ¼" from the seam line.

8. Right sides together, join the bottoms with a ½" seam. Press the seam open and topstitch ¼" from each side.

9. Right sides up, using a ¼" seam allowance, stitch the piping around the duffel ends.

Claire's Hint: Begin and end at the bottom notch.

10. Open the zipper.

11. Right sides together, join the duffel body and ends using a ¼" seam. Stitch again for security.

Claire's Hint: For neatness and additional strength, zigzag (W,4-L,4) over the edges of the seam or cover them with seam binding.

12. Turn right side out.

13. *Optional:* Insert the cardboard bottom.

• • •

BEACH BAG

Here's a beach bag any youngster will love. If your favorite child has a winter birthday, fill it with blocks, Legos, or boats.

Finished Size: 18" tall, 10" diameter

Materials

Fabric A (bag), ⅝ yard, 45" wide
Fabric B (lining), ½ yard, 45" wide
Remnant A (white—sails), 10" × 10"
Remnant B (yellow—boat), 9" × 8"
Scrap C (red—flag)
Fusible web, ¼ yard
Large eyelets, 2
Drawstring cord, 1¼ yard
Machine embroidery thread: white, red and blue
Optional: Cardboard, one 10" circle
Fabric Notes: For the bag, I used a lightweight terry velour. Other suitable fabrics include terry, nylon taffeta, canvas, and denim. For the bag lining, use a soft plastic, a water-repellent fabric, or a plain fabric treated with fabric protector.

Cutting Directions

1. Enlarge the appliqué and pocket patterns. (Illus. 251)

2. From Fabric A, cut one 32½" × 22½" bag and one 11" circle for the bottom.

3. From Fabric B, cut one 32½" × 16½" bag lining and one 11" circle for the bottom lining.

4. Using a release sheet, bond fusible web to the wrong sides of Remnant C and Scrap E.

5. Cut out the sails and flag.

6. From Remnant D, cut out the pocket.

Sewing Directions

1. All seam allowances are ¼".

2. Make the boat pocket. Right sides together, fold the fabric in half crosswise and trace the boat on the wrong side. Stitch around the boat, leaving a 2" opening on one side. Trim the seam allowances to ¼"; turn the boat right side out; and pin the opening closed.

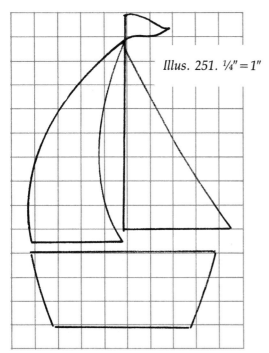

Illus. 251. ¼" = 1"

3. Apply the sailboat pocket to the bag. Right sides up, center the sailboat about 3" from the bottom. Pin and stitch the pocket in place.

4. Appliqué the sails and flag to the bag. Fuse to the bag; then satin-stitch (W,2).

Claire's Hint: For pucker-proof appliqués and embroidery, pin a piece of stabilizer to the back of the bag before beginning.

5. Embroider some waves below the boat with a satin stitch. (W,2–4)

6. Set two large eyelets on the bag, positioning them 3½" below the top and 1½" from each end.

7. Right sides together, join the two short ends to make a circle.

8. Divide and mark the bag and bag bottom into quarters.

Claire's Hint: Use short snips to mark the quarter points.

9. Join the bag and bag bottom. Right sides together, pin and stitch, matching the quarter points.

10. Fold the lining in half lengthwise and stitch the short ends, leaving a 6" section in the middle unstitched.

11. Join the lining and lining bottom.

12. Join the tops of the bag and lining. Mark and match the quarter points; stitch, leaving a 4"–6" opening. Turn right side out and close the opening.

13. Fold the top of the bag and lining to the inside so that the eyelets are on the outside ¼" below the fold line. (Illus. 252)

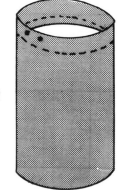

Illus. 252

14. Stitch the drawstring casing 1¼" from the fold.

15. Thread the cord into the casing and tie the ends together.

16. *Optional:* If desired, place a cardboard circle in the bottom.

HANDY TOTE BAG

Originally homemade by sailors from sail canvas, these handy tote bags are for kids any age. Large and sturdy, they can be used for carrying bulky clothing, odd-shaped gear, ice, wood, knitting, or books.
Finished Size: Small, 6″ × 13½″ × 12½″; Large, 8″ × 17″ × 17″

Materials

Fabric requirements are for a small bag; requirements for the larger bag are in parentheses.
Fabric A (bag), ½ yard (⅝ yard), 45″ wide
Contrast B (bag bottom), ¼ yard (¼ yard), 45″ wide
Webbing, 2¾ yards (3½ yards), 1″ width
Fabric Notes: Heavyweight canvas, duck, pillow ticking and Cordura nylon are excellent choices for heavy-duty, water-resistant bags. Poplin, denim, and rip-stop nylon are suitable for lighter-weight bags.

Cutting Directions

1. From Fabric A, cut two 20½″ × 18″ (26″ × 23½″) bag sections.
2. From Contrast B, cut one 20½″ × 10″ (26″ × 12″) bag bottom.
3. From the webbing, cut two handles 1⅜ yards long.

Sewing Directions

1. Seam allowances are ½″; the hem allowance is 2″.
2. Hem the bag sections. On one long edge of each bag section, fold the hem allowance to the wrong side. Turn the raw edge under 1″; stitch in place.
3. Mark the handle locations. Right side up, on the hemmed edge, mark a point 7″ (10″) from each end. On the opposite edge, mark a point 6″ (9″) from each end. Using a fadeaway marking pen, draw a line between these two points.
4. Stitch the handles to the bag. Align the outside edge of the webbing with the marked lines, beginning and ending at the unhemmed edge. Pin and edgestitch both sides of the handles to the bag sections. (Illus. 253)
Claire's Hint: For extra security, stitch a cross in a rectangle at the top of each strap.

5. Wrong sides together, join the sections at the bottom with a ½″ seam. Open the seam and zigzag (W,4-L,2) each side of the seam line.
6. Stitch the bag bottom to the bag. On the bottom section, make a notch at the center of each short end. On the long sides, press the seam allowance (½″) under.

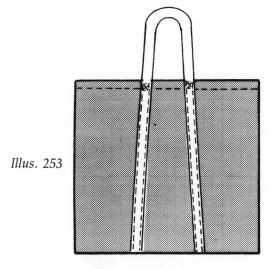

Illus. 253

Right sides up, pin the bottom to the bag, matching the notches to the seam line. Topstitch close to the folded edge and again ⅜″ away.

7. Right sides together, stitch the side seams. Stitch again ⅜″ from the raw edges. Trim close to the stitched lines.

8. Right sides together, fold the corners, matching the seam lines. Mark a point on each folded edge 4¼″ (5⅝″) from the corner; draw a line to connect them. Stitch on the marked line.

9. Turn the bag right side out.

• • •

QUILTED OVERNIGHT BAG

This is the perfect bag for overnight visits. The bag is large enough to hold the essentials, yet small enough for a child to handle. Any little girl or boy on your list will enjoy one.

Finished Size: 18″ × 12″ × 6″

Materials

Fabric A, quilted (bag), ⅝ yard, 45″ wide
Fabric B (lining), ⅜ yard, 45″ wide
Fabric Notes: To keep the inside of the bag from soiling easily, choose a water-repellent fabric or spray the lining with a fabric protector.

Cutting Directions

1. From Fabric A (quilted), cut two 13″ × 19″ bag sections and two 3½″ by 44″ handles.

2. From the lining fabric, cut two 13″ × 19″ lining rectangles.

Sewing Directions

1. All seam allowances are ½″ unless otherwise indicated.

2. Make the straps. Gauge-stitch along the long edges almost *but not quite* ½″ from the raw edges. Press the seam allowances to the wrong side.

Fold the strap in half lengthwise, wrong sides together, aligning the folds. Edgestitch both sides of the strips. Press. (Illus. 254)

3. Mark the strap locations. On the bag sections, make snips on one long edge (top) 6½″ from the ends. On the opposite edge (bottom), make snips 5″ from the ends. Using a fadeaway pen, connect the snips. (Illus. 255)

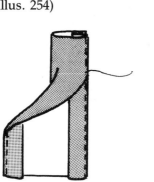

Illus. 254

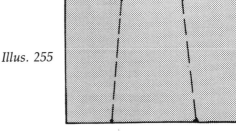

Illus. 255

4. Apply the straps to the bag. Right sides up, pin one strap to each bag section, aligning the outside edge of the strap with the marked line. Edgestitch both sides, stopping 2" from the top.

For extra security, stitch a rectangle on each strap section at the top of the bag. (Illus. 256)

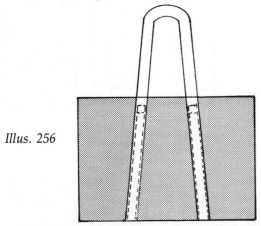

Illus. 256

5. Set the zipper. Right sides together, stitch the zipper to the top edge of each bag section with a ¼" seam.

6. Join the bag and lining. Right sides together and the zipper between, pin and stitch the tops together.

Press the bag and lining sections away from the zipper teeth.

7. Join the seams on the sides and bottom. Right sides together, stitch the bag. Then stitch the lining, leaving the lining bottom open 6"–8".

8. Topstitch through all layers ¼" from the zipper. *Claire's Hint:* To do this easily, turn the bag wrong side out. Stitch inside the bag.

9. Make the boxing at the bottom of the bag. Continuing with the bag wrong side out, fold the bag at the corners, aligning the seam lines on the sides and bottom. Mark a point on each fold line 2¾" from the corner. Draw a line to connect the points. Stitch on the marked line. Pin the seams together 2" from each corner. Stitch off a triangle from one fold line to the pin, continuing to the other fold line.

10. Turn right side out.

11. Close the lining seam.

12. Arrange the lining inside the bag.

● ● ●

DENIM KNAPSACK

Even school is fun for young scholars with a denim knapsack. Roomy enough for lots of books, crayons and pencils, or gym clothes. This is a particularly good learn-to-sew project for boys as well as girls.

Materials

Fabric, 1⅛ yards, 45" wide
Fleece, one 14" × 8"
Zipper, one 9"
Zipper, one 18"
D-rings, four 1¼" or 1½"

Cutting Directions

1. Trace the corner pattern. (Illus. 257a)
2. Cut two 13" × 17" rectangles for the back and front, one 5½" × 37½" side-bottom gusset, two 3 ¼" × 18½" tops, one 11" × 2¼" small pocket section, one 11" × 10¼" large pocket section, two 6" × 16" shoulder straps, two 4" × 16" adjustable

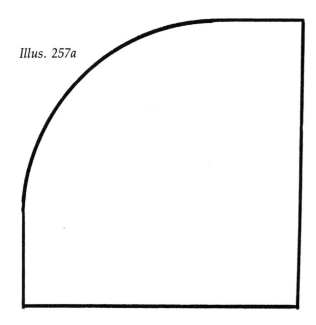

Illus. 257a

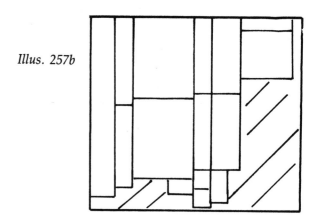

Illus. 257b

straps, two 4″ × 4″ tabs; one 3″ × 6″ hanging loop, and one 5″ × 3″ rectangle. (Illus. 257b)

3. Mark the midpoints on all sides of the front, back and side bottom gusset.

4. Using the pattern, shape the corners on the front and back.

5. From the fleece, cut two 14″ × 4″ rectangles.

Sewing Directions

1. Seam allowances are ¼″ and ½″ as indicated.

Claire's Hint: Narrow seam allowances are always easier to stitch accurately than wider ones; however, wide seam allowances are easier to turn under. On this gift, all seam allowances on the gusset and zippers are ¼″; the remaining seam allowances are ½″.

2. Make the pocket. Right sides together, pin and stitch the small pocket section to the 9″ zipper with a ¼″ seam. Repeat to join the large pocket section. (Illus. 258)

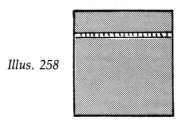

Illus. 258

3. Press the pocket. Press flat, wrong side up, with the zipper exposed; then press the ½″ seam allowances to the wrong side on all edges.

Claire's Hint: Place a line of gauge-stitching almost *but not quite* ½″ from the raw edges to use as a gauge before pressing.

4. Center the pocket on the knapsack front 4½″ from the top; pin and edgestitch around the pocket.

5. Right sides together, pin and stitch the tops to the 18″ zipper with ¼″ seams. Press and edgestitch close to the seam line.

6. Make the shoulder straps. On one long edge of each strap, press under ½″. Fold the fleece in half lengthwise; stitch. Center the fleece on the wrong side of the shoulder strap.

Fold and pin the unpressed side of the strap over the fleece; fold and pin the other side over the fleece. (Illus. 259)

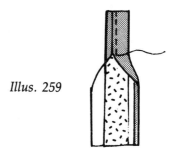

Illus. 259

Baste and topstitch the center of the strap through all layers.

Claire's Hint: Try a gluestick or water-soluble basting tape for basting.

7. Sew the D-rings to the shoulder straps. Wrong side up, thread the strap into 2 D-rings. Fold over ½" and stitch. Since the straps are already bulky, I don't try to turn the raw edges under.

Trim away any fraying on the ends. Straight-stitch first ¼" from the raw edge; then, using a zigzag (W,4-L,2), stitch over the raw edge.

8. Make the hanging loop. Wrong sides together, press in half lengthwise. Fold the raw edges to the fold line and press again. Edgestitch both sides.

9. Set the hanging loop to the knapsack back. Center and pin the loop 1½" below the top. Stitch ½" from the raw edges. (Illus. 260)

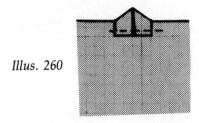

Illus. 260

10. Set the shoulder straps to the knapsack back. Right sides together, center and pin the straps over the hanging loop; stitch ½" from the raw edges.

11. Set the small rectangle (5" × 3") to the knapsack back. Press the seam allowances (½") to the wrong side. Center and pin the rectangle over the shoulder straps and loop, covering all raw edges. Edgestitch in place. (Illus. 261)

Claire's Hint: Fuse-baste the rectangle in place with a piece of fusible web 3½" × 1½".

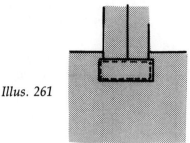

Illus. 261

12. Make the adjustable straps. Wrong sides together, press in half lengthwise. Fold the raw edges in to the fold line and press again. Edge-stitch both sides.

13. Stitch the adjustable straps to the knapsack sides about 2½" from the bottom.

14. Make the tabs, following the instructions for the adjustable straps. Fold them in half crosswise and machine-baste ¼" from the raw edges.

15. Join the tabs to the side/bottom gusset. Right sides up, center the tabs at each end of the side/bottom gusset; pin and stitch.

16. Join the tops and side/bottom gusset. Right sides together, pin, matching the zipper to the centers. Stitch ¼" seams.

17. Join the knapsack front and gusset. Right sides together, match and pin the centers. Stitch.

18. Open the zipper.

19. Join the knapsack back and gusset.

20. Finish the seams. Zigzag (W,4-L,3) the raw edges together. Press.

21. Turn the knapsack right side out.

TAKE-ALONG DUFFEL

Every kid needs at least one duffel for sports equipment, beach trips and overnight trips. This roomy bag has two outside pockets on the ends for small items.

Finished Size: Large, 20″ × 11½″ × 11½″; Small, 14″ × 8½″ × 8½″

Materials

Material requirements are for large bag; requirements for small bag are in parentheses.

Remnant, one 36″ square (45″ × 18″)

Zippers, one 20″; two 12″ (one 14″; two 9″)

Ribbon, twill tape, or braid, 3 yards (2½ yards), 1″–2″

Fabric Notes: Select a firmly woven fabric. I prefer lightweight materials such as nylon taffeta and rip-stop nylon; however, denim, pillow ticking, Cordura nylon, and corduroy are also good choices.

Cutting Directions

1. Cut one 36″ × 20½″ (26¾″ × 14½″) bag section and three 12″ (9″) circles for the ends.
2. Cut one circle in half for the pockets.
3. Mark the center of the bag. Fold the bag in half crosswise and press.
4. Mark the strap locations. Fold the bag lengthwise into quarters and press.

Sewing Directions

1. Join the straps and bag. Beginning at the bottom of the bag, pin and stitch, stopping 2″ from the top and allowing 18″ handles. (Illus. 262)
2. For strength, stitch a cross in a rectangle at the top of each strap.
3. Set the long zipper to the top of the bag. Press and topstitch.
4. Join the remaining zippers to the pockets. Right sides together, stitch ¼″ seam. Press and topstitch.
5. Set the zippers to the ends. Pin the pockets to the remaining circles, matching the raw edges. Topstitch the zipper tape close to the zipper and again at the edge.
6. Complete the pockets. Stitch around the bottom. (Illus. 263)
7. Press the bag and ends.

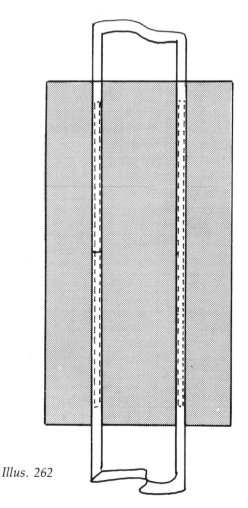

Illus. 262

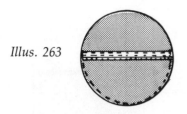

Illus. 263

8. Join the bag and ends. Quarter and mark all sections. Right sides together, pin and stitch one end, matching the quarter marks. Open the zipper. Complete the other end.
9. Finish and reinforce the seams with a zigzag (W,4-L,2).
10. Turn right side out.

— • • • —

BEDSIDE ORGANIZER

Designed just for kids, this bedside organizer is perfect for keeping a couple of comic books, writing paper, and a pen close to the bed without night table clutter. It is a particularly thoughtful gift for a sick child.

Materials

Fabric A (caddy and pockets), ½ yard, 45″ wide
Bias binding, 3¼ yards
Cardboard, 12″ × 5″
Fabric Notes: Select a firmly woven fabric with body. I used pillow ticking.

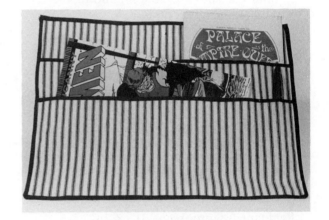

Cutting Directions

1. From Fabric A, cut one 14″ × 10″ caddy, one 14″ × 6″ Pocket A, one 14″ × 8″ Pocket B, and one 14″ × 15″ Pocket C. (Illus. 264)

Sewing Directions

1. Bind one long edge on Pockets A and B.
2. Right sides up, stack Pocket A on Pocket B. Stitch a pocket 2″ from one end. (Illus. 265a)

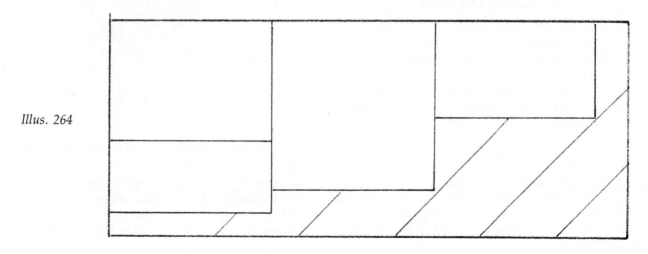

Illus. 264

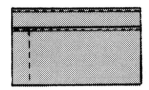

Illus. 265a

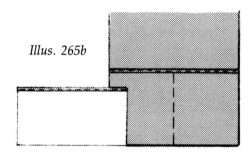

Illus. 265b

3. Right sides up, stack and pin the pocket stack to the caddy body. Fold Pocket A out of the way and stitch through the center of Pocket B, creating two equal-sized pockets. (Illus. 265b)
4. Machine-baste the sides and bottom together ¼" from the raw edges.
5. Bind the sides and bottom, mitring the corners at the bottom.

6. Make Pocket C. Bind one short end. Fold the pocket end under 6"; machine-baste the sides together. Bind the sides.
7. Wrong sides together, machine-baste the raw edges of the caddy and Pocket C together. Bind the edge.
8. Insert the cardboard.

● ● ●

GINGERBREAD APRON

They're never too young to learn to cook and your favorite little chef will love this special apron.
Finished Size: 14½" × 17"

Materials

Remnant A (apron), one 31" × 18"
Remnant B (gingerbread man), one 5" × 7"
Fusible web, 4½" × 6½"
Rickrack, 1⅞ yards
Machine embroidery thread: white and dark brown

Cutting Directions

1. Enlarge the apron pattern. (Illus. 266a)
2. Trace the appliqué pattern. (Illus. 266b)
3. From Remnant A, cut the apron and four 4" × 18" ties.
4. Using a release sheet, bond the fusible web to the wrong side of Remnant B. Cut out the gingerbread man.

Sewing Directions

1. All hem allowances are ½".
2. Center the gingerbread man 1½" below the top and fuse in place. Satin-stitch (W,2), using an embroidery foot so the stitches won't pile up under the foot.

3. Remove the embroidery foot; and, using white thread, embroider the buttons.
4. Make the straps. Wrong sides together, press in half lengthwise. Fold the raw edges in to meet the fold line. Edgestitch the folded edges together. Edgestitch the other side of the tie. Repeat for all ties.

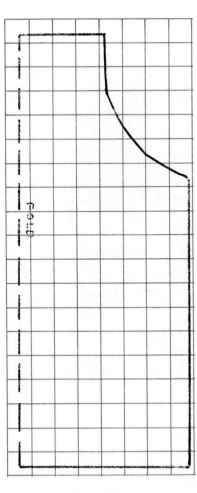

Illus. 266. ¼" = 1"

Illus. 266a

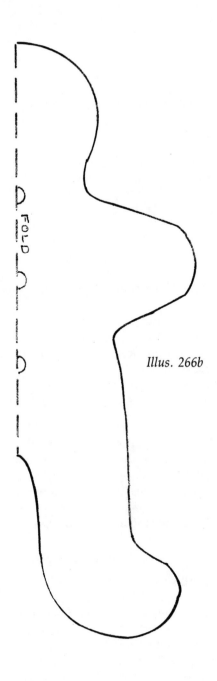

Illus. 266b

5. Baste the ties to the wrong side of the apron, positioning the neck ties ½" from each side and the waist ties ½" from the top. (Illus. 267a)

6. Make a narrow machine hem around the apron, folding the ties into position as you hem.

7. Pin and stitch the rickrack in place.

Claire's Hints: For a more attractive finish, leave the top edge until last. (Illus. 267b) Since rickrack doesn't have a right and wrong side, mitre the corners by turning the rickrack "wrong side up."

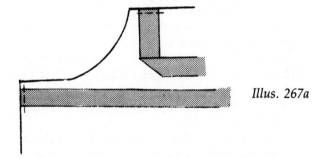

Illus. 267a

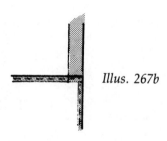

Illus. 267b

ICE CREAM APRON

Finished Size: Apron front, 13″ × 19″; Total measurement, 22″ × 22″

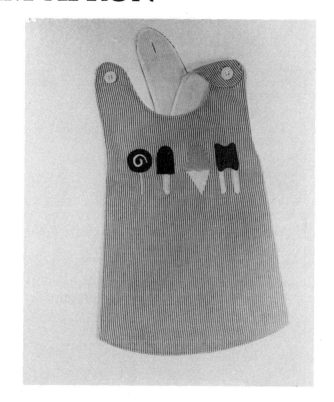

Materials

Remnant A (apron), one 24″ square
Remnant B (lining), one 24″ square
Remnant C (lollipop—blue), one 3″ square
Remnant D (fudgescicle—green), one 3″ square
Remnant E (ice cream—white), one 3″ square
Remnant F (Popsicle—orange), one 3″ square
Remnant G (sticks and cones), three 3″ square
Fusible web, 18″ × 6″
Embroidery thread: blue, green, yellow, orange, white
Buttons, two 1″
Fabric Notes: Select firmly woven cotton or polyester/cotton blends for this gift. I used a gingham stripe.

Cutting Directions

1. Enlarge the apron pattern. (Illus. 268a)
2. Trace the appliqué designs. (Illus. 268b)
3. Using the apron pattern, cut one apron and one lining.
4. Using a release sheet, bond the fusible web to the wrong sides of Remnants C, D, E, F, and G.
5. Cut out the appliqué designs.

Sewing Directions

1. All seam allowances are ¼″.
2. Center the appliqués on the front about 2¼″ below the neckline, and fuse in place.
3. Satin-stitch (W,2.5) around each appliqué.
4. Satin-stitch (W,4) the stick and the swirl on the lollipop. To make a point on the ends of the swirl, narrow the stitch width while stitching.
5. Right sides together, pin and stitch around the apron and lining, leaving the bottom open.
Claire's Hints: For a smooth finish, clip the seams in the concave curves around the neck and armholes. I clip every ¼″. Using pinking shears, trim around the tops of the straps.
6. Turn the apron right side out; press. If the lining is longer than the apron in the unstitched section, trim away the excess.
7. Close the opening. You can stitch most of it by machine. Fold just the unstitched section right sides together. Pin as much as possible; the top of the apron will be sticking out at the bottom so that you won't be able to pin the entire opening. This really looks messy. Stitch as far as possible.

Pull the apron through the opening. Press again, folding the seam allowances in the unstitched section to the inside.
8. Edgestitch around the apron, finishing the opening as you stitch.
9. On the back straps, center a 1⅛″ buttonhole about 1″ from the end.
Claire's Hints: For a more attractive buttonhole, loosen the upper tension.

If the fabrics are lightweight, place a piece of stabilizer under the buttonhole before stitching to prevent tunnelling.
10. Sew the buttons on the front straps about 1″ below the top.
Claire's Hints: Stitch the buttons on by machine using transparent tape to hold them in place. Lower the feed dogs and zigzag slowly.

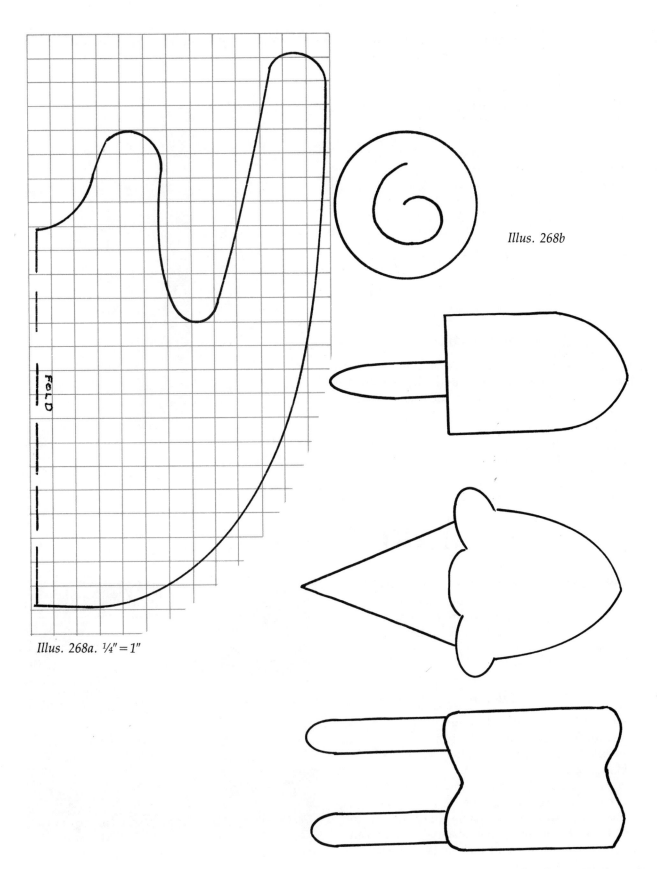

Illus. 268b

Illus. 268a. 1/4" = 1"

FOLD

QUICK-AND-EASY ELASTIC BELT

Need an inexpensive birthday gift that's quick and easy to make? This elastic belt is the perfect solution.

Elastic belting is available in a variety of designs and colors; and many don't even look like elastic. This heart design is a favorite of little girls.
Finished Sizes: Children and girls: 2–5, 20"; 6–8, 22"; 10–14, 24"; Misses: XS, 22"; S, 24"; M, 27"; L, 30"; XL 34"; Men: XS, 26"; S, 28"; M, 32"; L, 36"; XL, 42".

Materials

Buckle, one 1" wide
Elastic belting, amount equal to the finished belt length. *Example:* 24" belt requires 24" elastic.

Sewing Directions

1. Thread one end of the elastic into one side of the buckle. Pull it through 1" and machine-stitch. Use a zipper foot so you can stitch close to the buckle ridge.
2. Repeat on the other end.
Claire's Hint: Before stitching, check to be sure the buckle will close properly.

• • •

FAKE FUR MUFF

This fake fur muff will thrill most little girls. Knit cuffs hug the wrist and the muff completely envelops her hands to keep them warm and cozy. And, if you haven't sewn on fake fur before, you'll see just how easy it is.
Finished Size: 10" long.

Materials

Remnant A (muff), one 11" × 15"
Remnant B (lining), one 36" × 13½"
Optional: Needlepunch insulation, one 11" × 15"
Ribbing, one 14" × 7"
Fabric Notes: I used a fur fabric. Velvet, velveteen, and corduroy are also suitable.

For extra warmth, interline the muff with needlepunch, an insulating material. Fleece can also be used but the muff will not be as warm.

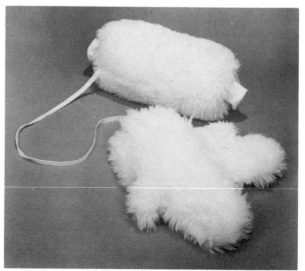

Photo also shows pressing cloths and wrist pincushion.

Cutting Directions

1. From the fur fabric, cut one 11″ × 15″ muff. Carefully cut through the backing only.
2. from the lining fabric, cut one 11″ by 12″ lining and one 36″ × 1½″ strap.
3. From the ribbing, cut two 7″ × 6″ knit cuffs.
4. *Optional*: From the needlepunch, cut one 11″ × 15″ interlining.

Sewing Directions

1. All seam allowances are ¼″ unless otherwise noted.
2. Make the strap.
3. Mark the strap locations on one short side 2″ from each end. Right sides together, pin the strap to the muff so that the strap ends overlap the muff edge ½″. Stitch.
4. Pin the interlining to the wrong side of the fur fabric; stitch ¼″ from the raw edge. To avoid losing the pins in the fabric, use extra-long pins.
5. Right sides together, zigzag (W,4-L,2) the short ends together, allowing the needle to swing off the fabric when it swings to the right. (Illus. 269) (If your machine doesn't zigzag, stitch a ⅛″ seam.)
Claire's Hint: From the wrong side, press the seam line with the handles of your cutting shears so the edges will butt together when the muff is turned right side out.

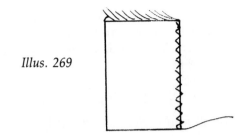

Illus. 269

6. Make the wrist cuffs. Right sides together, join the ends of the ribbed wrist cuffs to make a circle; press. Wrong sides together, fold the cuffs in half crosswise, matching the raw edges.
7. Stitch the cuffs to the ends of the muff. Divide and mark the raw edges of the cuffs and muff into quarters. Right sides together, match the marked points and zigzag (W,2-L,2) the cuffs to the muff.
8. Right sides together, join the short ends of the lining. Divide and mark the raw edges into quarters.
9. Join the muff and lining. Right sides together with the cuff sandwiched between, match the seam lines and stitch the lining to one end of the muff.
10. Turn the lining to the inside. Fold under the raw edge and hand-sew the lining to the other end of the muff.
11. Turn right side out; and using a comb or tapestry needle, pull the fur out of the seam line.

• • •

FAKE FUR MITTENS

Pretty and practical, these fake fur mittens make fantastic gifts for Christmas and winter birthdays. With just a little assistance, your daughter can make a pair for herself and all her friends.

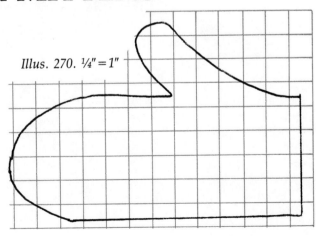

Illus. 270. ¼″ = 1″

Materials

Fur fabric, one 36″ × 13½″
Optional: Needlepunch insulation, one 36″ × 13½″

Cutting Directions

1. Enlarge the pattern. (Illus. 270) To make the mittens for a larger child, add ⅜″ to all edges.

2. Cut two mittens with the pattern right side up and two mittens with the pattern reverse side up.
3. *Optional:* Cut four mittens from needlepunch insulation.

Sewing Directions

1. All seam allowances are ¼"; hem allowances are ¾".
2. *Optional:* Pin the interlining to the wrong side of each mitten. Machine-baste ¼" from the edge.
3. Right sides together, pin the mittens together. *Claire's Hint:* To avoid catching the excess fur in the seam line, push it to the inside.
4. Zigzag (W,4-L,2) all edges except the bottom.

Claire's Hints: If straight-stitching is preferred, shorten the stitches at the inner thumb point and take two short stitches across the "V". (Illus. 271) Clip to the stitched line.

Illus. 271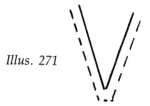

5. Turn right side out and pull the fur out of the seam.
6. Hem the bottom by hand.

PAMPERED PETS

ROCKY'S LEASH

When Rocky came to live with us we found we were one leash short for "family" outings. After he chewed up several hand-me-downs, I decided he was ready for a leash of his own; hopefully, one he wouldn't turn into shreds the first week. This is the leash Rocky received on his six-month birthday.

Finished Length: 6 feet

Materials

Webbing, 1⅜ yards, 1" wide
Spring swivel hook, one 3"
Material Notes: Spring swivel hooks are available at hardware dealers or they can be ordered from a handbag supplier. I prefer the webbing made by Offray.

Sewing Directions

1. Use a polyester topstitching thread, a size 14 (90) or 16 (100) needle, and a stitch length of 8 spi (3mm).
Claire's Hint: To prevent fraying, dab a little fray retardant on the ends of the webbing.

2. Make the hand-loop. Measure and fold the webbing 9½" from one end. Turn under the raw edge ¾" and stitch a cross in a rectangle.
3. Thread the other end of the webbing into the loop of the spring swivel hook. Fold about 4" from the end and turn under the raw edge. Stitch a cross in a rectangle.

• • •

PET BED

Go ahead and pamper your pet. He will love this comfortable bed and appreciate the security of always knowing where he is supposed to sleep. The polyester fibrefill and cedar chips will discourage fleas and odor and protect your expensive carpets from dirt and dog hair.

The bed has two covers: one a permanent casing for the fibrefill, the other a decorative zip-off cover for easy washing.

Finished Sizes: Small, 20"; Medium, 35"; Large, 42"

Materials

Material requirements are for small bed. Requirements for medium and large bed are in parentheses.
Fabric A (zip-off cover), ⅝ yard (2 yards; 2⅜ yards), 45" wide

Fabric B (stuffing cover), ⅝ yard (2 yards; 2⅜ yards), 45" wide
Zipper, one 24" (20", 2; 24", 2)
Bonded batting, 1⅞ yards (3 yards, 3⅝ yards)

Fabric Notes: Select firmly woven, medium-weight, washable fabrics. Fabrics like poplin, corduroy, denim, and cotton flannel are good choices for the zip-off cover. Coordinate color and pattern of the fabric with the decor in your home.

Heavyweight muslins and drill are good choices for the stuffing liner.

Extra-loft is a bonded polyester batting by Fairfield Processing Corporation, has extra loft and is easy to handle. Fibrefill, old pillows, and cedar chips are also suitable stuffing materials. Styrofoam (expanded polstyrene) chips make a noisy bed.

Pattern Directions

The directions are for the small bed. Directions for the medium and large beds are in parentheses.
1. Make the pattern for a 20″ (35″, 43″) circle.
Claire's Hint: Cut a large piece of pattern paper. Fold the pattern paper into quarters. If the paper isn't wide enough, tape two pieces together. Then, with a measuring tape pinned securely to the fold corner, measure and mark a quarter circle 10½″ (18½″, 22½″) from the pin.

Connect the marked points and cut out the pattern.

Cutting Directions

1. Cut two 21″ (36″, 43″) circles from Fabric A and Fabric B.
2. Cut two 20″ (35″, 42″) circles from the batting.

Sewing Directions

ZIP-OFF COVER
1. All seam allowances are ½″.
2. Join the top and bottom. Right sides together, pin and stitch, leaving 24″ (40″, 48″) unstitched for the zipper placket. (Illus. 272)

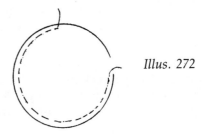

Illus. 272

3. Press and turn right side out.
4. Set the zipper. Fold the raw edge of the opening under ½″. Open the zipper; pin and stitch in place. (Illus. 273)

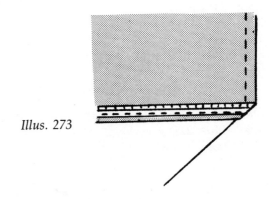

Illus. 273

Claire's Hint: This is unbelievably easy when you align the folded edge of the fabric with the zipper teeth.

BED INSERT
1. All seam allowances are ½″.
2. Right sides together, stitch the circles together, leaving 10–12″ open for turning.
3. Turn the bed right side out.
4. Insert and smooth the batting.
Claire's Hint: To keep the batting from shifting, tack in several places.
5. Close the opening.
6. Put the stuffing in the zip-off cover.

PET NECKERCHIEF

Pets like gifts too; and this personalized neckerchief will make any pet feel special. Our dogs wear their neckerchiefs when we have guests because their people-friends have difficulty identifying them.

If you're a novice at machine embroidery, this is an excellent first project.

Finished Size: 22" × 22" × 31½"

Materials

Remnant, 23" square
Stabilizer, one 12" square
Embroidery hoop, one 10"
Machine embroidery thread: white

Cutting Directions

1. Enlarge the pattern, placing the broken line on a bias fold. (Illus. 274)
2. Cut one neckerchief.

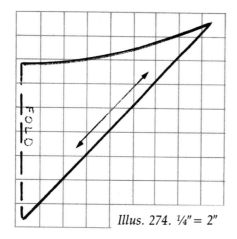

Illus. 274. ¼" = 2"

Sewing Directions

1. All hem allowances are ½".
2. Write the pet's name on the corner of the neckerchief, placing it at least 2" from the sides.
3. Pin the stabilizer under the corner to be embroidered and put the neckerchief in the embroidery hoop. If this is your first experience with embroidery, put the hoop on so the fabric will be flat against the machine bed.
4. Embroider the name in white. Use thread to match the neckerchief in the bobbin. Satin-stitch (W,3).
Claire's Hints: Loosen the upper tension; lower the feed dogs; remove the presser foot, and lower the presser foot bar. Stitch slowly.

Rest your arms on the machine base and move the hoop from side to side and up or down but do not rotate it.

Retrace the name to fill in any gaps.
5. Hem the edges of the neckerchief with a narrow machine hem.

APPENDICES

GLOSSARY

Appliqué. 1. A design sewn on top of another fabric. 2. To apply smaller designs to another fabric.

Appliqué Scissors. Specially designed scissors which trim close to the stitch line. One blade looks like a pelican's beak. Manufactured by Gingher, Inc.

Apply. To stitch.

Backtack. To fasten the threads securely. Generally used at the beginning and ends of seams.

Basting. A temporary method for holding the fabric layers together for permanent stitching. Easy-to-use basting aids include washable gluesticks, water-soluble basting tape, and pins.

Batting. A soft material used to add softness, insulate, and/or give body.

Beadings. Lace or eyelet trim with holes through which ribbon is threaded. Can be insertions, edgings, or galloons.

Bias Binding. A narrow bias-cut fabric used to finish edges.

Bonded Batting. Batting coated on both sides with a light resin. More loft and easier to handle than regular batting. I used Poly-fil Extra-Loft Batting, manufactured by Fairfield Processing Corporation.

Butt. To match the edges or folds so they meet but don't overlap.

Canned Air. Available from camera stores and sewing machine dealers. An excellent aid for keeping the sewing machine free from lint and fuzz.

Casing. A hem or tuck, open on both ends, through which elastic or ties are threaded.

Chain Stitch. To sew from one fabric section to another without lifting the presser foot or breaking the threads.

Close. To finish stitching a seam by hand or machine.

Cording. A narrow, corded strip—generally bias-cut—inserted into a seam. Sometimes called corded piping.

Craft Fuse. A crisp, nonwoven fusible interfacing. Manufactured by Stacy Fabrics Corp.

Crimping. A method of easing more fabric into the line of stitching. Sometimes called crowding, ease plus, or staystitching plus.

Crossgrain. The woof or filling, which runs from selvage to selvage.

D-Rings. Metal rings shaped like the letter D.

Dressmaker's Carbon. Special tracing paper for marking fabrics.

Edgestitch. To stitch, on the right side of the item, as close (about 1/16") to the edge or seam line as possible.

Edgings. Lace or embroidery with one straight edge and one finished or scalloped edge. Can be very narrow or very wide. Used to finish edge.

Elnapress. An ironing device with a large heating sole approximately eight times the size of an ordinary iron. Manufactured by Tavaro S.A. and marketed by Elna/White sewing machine dealers.

Embroidery Foot. Special sewing machine foot with a wide slot or V shape on the bottom which allows it to move freely over satin-stitching.

Embroidery Hoop. A special hoop for machine-embroidery.

Entredeux. French word meaning "between the two." A row of embroidered rectangles 1/8" to 1/2" wide. Looks like a small ladder. Right side is raised and shiny; wrong side is dull and flat. Frequently inserted between fabric and lace to prevent stretching.

Fabric Protector. A chemical spray which protects fabric from soil and moisture. I prefer Tectron, which is also nontoxic and will last through several launderings. Scotchgard is the name of another fabric protector.

Facile. Trade name of a soft, synthetic suede (made by Spring Industries, Inc.).

Fadeaway Marking Pen. A fabric marker which usually disappears in 48 hours or less. Sometimes called an air-erasable or 48-hour pen.

Fibrefill. A synthetic stuffing material. I prefer Poly-Fil polyester fibrefill which retains its fluffiness.

Fleece. An easy-to-handle needlepunch batting. Recommended to add thickness, softness, and/or body. Looks like needlepunch insulation but doesn't have the same insulating qualities. Sometimes called polyester fleece.

Fray Retardant. Lacquer-like liquid which prevents ravelling. Will discolor some fabrics. Fray Check is a popular brand. Clear, diluted fingernail polish can be used as a substitute.

Fusible Web. A weblike material used to bond two fabrics together. When a release sheet is used, it can be applied to a single layer of fabric. Fusible Web, Jiffy Fuse, Magic Polyweb, Sav-a-Stitch, and Stitch Witchery are some of the well-known brand names.

Galloons. A lace trim with two scalloped edges. Two edgings can be combined to simulate a galloon.

Gluestick. A washable glue useful for basting.

Grain. The warp or lengthwise grain which runs the length of the fabric, parallel to the selvages.

Holiday. An unstitched section.

Insertions. Narrow lace or embroidery with two straight sides. Used to join fabrics and other trims. Can be used instead of seams.

Join. 1. A seam line. 2. To stitch together.

Lamaire. A synthetic leather manufactured by Uniroyal, Inc.

Lip Braid. Sometimes called piping.

Loft. The thickness of the batting.

Machine Embroidery Thread. Thread made for machine embroidery.

Mitre. 1. A diagonal seam at a corner. 2. To join two edges at an angle. Generally a 45° angle.

Needle Lubricant. A silicone-like liquid. Eliminates skipped stitches on fabrics and sticking or stitch pile-up on leathers and vinyl. Brand names include Sewers' Aid, Needle Glide, and Needle-Lube.

Needlepunch Insulation. Made by punching polyester fibres into a stable core. Can be used for insulating and generally recommended for hot pads and pot holders. More expensive than fleece.

Patchwork. Term used to describe fabric seamed together with many smaller pieces.

Pattern Cloth. Nonwoven fabric. Plain or grid for making patterns.

Piping. A decorative strip, generally bias-cut, sewn into a seam line. Frequently corded.

Pivot. To turn a corner with the needle inserted into the fabric.

Raw Edge. Unfinished edge.

Release Sheet. A plastic film that allows you to bond fusible web to the fabric to create an iron-on fabric. Trade names include TransFuse (made by Stacy Fabrics Corp.) and Appliqué Pressing Sheet (made by Solar-Kist Corp.).

MM. Used on newer machines, the number of millimetres in a single stitch to indicate the length and width.

Rotary Cutter. A cutting tool with a round cutting blade. Must be used with a cutting mat.

Satin Stitch. A zigzag stitch with a very short (L,.5 or less) stitch length and variable stitch width.

Seam Allowance. Width of fabric between the seam line and raw edge.

Seam Line. The stitching line.

See-through Ruler. Plastic ruler with a 1/8" grid. Manufactured by C-Thru Ruler Co.

Set. To apply or stitch to another fabric.

Shank Button. A button that is smooth on top with a stem on the bottom.

Silk-screen. A printing process used on fabrics.

Spi. Stitches-per-inch. Used on older machines, the number of stitches the sewing machine makes in one inch.

Spot Tack. Stitch in place several times to fasten stitches.

Spring Swivel Hook. A snap latch. Sometimes called a harness latch.

Stabilizer. Nonwoven interfacing material used under fabric to prevent puckering and skipped stitches. Stitch 'n Tear, Tear-Away, and Trase Erase. A water-soluble material which disappears when dipped or sprayed with water. (Aqua-Solv)

Stabilizer Substitutes. Strips of regular (2mm) plastic or typing paper.

Style-A-Shade. Very crisp nonwoven fusible interfacing. Used to stiffen fabrics. Made by Stacy Fabrics Corp.

Topstitch. To stitch on the right side of the item.

Transfer Pencil. A marking pencil. Used to transfer designs by pressing.

Trim. To cut away excess fabric.

Ultrasuede. Trade name for synthetic suede made by Spring Industries, Inc.

Water-soluble Basting Tape. Double-sided basting tape which will dissolve in water.

Water-soluble Marking Pen. A pen for marking fabrics. Mark will disappear when dampened.

Velcro. Hook and loop fastener.

Yarn Needle. A long (3"–6") needle with a large eye.

Zigzag. The sideways movement of the needle.

• • •

TROUBLESHOOTER FOR MACHINE STITCHING PROBLEMS

The three most common reasons for stitching problems are improper threading, a dirty machine and a damaged needle.

If you keep your machine clean and well oiled, it will reward you with many years of trouble-free pleasure.

Clean your machine when you finish sewing each day. This really isn't too often. In fact, some days your machine will require cleaning during the day also.

Many materials such as synthetic fabrics, embroidery thread, fleece and needlepunch insulation leave large deposits of lint between the throat plate and feed dogs. This deposit accumulates much faster in zigzag machines than the old-fashioned straight-stitch variety, perhaps because of the larger hole in the throat plate. In any event, in addition to causing puckered seams and skipped stitches, lint and fibres can permanently damage the machine.

My machine actually talks to me. Don't laugh! It starts with a little noise which gets louder, if ignored, while lint is collecting. Listen to your machine; it may have a voice you haven't previously noticed.

Oil your machine after every eight hours of stitching. And, of course, you should always clean it before oiling.

Change the needle frequently. Universal ballpoint needles in small sizes are best for most stitching. I prefer those made by Schmetz and J.P. Coats/Coats and Clark.

Whether you sew a lot or a little, you can expect to have stitching problems. Many are directly related to the variety and kinds of fabrics used today. Most of these can be solved with a little knowledge and patience and without the services of an expensive repairman.

NORMAL, EVERYDAY PROBLEMS

Machine Doesn't Run

Machine not plugged in.

Machine not turned on.

Machine clogged with unsuitable oil.

Machine clogged or rusted because of improper storage. To prevent this, do not store the machine in an unheated, unairconditioned, or damp garage.

TENSION FAULTS

Tension is the amount of pull or stress on the needle and bobbin threads. The right amount of tension for one fabric may not be right for another. The fabric thickness, weight and softness; the number of fabric layers; different weight threads on the top and bobbin; and the stitch type, length, and width may cause the tension to be unbalanced—too tight, too loose.

A perfect stitch is formed when the threads interlock in the center of the fabric layers. (Illus. 275)

If the upper tension is too tight, the needle thread will lie flat on top of the fabric. (Illus. 276)

If the bobbin tension is too tight or the upper thread too loose, the lower thread will lie flat along the surface. (Illus. 277)

The tension on the needle thread is regulated by two concave discs and a tension screw or dial. When the screw is turned clockwise or tightened, the discs move closer together creating a greater pull and more tension on the thread. For regular sewing, most adjustments are made to upper tension. However, this is not true for machine embroidery and machine appliqué.

If the tension disc on your machine has numbers, the higher the number, the greater the tension. When the presser foot lever is raised, there is no tension.

The bobbin or lower tension is regulated by adjusting the screw on the bobbin case. If your machine has a separate bobbin case, the tension screw is easy to find at the rear of the flat spring. If the machine doesn't have a separate case, consult the machine manual or your local dealer.

To change the bobbin tension, turn the screw clockwise to tighten and counterclockwise to loosen.

Claire's Hint: This is a very short screw and a 1/4 or 1/2 turn will correct most problems. If you turn it too much, the screw may fall out and be lost forever.

Some bobbin cases have a small hole at the end of the metal finger. When the bobbin thread is threaded into the eye on the finger, the bobbin tension is increased without changing the balance of the upper and lower tension.

To test the tension, fill the bobbin and replace it in the machine. Thread the upper machine with the same type and weight thread in a different color. Set the upper tension on 5. Stitching with the grain through two layers of starched organdy, zigzag (W,4-L,4).

Examine the stitched line. There should be no puckers and it should look the same on the top and bottom with only one color thread showing on each side of the fabric.

If the needle thread floats, the upper tension is too tight and needs to be loosened. If the bobbin thread floats, the upper tension is too loose and needs to be tightened. Adjust and stitch again. Continue fine tuning until the stitch is perfect.

If the tension is balanced but the seam puckers, loosen both tensions.

If you can't decide if the tension is balanced just by looking at the stitched line, hold each end of the stitched line between your thumb and forefinger and pull sharply. The threads should break evenly. If they don't, the one which breaks is the tighter of the two. If neither thread breaks, both tensions may be too loose. Adjust as needed.

Here are some common reasons for tension problems:

Dirty machine. Lint between the tension discs, in the bobbin case, around the bobbin, and under the throat plate is the number one troublemaker.

Illus. 275

Illus. 276

Illus. 277

Wrong size or type needle.
Bent or damaged needle.
Incorrectly set needle.
A bent, rusted, or damaged bobbin.
Wrong bobbin for the machine.
Improperly wound bobbin. Polyester thread will stretch when wound on the bobbin at high speed. Once it is stitched into a seam, it relaxes; and the seam puckers. To correct, wind the bobbin on slow speed.

Layers of different threads on the bobbin.

The bobbin pigtail—the thread end sticking out of the bobbin—was left on. Cut it off.

The bobbin case screw has worked out.

Thread too coarse, too fine, old, brittle, or poor quality with slubs and knots.

Different weight threads on the top and bobbin.

The thread has slipped out of the tension discs and/or take-up lever.

The thread is catching on rough surfaces on the machine, thread guides, throat plate, or thread spindle.

The thread is catching in the slash on the thread spool. Turn the spool upside down to avoid this.

Damaged spring on the bobbin case. To prevent this, cut the bobbin thread close to the spring before removing the bobbin from the case. Pulling the thread through the spring over a period of time can damage the spring.

NEEDLES BREAKING

Eliminate needles breaking by identifying the cause of the problem.

Stitching over pins or zipper.
Needle bent.
Changing the needle position with the needle in the fabric.
Changing from straight stitch to zigzag with the needle in the fabric.
Needle too fine for the material.
Wrong needle for the machine.
Needle improperly set or not set tightly.
Loose presser foot.
Bobbin or bobbin case incorrectly inserted.
Zigzag stitch with incompatible foot.
Zigzag stitch with small hole needle plate.
Pulling fabric away from needle without raising presser foot lever.
Pulling fabric towards the front.
Pulling fabric with the needle down.

NEEDLE BECOMES UNTHREADED

Some common causes for this problem include:
Thread ends too short.
Take-up lever not in the highest position.
Threads not held to side when starting. Chaining from one seam to another or to a fabric scrap between seams eliminates this.

NEEDLE THREAD BREAKING

This is not a difficult problem to correct. Here are some common reasons for the needle thread breaking:
Dirty machine. Lint or thread ends around the bobbin or bobbin case.
Tension too tight.
Improperly threaded machine.
Poor quality needles.
Bent or damaged needle.
Improperly set needle.
Too coarse or fine thread for the needle or fabric.
Old, brittle, or poor-quality thread with slubs or knots.
Starting with the take-up lever in the wrong position.
Damaged surfaces (guides, tension disc, take-up lever) on the machine.
Improperly positioned thread spool and the thread is catching on the slash.

BOBBIN THREAD BREAKING

Eliminate bobbin-thread breaking by finding the cause in this list.
Dirty machine. Lint or dust in or around the bobbin case.
Bobbin tension too tight.
Improperly wound bobbin.
Bobbin set into bobbin case backwards.
Improperly threaded machine.
Damaged throat plate.
Bobbin-screw has worked out and is catching the thread as the bobbin turns.
The bobbin's pigtail is caught in the bobbin case.

PUCKERED SEAMS

Puckered seams are most common on lightweight, permanent press, and tightly woven fabrics. All fabrics pucker most when stitched in the direction of least stretch—lengthwise.
Use one or more of these suggestions to eliminate puckered seams.
A new needle.
A universal ballpoint needle.
A smaller needle.
Finer thread.
The same size and kind of thread on the needle and bobbin.
Correct the tension.
Lighten the pressure.
Shorten the stitch length.
Use a straight-stitch foot and small-hole throat plate.

Set the needle position in the right-hand position if the machine doesn't have a straight-stitch foot.
Use an all-purpose zigzag foot, instead of an embroidery foot, except when embroidering or appliquéing.
Hold the fabric firmly in front and back of the needle to prevent the machine from feeding the fabric too quickly.
Change to low speed or stitch slowly.
Place stabilizer between the fabric and feed dogs. (Strips of Ziploc bags work very nicely.)

SKIPPED STITCHES

Understanding the cause of skipped stitches will generally solve this problem. The fabric clings to the needle as the needle penetrates the needle hole in the throat plate. This causes the thread to stay so close to the needle that it doesn't make a loop large enough to be caught by the shuttle hook on the bobbin case and make a stitch.
Use one or more of these suggestions to eliminate skipped stitches.
Wash fabrics to remove undesirable finishes.
Thread the machine properly.
Use a new needle.
Use the smallest needle possible for the fabric.
Use a larger needle. A small needle may not make a large enough hole in a resilient fabric. Usually the reverse is the case—a too-large needle causes fabric distortion.
Use a universal ballpoint needle or a topstitching needle.
Use a different type needle, i.e., leather, lingerie.
Set the needle properly.
Use a straight-stitch foot and small-hole throat plate.
Set the needle position in the right-hand position if the machine doesn't have a straight-stitch foot.
Use an all-purpose zigzag foot, instead of an embroidery foot, except when embroidering or appliquéing.
Cover the large hole in the zigzag throat plate with transparent tape if the machine doesn't have a small-hole plate.
Hold the fabric firmly in front and back of the needle to prevent the machine from feeding the fabric too quickly.
Increase the pressure.
Change to low speed or stitch slowly.
Stitch evenly.
Loosen the upper tension.
Place stabilizer between the fabric and feed dogs.
Use a needle lubricant on the needle, thread, bobbin, and fabric. Test first for spotting.
Level the presser foot. Hold the toes of the presser foot down as you stitch. When this doesn't solve the problem, make a leveller of lightweight cardboard; place it under the presser foot as needed to balance the foot.
Rub the section to be stitched with a sliver of soap.
Use a hammer to pound the seam or hem before stitching. This is particularly effective when stitching through multiple layers of denim.

CREEPING UNDERLAYER AND DRAG LINES

This is a very common problem because of the basic design of the sewing machine. The feed dogs move the fabric to the back of the machine each time a stitch is made. The fabric is held in place by the presser foot which pushes the upper layer forward while the feed dog pulls the lower layer backward.

Use one or more of these suggestions to prevent creeping and drag lines.

Stitch with the grain.

Use an even-feed foot or a roller foot.

Stitch and rest. Stitch a few inches; stop; raise the presser foot to relax the fabric; lower it; and continue stitching.

Lighten the pressure on the presser foot.

Hold the fabric firmly in front and back when stitching.

Hold the fabric firmly on either side of the presser foot.

Pull the bottom layer forward with the right hand while pushing the upper layer back with the left hand.

Use the points of the scissors or end of a screwdriver to push the upper layer towards the needle or to hold the upper layer firmly against the lower layer.

If the two sections are uneven in length, position them so the longer one is on the bottom.

Stitch with a piece of stabilizer between the fabric and feed dogs.

When topstitching, baste. Use the points of the scissors to gently push the top layer towards the needle.

When topstitching leather (real or synthetic), rub the surface with a needle lubricant before stitching.

MACHINE JAMS

Some common causes for the machine to jam.

Dirty machine.

Lint or thread around the bobbin case.

Threads not held to the side when beginning.

Bobbin incorrectly inserted.

Damaged needle.

Needle incorrectly inserted.

Presser bar lever in the up position.

Pressure too heavy on the presser foot.

Machine incorrectly threaded.

Fabric not far enough under presser foot.

Fabric pulled into needle hole. To correct, use stabilizer at the beginning of seams. Start stitching on the stabilizer; cover with fabric; and continue stitching.

Needle hole too large.

Wrong foot. Change to an embroidery foot for satin stitching.

Too many stitches. Do not backstitch at the beginning or end of seams on lightweight fabrics.

FABRIC DOESN'T FEED PROPERLY AND UNEVEN STITCH LENGTH

Review this list of common causes when the fabric doesn't feed.

Machine not plugged in.

Machine not turned on.

Feed dogs down.

Stitch length on 0.

Presser foot lever not down.

Foot sticks to fabric (leather and vinyl). Rub the material surface with needle lubricant or talcum powder. Or use a Teflon-coated foot.

Incorrect foot. Change to an all-purpose zigzag foot or straight-stitch foot.

Pressure too light.

Dirty machine. Lint packed under the feed dogs.

Pulling on the fabric.

Speed setting too fast.

Machine clogged by unsuitable oil.

Greater fabric thickness. Try holding the toes down, using a leveller at the back of the foot, rubbing the area with a sliver of soap, or pounding with a hammer to break down the fibres (denim).

NOISY MACHINE

Some common reasons for a noisy machine:

Dirty machine.

Poor-quality or wrong-type machine oil.

Loose part.

Punching noise frequently caused by a dull needle.

FABRIC TUNNELS ON ZIGZAG

If the fabric rolls or tunnels when zigzagging, try one or more of these solutions.

Use stabilizer.

Change to a machine overcast foot.

Shift to slow gear or stitch slowly.

● ● ●

METRIC EQUIVALENCY CHART

MM—MILLIMETRES   CM—CENTIMETRES

INCHES TO MILLIMETRES AND CENTIMETRES

INCHES	MM	CM	INCHES	CM	INCHES	CM
⅛	3	0.3	9	22.9	30	76.2
¼	6	0.6	10	25.4	31	78.7
⅜	10	1.0	11	27.9	32	81.3
½	13	1.3	12	30.5	33	83.8
⅝	16	1.6	13	33.0	34	86.4
¾	19	1.9	14	35.6	35	88.9
⅞	22	2.2	15	38.1	36	91.4
1	25	2.5	16	40.6	37	94.0
1¼	32	3.2	17	43.2	38	96.5
1½	38	3.8	18	45.7	39	99.1
1¾	44	4.4	19	48.3	40	101.6
2	51	5.1	20	50.8	41	104.1
2½	64	6.4	21	53.3	42	106.7
3	76	7.6	22	55.9	43	109.2
3½	89	8.9	23	58.4	44	111.8
4	102	10.2	24	61.0	45	114.3
4½	114	11.4	25	63.5	46	116.8
5	127	12.7	26	66.0	47	119.4
6	152	15.2	27	68.6	48	121.9
7	178	17.8	28	71.1	49	124.5
8	203	20.3	29	73.7	50	127.0

YARDS TO METRES

YARDS	METRES	YARDS	METRES	YARDS	METRES	YARDS	METRES	YARDS	METRES
⅛	0.11	2⅛	1.94	4⅛	3.77	6⅛	5.60	8⅛	7.43
¼	0.23	2¼	2.06	4¼	3.89	6¼	5.72	8¼	7.54
⅜	0.34	2⅜	2.17	4⅜	4.00	6⅜	5.83	8⅜	7.66
½	0.46	2½	2.29	4½	4.11	6½	5.94	8½	7.77
⅝	0.57	2⅝	2.40	4⅝	4.23	6⅝	6.06	8⅝	7.89
¾	0.69	2¾	2.51	4¾	4.34	6¾	6.17	8¾	8.00
⅞	0.80	2⅞	2.63	4⅞	4.46	6⅞	6.29	8⅞	8.12
1	0.91	3	2.74	5	4.57	7	6.40	9	8.23
1⅛	1.03	3⅛	2.86	5⅛	4.69	7⅛	6.52	9⅛	8.34
1¼	1.14	3¼	2.97	5¼	4.80	7¼	6.63	9¼	8.46
1⅜	1.26	3⅜	3.09	5⅜	4.91	7⅜	6.74	9⅜	8.57
1½	1.37	3½	3.20	5½	5.03	7½	6.86	9½	8.69
1⅝	1.49	3⅝	3.31	5⅝	5.14	7⅝	6.97	9⅝	8.80
1¾	1.60	3¾	3.43	5¾	5.26	7¾	7.09	9¾	8.92
1⅞	1.71	3⅞	3.54	5⅞	5.37	7⅞	7.20	9⅞	9.03
2	1.83	4	3.66	6	5.49	8	7.32	10	9.14

INDEX

accessories
 adjustable twist, 90
 classic obi, 93–94
 clutch bag, 98–99
 collage belt, 88–89
 corduroy tote bag, 95–96
 cummerbund variation, 91
 easy designer, belt, 92
 easy fashion belt, 92–93
 fancy comb, 100
 hobo bag, 97–98
 lace scarf, 99–100
 Marcy's belt, 88
 quick-and-easy tie, 94–95
 ribbon belt, 91–92
adjustable twist, 90
appliqué
 applying, 17–18
 enlarging, 8
 machine, general tips and
  techniques, 16–18
 place mats, 33–34
 scissors, 9
 teddy, 158
apron(s)
 chef's delight, 26–27
 country, 27–28
 eyelet hostess, 29–30
 gingerbread, 170–171
 ice cream, 172–173
 no-nonsense, 25–26

baby gifts
 baby bonnet, 154
 baby pillow, 151
 bib and burp cloth, 144–145
 christening pillow, 152
 hooded bath towel and wash
  mitt, 152–153
 pram coverlet, 155
 quilted bib, 147–148
 receiving blankets, 156
 stroller bag, 148–151
 teddy bear bib, 145–146
backtack, 9
bag(s)
 beach, 161–162
 clutch, 98–99
 corduroy tote, 95–96
 denim knapsack, 165–167
 handy tote, 163–164
 hanging garment, 118–119
 hobo, 97–98
 lacy lingerie, 106–107

mushroom, 51
 quilted overnight, 164–165
 shoe, 130
 silver care, 60
 stay-fresh bread, 52
 stroller, 148–151
 teddy's duffel, 160–161
 travelling, 122–123
 travel mesh, 128
 weekend duffel, 119–121
 wine-bottle, 23
 wineglass, 24
bandana pillow, 64
basket liner, 50
 quilted for picnic basket, 22–23
beach bag, 161–162
bed, pet, 178–179
bedside caddy, 109–110
bedside organizer, 169–170
belt(s)
 adjustable twist, 90
 classic obi, 93–94
 collage, 88–89
 easy designer, 92
 easy fashion, 92–93
 Marcy's, 88
 money, 133
 quick-and-easy elastic, 174
 quick-and-easy tie, 94–95
 ribbon, 91
bias, 9–10
bias binding, 11–12
bib
 and burp cloth, 144–145
 quilted, 147–148
 teddy bear, 145–146
bindings, 10–12
 bias, 11–12
blankets, receiving, 156
bobbin-thread breaking, 185
bonnet, baby, 154
bordered napkins, 30–31
bound coasters, 50
box, flop, 53–54
boxing, 12
bread
 bag, stay-fresh, 52
 French bread warmer, 53
breakfast pillow, 78–79
bridal hankerchief and garter,
  112–113
briefcase
 computer, 84–85
 teddy's, 159

bull's-eye pillow, 67
business, gifts for. see executives,
  gifts for

caddy
 bedside, 109–110
 place mat, 40
 silverware, 24–25
 stationery, 111–112
 tie, 128–129
camisole, 102–103
candy wrapper pillow, 67–68
cardcase and table cover, 58–59
car organizer, 130–131
case(s)
 cardcase and table cover, 58–59
 cosmetics, 121
 map, 132
 tire-gauge, 131
casserole jacket, 41–42
cat(s)
 fancier ensemble, 36–37
 leash, 178
 meow pillow, 72–73
 neckerchief, 180
 pet bed, 178–179
chef's delight apron, 26–27
children's gifts. see also baby gifts
 beach bag, 161–162
 bedside organizer, 169–170
 denim knapsack, 165–167
 fake fur mittens, 175–176
 fake fur muff, 174–175
 gingerbread apron, 170–171
 handy tote bag, 163–164
 ice cream apron, 172–173
 quick-and-easy elastic belt, 174
 quilted overnight bag, 164–165
 take-along duffel, 168–169
 teddy bear ensemble, 158–161
christening pillow, 152
classic obi, 93–94
clipping, 9
close the opening, 12–13
closet luxuries, 103–106
cloth
 bib and burp, 144–145
 picnic, 23
 pressing, 139
clothes hanger
 luxury, 103–104
 padded, 82
clutch bag, 98–99

coasters

ABOUT THE AUTHOR

Claire Shaeffer is known for her innovative sewing techniques and easy-to-read instructions.

She is a college instructor, nationally known lecturer, and regular contributor to *Sew News*, *Needle and Thread* and *Handmade*.

Her book, *The Complete Book of Sewing Short Cuts* (New York: Sterling Publishing Co., 1981) described as "invaluable and highly recommended" by *Library Journal* has been a best-seller in the home-sewing field since publication.

Claire graduated with honors from the Peralta Colleges with certificates in Fashion Design and Industrial Sewing and summa cum laude from Old Dominion University with a degree in Art History.

She is a member of the American Home Economics Association, Costume Society of America, Costume Council—Los Angeles County Museum of Art, and Friends of Fashion—City of London Museum.

Her biography is listed in *Personalities of America*, *Directory of Distinguished Americans*, *World Who's Who of Women*, and *Dictionary of International Biography*.